"*Promoting Activity and Participation in Individuals with Serious Mental Illness* is required reading for all mental health trainees and practitioners from any discipline, as well as peer specialists, who are committed to supporting people in pursuing meaningful, self-directed lives in the community. The evidence-based approach is built on solid conceptual frameworks and has been further refined in this second version as a result of the extensive practice and research knowledge of an accomplished group of authors. Community inclusion and participation are increasingly being recognized as a medical necessity. *Promoting Activity and Participation in Individuals with Serious Mental Illness* provides a roadmap for making it happen that can be embedded in any mental health program or service."

—**Mark Salzer, PhD**, *professor, Department of Social and Behavioral Sciences at Temple University and director of the Temple University Collaborative on Community Inclusion of Individuals with Psychiatric Disabilities*

"*What people do in their everyday lives matters to their health and well-being*! *Promoting Activity and Participation in Individuals with Serious Mental Illness* starts with empirical evidence about the power of participation in daily activities and translates this into practical tools for mental health practitioners. It combines the art and science of supporting individuals with serious mental illness, and is an important addition to every therapist's toolbox for recovery-oriented practice."

—**Sandra Moll, PhD, OT Reg (Ont)** and **Rebecca Gewurtz, PhD, OT Reg (Ont)**, *associate professors, McMaster University, Canada and members of the Do-Live-Well Framework development team (www.dolivewell.ca)*

"Developed from the knowledge base of occupational science and occupational therapy, *Promoting Activity and Participation in Individuals with Serious Mental Illness* is a quantum leap for the development of practices focused on promoting activity and participation in the mental health field. It is an intervention that consistently combines client-centering and the systematisation of services. Both clients and service providers confirm this through high demand and the benefits they realize from the success of their own doing."

—**Andreas Pfeiffer**, *president, German Occupational Therapy Association*

"With the first version of this book, it became no longer acceptable to blame the inertia that may be associated with a serious mental illness on the person struggling with it, as the reader was led down a path that broke through what at times could be an impasse in treatment. With the addition of the capabilities framework as a foundation, culture as a context, and community inclusion as a primary goal, this second version takes additional steps in laying out concrete practices which can support the person in identifying and pursuing engagement in the kinds of activities that give meaning and purpose to all of our lives. What results is an invaluable resource for promoting recovery-oriented practice."

—**Larry Davidson, PhD**, *professor of Psychiatry and director, Program for Recovery and Community Health, Yale University*

Promoting Activity and Participation in Individuals with Serious Mental Illness

This book presents 'Action Over Inertia', a recovery-orientated, strengths-based approach to address the profound disruptions in daily activities and community participation often experienced by those living with serious mental illness.

With a focus on supported 'doing', the Action Over Inertia approach engages individuals in small activity and participation efforts as an opening to making longer term and sustained changes that offer meaning and well-being. The book helps service providers develop their own knowledge of activities and the health and well-being benefits an individual might receive from activities. It also asks them to consider the biases, assumptions, and constraints that might impact their ability to implement interventions related to activity and participation. A range of worksheets, resources, vignettes, and other tools are provided to support this practice.

The manual was developed from the knowledge and practice of occupational science and therapy, but it will be of interest to any mental health professional, peer-provider, administrator, or policy maker interested in promoting recovery for people with serious mental illness.

Terry Krupa, PhD, is professor emerita, School of Rehabilitation Therapy, Queen's University, Canada. Her research and practice have focused on promoting the community participation of people living with serious mental illness.

Megan Edgelow, EdD, is assistant professor, School of Rehabilitation Therapy, Queen's University, Canada. She has clinical, teaching, and research experience in mental health and activity participation.

Shu-Ping Chen, PhD, is associate professor, Department of Occupational Therapy, University of Alberta, Canada. Dr. Chen's teaching and research focuses on empowerment, recovery, and social inclusion for people with mental health issues.

Carol Mieras, MScOT, is adjunct academic staff and co-manager of the MasterCard Scholars Program, Queen's University, Canada. Her research and practice focus on inclusion and disability, particularly related to mental health.

Promoting Activity and Participation in Individuals with Serious Mental Illness

The Action Over Inertia Approach

Terry Krupa, Megan Edgelow, Shu-Ping Chen, and Carol Mieras

Routledge
Taylor & Francis Group

NEW YORK AND LONDON

First published 2022
by Routledge
605 Third Avenue, New York, NY 10158

and by Routledge
2 Park Square, Milton Park, Abingdon, Oxon, OX14 4RN

Routledge is an imprint of the Taylor & Francis Group, an informa business

Library of Congress Cataloging-in-Publication Data
Names: Krupa, Terry, 1956-author. | Edgelow, Megan, author. | Chen, Shu-Ping, author. | Mieras, Carol, author.
Title: Promoting activity and participation in individuals with serious mental illness: the action over inertia approach/Terry Krupa, Megan Edgelow, Shu-Ping Chen, Carol Mieras.
Description: New York, NY: Routledge, 2022. | Includes bibliographical references and index. |
Identifiers: LCCN 2021015151 (print) | LCCN 2021015152 (ebook) | ISBN 9780367629007 (hardback) | ISBN 9780367629021 (paperback) | ISBN 9781003111368 (ebook)
Subjects: LCSH: Mentally ill–Rehabilitation. | Community mental health services.
Classification: LCC RC439.5 .K78 2022 (print) | LCC RC439.5 (ebook) | DDC 362.2/2–dc23
LC record available at https://lccn.loc.gov/2021015151
LC ebook record available at https://lccn.loc.gov/2021015152

ISBN: 978-0-367-62900-7 (hbk)
ISBN: 978-0-367-62902-1 (pbk)
ISBN: 978-1-003-11136-8 (ebk)

DOI: 10.4324/9781003111368

Typeset in Times New Roman
by Deanta Global Publishing Services, Chennai, India

Contents

Authors and Contributors

Terry Krupa
School of Rehabilitation Therapy
Queen's University
Kingston, Ontario

Megan Edgelow
School of Rehabilitation Therapy
Queen's University
Kingston, Ontario

Shu-Ping Chen
Department of Occupational Therapy
Faculty of Rehabilitation Medicine
University of Alberta
Edmonton, Alberta

Carol Mieras
Mastercard Foundation Scholars Program
School of Rehabilitation Therapy
Queen's University
Kingston, Ontario

With contributions from:

Renee Bucci
Heads Up! Early Psychosis Intervention Program
Kingston Health Sciences Centre
Kingston, Ontario

Allison Casteels
KidsInclusive
Kingston Health Sciences Centre
Kingston, Ontario

Sarah Goodfield Weinstein
CBI Health Group – Toronto Eglinton
Toronto, Ontario

Cate Preston
Back in Motion Rehabilitation
Surrey, British Columbia

Allie Rogers
School of Health, Community Services & Creative Design
Lambton College
Sarnia, Ontario

Tanya Schoenhals
Belleville, Ontario

Tina Siemens
Providence Care Hospital
Kingston, Ontario

Sara Ubbens
Modern OT – Occupational Therapy Services
Ottawa, Ontario

Foreword I

For so many of my years working as a mental health occupational therapy practitioner and educator (in the US), I have been so inspired and impressed by the work of Dr. Krupa and colleagues in Canada. For decades they have crafted and disseminated practical, accessible, evidence-based interventions widely available to occupational therapists and other professionals, paraprofessionals, and peer support providers which are aligned with a client centred recovery and wellness orientation that I believe to be so important.

In my estimation, the updated intervention approach described in *Promoting Activity and Participation in Individuals with Serious Mental Illness* will continue to benefit those with serious mental illness worldwide who face disparities, discrimination, comorbidities as well as demonstrate lifestyle habits that lead to poorer quality of life and reduced lifespan. We have known for far too long that in addition to living with a major mental disorder, people are at risk of developing or living with other medical and mental health comorbidities. Additionally, far too many of these individuals are negatively impacted by issues of poverty, under and unemployment, trauma, limited health literacy, reduced social support, and more. This updated version of the intervention approach considers these factors and provides a structure for practitioners to collaborate to co-create plans to lead to positive individual level outcomes. This book offers new foundational, structural, and practical features for an occupational time-use intervention that can enhance occupational balance and engagement for people with serious mental illness.

The updated Action Over Inertia intervention approach more robustly recognizes the social determinants of health and formidable disparities so many people encounter in creating and enjoying a life of meaning and well-being through activity and participation.

The Do-Live-Well framework provides a proactive lens to consider the importance of activities and participation to health and well-being. The increased attention to factors such as race, ethnicity, age, gender, and more allows the practitioner to gain a full picture of the individualized experiences, needs, context, and preferences to offer a person-centred approach. Increased attention to systemic factors can help practitioners to systematically consider the effects of social determinants, disadvantage, and structural factors that impact lifestyle, quality of life and lifespan. Asking the right questions can help the client express what is important to create an effective plan leading to favourable outcomes.

Despite decades of recovery-oriented research, far too often mental health intervention approaches, including those offered by occupational therapists, continue to be deficit focused. Action Over Inertia however is based on the capabilities framework offering therapists a positive lens to connect with people, to explore, engage, and involve them in personally meaningful activities of their choice. I have witnessed the importance of focusing attention on activity and helping a person to create and sustain structure and routine by planning activities that have meaning and purpose, and are personally satisfying. The increased attention to family, culture, and social context promotes an approach which taps into client choices and actions that are truly motivational and enhance client engagement which I believe can positively impact health and well-being outcomes. In this book there is explicit attention to inclusion and citizenship as principles guiding practice; this is so important because of the social exclusion, discrimination, and self-stigma faced by far too many people.

This book includes more robust descriptions of approaches and strategies to enable people to connect with meaningful activities and increase participation. Service providers are provided a structured approach they can flexibly adapt to help them collaborate with clients, to co-create opportunities and foster community capacity building. It promotes a message of optimism – that a fulfilling life is possible. In addition to case studies and focused questions to engage practitioners, key competencies are identified to help practitioners to be recovery focused, curious, and ensure there is a collaborative approach.

This book is truly a practical intervention that embodies the recovery and wellness models espoused as very important by people in recovery and peer providers internationally. This intervention provides a structure whereby the practitioner and individual can collaborate to overcome the often-formidable barriers preventing them from deriving meaning and enjoyment from the wide range of activities and participation that make up their daily life.

Peggy Swarbrick
PhD, OT, CPRP, FAOT
Associate professor and director of Practice
Innovation and Wellness
Rutgers University Behavioral Health Care
Wellness Institute director
Collaborative Support Programs of New Jersey

Foreword II

I am excited to see that *Promoting Activity and Participation in Individuals with Serious Mental Illness* provides the updated version of the Action over Inertia approach and to share that excitement with you. Action Over Inertia set out a clear vision and practices to address profoundly disrupted patterns of activity and participation among people living with ongoing health conditions, and positioned these practices in the context of recovery-oriented mental health care. This book builds on this vision and further articulates Action Over Inertia as a distinct intervention for enabling the development of activity and participation patterns that support health and well-being. That is, Action Over Inertia focuses on what individuals do in their daily lives, how, why, and the potential of activity and participation experiences to contribute to health and well-being.

Involvement in self-chosen, personally, and culturally meaningful activities is widely recognized in the mental health field as contributing to recovery and well-being. Yet, practices for enabling meaningful engagement, social connection, and participation as part of one's community are among the least defined and developed aspects of recovery oriented practice approaches. Action Over Inertia is a person centred practice grounded in knowledge from the fields of occupational science and occupational therapy about the qualities and organization of daily activities and participation, their personal and sociocultural meanings and expression, and their relationships to health, well-being, and recovery. Action Over Inertia makes visible practices that have historically been poorly described and understood in the mental health field. In so doing, it opens doors to new understanding and strategies that are important to address the struggles in daily life all too frequently faced by people living with ongoing mental health issues around the world. It also invites possibilities for collaboration, consultation, and sharing of knowledge related to activity, participation, health, and well-being with consumers, families, and service providers in the interest of overcoming obstacles to participation and inclusion.

Action Over Inertia was designed for *working with* people whose disrupted patterns of activity and participation are significant issues for health and well-being. Over my career as an occupational therapist, I have worked with many people who shared with me their challenging experiences of everyday life in the context of living with mental health issues, and often we struggled together to create activity and participation experiences that might increase their sense of well-being. These experiences have taught me much – not only about lived experiences of disrupted lives and accompanying struggles, successes, and setbacks – but also about the many possibilities for finding strengths and resources to draw on in moving forward. Had I had the tools and resources of Action Over Inertia available to me at the time, I might possibly have offered more effective supports, but I certainly would have had tools to make more explicit how activity and participation patterns, health, and well-being are connected. When I first learned about Action Over Inertia, I had long been interested in time use (or how people spend their time) as an indicator of health and well-being, so what excited me were the tools and resources for supporting individuals to explore possibilities and to create and sustain personally meaningful and satisfying activity patterns associated with recovery and well-being.

Promoting Activity and Participation in Individuals with Serious Mental Illness makes the person-centred, strengths- and capabilities-focused elements of this intervention approach explicit. In so doing, it connects Action Over Inertia with the Do-Live-Well framework focused on evidence-based links between activities and participation and health and well-being; and the Capabilities approach, a social justice framework focused on situations that compromise people's opportunities, resources, and power to live the kinds of lives they value. Importantly, this means this book gives more attention to the complex and interacting social forces (for example, poverty, stigma and discrimination, social isolation) that situate many of the disruptions to activities and participation experienced by people living with persistent mental health issues in our communities. Recognizing their impacts on activity and participation patterns is essential in developing strategies to address these obstacles to inclusive participation. More robust descriptions of approaches and strategies to enable people to connect with meaningful activities and participation are also included in the new version, along with more extensive illustrations of the use of Action Over Inertia in practice scenarios.

In Australia, the potential of Action Over Inertia has been explored in several contexts. In youth and adult community mental health services, this intervention approach has been offered to provide individuals with support for re-engagement in self-chosen activity and participation patterns as part of their recovery; it has also been offered as an individualized support intervention within community support services for people with psychiatric disabilities. In this way, Action Over Inertia can be used in working alongside individuals to explore what they do in their daily lives, why, and how current patterns of activity and participation may connect to meaning, health, and well-being, as well as to develop strategies differently constructing patterns of activity and participation to better support well-being. In supported accommodation services, Action Over Inertia has also been used to align interventions focused on activities and participation with recovery-oriented practice. In this context, the occupational therapists collaborated with a Consumer Advisory Group, and management of the mental health services to develop and implement Action Over Inertia in a time-limited group format. Offering Action Over Inertia in a group format aimed to not only promote understanding of the contribution of activity participation in recovery and well-being, but also to foster group support for self-development and effecting change. This approach has highlighted the power of sharing – nothing counters a sense of isolation and aloneness like being among people whose experiences we recognize as like theirs, as the peer support literature attests. It also indicates the potential usefulness of offering Action Over Inertia within a peer support context, in collaboration with occupational therapists, whether as co-facilitators, supervisors, or consultants in the process.

The new version of Action Over Inertia also reflects a depth of practice wisdom that comes from having explored the philosophical, theoretical, and practice elements of this approach with many practitioners, including occupational therapists, peer support workers, and others in the mental health field around the world. Having witnessed some of these conversations at interactive workshops in Australia, it is evident that the authors have sought to share these learnings. In particular, the book offers further practical strategies for how to enable people to construct activity and participation patterns in daily life that hold meaning and contribute to health and well-being. The power of Action Over Inertia to practically and tangibly bring about practice change will be further enhanced by its use in collaborative practice with experts by experience, whereby dialogue across occupational and lived experience perspectives could move forward authentic recovery-oriented care.

While primarily described for working alongside people with persistent mental illness with patterns of activity and participation as the focus for strategies to support health and well-being, Action Over Inertia is not an intervention focused on mental illness per se. There are many other populations for whom struggles with disrupted activity and participation patterns are very real and for whom the Action Over Inertia approach and practices also have much to offer in more fully addressing disruptions to activities and participation patterns that undermine health and well-being.

I hope that *Promoting the Activity and Participation of Individuals with Serious Mental Illness* serves to inspire many occupational therapists, and others who provide mental health care and support, to a deeper understanding of patterns of activity and participation as a focus for interventions to support health and well-being. With the right supports, people can construct diverse experiences with activity and participation that enable meaningful engagement and influence their own possibilities for health, well-being, and recovery.

Ellie Fossey
PhD, MSc (Health Psychol), DipCOT(UK)
Professor and Head
Department of Occupational Therapy
Monash University
Melbourne, Australia

Foreword III

When the first version of the Action Over Inertia intervention approach was published in 2010, I found myself more excited about this workbook than other publications that I had seen over the years. It was seminal in providing a manual for practitioners that allowed them to critically look at their practices and ensure that clients become participants in their own journey towards recovery. It also bridged theory and practice in a way that helped professions engage their clients as partners within their own life changes rather than participants. Its approach was simple; we followed Alex and Jamie on the journey towards active societal participation through activity, which allowed Alex to discover his own strengths and solutions from a capability perspective. It provided something that was missing from not only my life as an educator but also working within the inner city community. Students, clinicians, and, more importantly, clients responded to its user-friendly format, and it gave a starting point for recovery-based interventions with clients. The workbook became a permanent fixture in most conversations with clients, students, families, or program funders. It truly was a gift to propel recovery practice forward and filled a need to support clinicians to change their approach to practice. Utilized by multiple professions, it provided a structure that bridged many clinical conversations to the benefit of clients.

In writing this foreword, I was excited to be able to review the changes, but held a little scepticism of what a new version could offer, and concern that it would be less user-friendly. That simply was not true. The changes and additions offered in this book, *Promoting the Activity and Participation of Individuals with Serious Mental Illness*, are refreshing and add essential components to the complexity of our practices. Useful for all practitioners in mental health, it clearly establishes the lens of occupational therapy in recovery thus supporting an occupational base and adds additional strategies to apply this knowledge. Alex and Jamie are still there, however their journey matches the complexity that is found in the practice environment. In addition, this workbook addresses the frustration and challenges faced by all partners in mental health systems as funding continues to evolve. There is special attention to family, culture, and social context in relation to choice and actions related to activity and participation that are clearly challenges in this time in our history. The workbook has added core frameworks that lead to better outcomes. Added to this version is the Do-Live-Well framework, which clearly links activities and practice to health and well-being, a concept often left out of a medical model. In addition, the Capabilities Framework supports practice to engage services in considering their role in promoting activity and participation. To support the use of these two frameworks effectively, there are clear examples of approaches and strategies embedded within the workbook. In addition, strategies to address systematic factors that lead to disincentives are introduced which will assist practitioners and their clients. The worksheets have continued to evolve and are multi layered for those moments when inertia or frustration begins to interfere with activity so the client has the incentive to move forward and the service provider has support in analyzing those moments in practice.

This new version of the workbook is one of those practice supports that should be on every practitioner's desk, wherever their mental health practice is. Whether an early or seasoned practitioner, it provides confidence-focused questions and provides opportunities for clinicians to reflect on their own practices, as well as evaluate their own service delivery. It helps challenge the concepts and social environment that most interfere with client success, and helps put clients in charge of their own destiny through actively engaging them in making their own choices. It may follow Alex and Jamie, but I suspect every practitioner will relate to the issues presented, and be able to benefit by utilizing the strategies put forward to enhance everyday practices and ensure they empower every client to own their own life possibilities.

Elizabeth Taylor PhD
OT(C) FCAOT
Clinical professor emeritus
University of Alberta
Edmonton, Alberta

Preface

It has been over ten years since the first version of the Action Over Inertia intervention approach was published. When it was released, we hoped that our efforts to articulate practices related to activity and participation would resonate with occupational therapists, other service providers, and people with lived experience in the mental health field. We were pleased to see the positive reception to the work. Dissemination occurred rapidly through its translation into several languages, the integration of the approach in recovery-related research projects, its inclusion in curricula for students in occupational therapy and psychosocial rehabilitation, and the offering of many workshops internationally. Besides affirming that we had addressed a need, these dissemination initiatives also provided us the opportunity to gather new ideas, and to consider further the complexities of delivering this intervention approach in practice.

Since publication of the first version, we have heard many stories about the multiple factors at play in facilitating engagement of people with serious mental illness in meaningful activity and participation and of the impacts (anticipated and unanticipated) of this engagement. For example, in Singapore and Taiwan we heard how choices and initiatives related to activity and participation had to be understood and negotiated in a family context, both for cultural and economic reasons. In Qatar we talked with occupational therapists about how activity and participation patterns varied across different populations and we also had the opportunity to consider the application of the approach in substance-use treatment settings. In Kenya we heard about the distress caused by 'idleness' and the pressures this placed on families – but we also heard how changes in activity and participation patterns could contribute to well-being of families, mend damaged social relations, and reduce stigma in the community. In Canada, Australia, Europe, and Israel we learned about how the intervention practices were being adapted to better fit with the local mental health system context. We learned of innovative efforts to adapt the intervention for online delivery by peer providers, to support the transition from homelessness to stable housing, and to address the needs of veterans dealing with mental illness in their transition to civilian life. In this book, we tried to capture these stories as critical elements of the intervention approach.

We also found that discussions of activity and participation in serious mental illness often defaulted to interpretations of the problems as 'negative symptoms', with challenges framed in biomedical and psychological perspectives, leading to a narrow focus on individual-level interventions. For us, it indicated the need to more fully ground the focus of the approach in the understanding of 'what people do', 'how do they do these things', and 'why are people motivated to do what they do – what do they 'get' from this doing?' It pointed out the need to more explicitly develop the theoretical grounding of the intervention approach, and more fully describe how interventions could influence social level factors impacting an individual's activity and participation. We hope that this book, *Promoting the Activity and Participation of Individuals with Serious Mental Illness*, will continue to spark dialogue, motivate implementation of holistic initiatives, and advance innovations in practice.

Finally, we wrote this book in the middle of a global pandemic – and we are still counting down the days until the pandemic-related restrictions can be loosened without ill-effects. Interestingly, the pandemic seems to have generated broad public appreciation for the negative personal and social consequences that can arise with significant disruptions in daily activity and participation patterns. We hope that the lessons learned from the pandemic will continue to advance the profile of health and well-being through activity and participation.

Terry, Megan, Carol, and Shu-Ping

Acknowledgements

We are fortunate to have had many people contribute to this work.

We would like to acknowledge the authors of the first version of the Action Over Inertia intervention approach for their efforts in pioneering this work – Andrea Almas, Andrea Perry, Debbie Radloff-Gabriel, Jennifer Jackson, and Marla Bransfield.

Thanks are extended to the many occupational therapists and other service providers who provided invaluable feedback about the implementation of this intervention approach.

We would like to thank philosopher Dr. Christine Overall for her assistance with unpacking issues related to the ethics of delivering services related to activity and participation.

Finally, we would like to extend our thanks to the many people with lived experience of serious mental illness who informed our understanding of activity and participation in daily life.

Introduction

Alex

Alex is 38 years old and lives in a shared-living home located in a poorer socio-economic district of a mid-sized city. He shares his room with another man. Alex pays for this living arrangement with the money he receives from his government disability pension. His parents live about two hours away by bus and his sister and her family live in his city.

Alex has been hospitalized for treatment of a mental illness twice in the last four years. During his last hospital admission, the community team connected with him to engage him with follow up services in the community. Jamie works for the community mental health team and is one of Alex's primary service providers.

During their first meetings, Jamie tried to get a sense of who Alex was – and what he liked to do. It was difficult for Alex to offer a picture of himself through his activities. He identified few activities in which he regularly engaged beyond basic self-care. In these first meetings Jamie became aware that Alex, like all residents in his home, has no responsibility for the care of house, for the preparation of the meals, or for much of his own living space. Jamie became aware that Alex is socially isolated, despite the almost continual presence of other people in his home. Alex sees his parents and sister infrequently but they speak at least once a week by phone.

At first Alex had trouble talking about his activities today or in the future. He responded to Jamie's conversations with short answers and rarely initiated conversation. He was friendly but rarely smiled or offered much emotion and expression. Generally, he presented as easily overwhelmed during interactions. Sometimes their discussions made him anxious and Jamie was left with mixed feelings from Alex – both that he wanted to be left alone and to receive assistance at the same time.

As Jamie and Alex got to know each other, Alex opened up about his own experience of his daily activities. He described his lifestyle as 'empty' and recalled that it had been a long time since he had anything he could describe as an 'interest'. Indeed, he was unable to spontaneously offer information about his preferences and values in activity. He could remember a time back in his teens when he was involved in leisure activities with his friends, but stated that even then his friends would plan and initiate the activities.

Focused questions:

1. Why are you interested in this intervention approach?
2. How familiar are you with an activity and participation-oriented intervention approach?
3. Have you worked with people who have had activity and participation patterns that you are concerned about? How would you describe these patterns? Why do they raise concerns?
4. Have you worked with people who have activity and participation patterns similar to those demonstrated by Alex? How common are these types of activity and participation issues in your practice?

I.1 Health and Well-Being through Activities and Participation: the Focus of This Intervention Approach

This intervention approach has been designed to address the significant disturbances that people with serious mental illness can experience in finding meaning, health, and well-being from their daily activities and participation.

The philosophical and knowledge foundations of the intervention approach are grounded in the fields of occupational science and occupational therapy. Within these fields the construct of 'occupation' captures the complexity of daily activities and participation: the inherent occupational nature of humans, the qualities and organization of daily activities and participation, their personal and socio-cultural meanings and expression, and their relationship to health, well-being, and human adaptation (Wilcock, 1998; Christiansen & Townsend, 2004).

The focus of this intervention manual is on enabling engagement in patterns of activity and participation that contribute to health and well-being applied to people with serious mental illness. Enabling engagement refers to facilitating the capacity and opportunities for individuals to become 'involved in doing', particularly in a way that promotes experiences of well-being, quality of life, belonging, and personal development (Townsend, Beagan, et al., 2007). The approach highlights several important aspects of this engagement, including the following:

- *Emotional connection* to activities and participation through the experience of 'meaning' are important. A series of guided approaches for systematically considering different dimensions of meaning that might be further developed to facilitate this emotional connection are provided.
- An individual's activity and participation patterns should be considered as an *integrated 'whole'*. This means that rather than attending to discrete activities or specific examples of activity and participation, the focus is on how activity and participation patterns are represented over the course of typical days and weeks, and also over the life course.
- For every individual, today's *activity and participation patterns evolved from a past, and will evolve into future patterns*. The intervention approach considers activity and participation histories to be a foundation for change, and also expects that even small positive changes can influence future activity and participation patterns.
- Any individual's activity and participation patterns have the potential to connect people meaningfully to *the community*. While it is recognized that people naturally demonstrate considerable variation in their social and community connections, the intervention approach does attend to helping people find meaning, health, and well-being through social connection. An important goal is to positively influence the potential for their presence to be respected and their voices to be heard – and counted in their communities.
- The intervention approach considers the location and social position of daily activities and participation, valuing patterns that contribute to making people '*of their community*' rather than just 'in the community'.

Engagement is a complex phenomenon complicated by the fact that the forces that motivate individuals to select and sustain their participation in particular activities and participation patterns are both highly individual and socially bound. There is no one ideal representation of positive engagement, and this always needs to be considered when weighing the extent to which patterns reflect well-being.

I.2 A Word about Language

The concepts of activity and participation are used to describe the focus of this intervention approach. This is in keeping with the framework of the International Classification of Functioning (World Health Organization [WHO], 2001) which distinguishes between activities (execution of tasks or actions by individuals) and participation (involvement in life situations) but ultimately merges them under one heading, 'activities and participation'. We have chosen to maintain this merged concept. Of course, applied in practice, the concepts used should be sensitive to the situation and people involved. For example, occupational therapists use the term 'occupation' to refer to the broad range of meaningful human activity and participation. Conversations with individuals receiving mental health services may see a range of language used to ensure a shared understanding. For example, 'the things you do over your days and weeks' is a phrase that is descriptive and broadly understood.

The focus of the intervention is on activity and participation '*patterns*' rather than on a specific type of activity or participation option. The idea of patterns indicates the importance of focusing on routine, consistency, structure, and trends in activity and participation involvement. It considers not only the types and amount of activity and participation, but also how they are organized in daily life.

Service providers using this intervention in practice are encouraged to find a language for change that resonates with individuals served. For example, some individuals may be familiar with and connect with the concept of setting goals for change in activity and participation patterns. Others may connect more with language such as 'personal projects', 'lifestyle changes', or 'making changes to the way I spend my time'. The important point is to remain sensitive to the experiences and needs of individuals served and to agree on language that will motivate and focus change.

I.3 Assumptions Underlying the Intervention Approach

There are six assumptions that underlie this intervention approach.

1. Disengagement from the activities and participation that are linked to human health and well-being is viewed as a significant issue for those with serious mental illness. First, the sheer number of people with serious mental illness impacted is significant. Larry

Davidson has described the prevalence of this among community mental health programs:

> It is one of the first and most common complaints … clients are not motivated, they don't want to change their behavior, they won't follow through with their plans or recommendations, and, to be blunt, it is hard to rouse their clients from the 'inertia' that appears to have settled in.
>
> (Krupa et al., 2010, p. vi)

Research examining the activity and participation patterns of people with serious mental illness shows patterns such as high levels of inactivity, limited participation in productive activities, passive leisure pursuits, and reversal of day/night activities to name a few (Eklund et al., 2009). In addition, first person narratives often highlight the distress and despair associated with the lived experience of problematic activity and participation patterns. Perhaps the most well-known example of this comes from Patricia Deegan (1988) who, in her seminal writings on recovery, wrote of this despair: 'As for the present it was a numbing succession of meaningless days and nights, in a void in which we had no place, no use and no reason to be' (p. 12).

2. The second assumption is that, historically, practice that has focused on the activity and participation experiences of people with serious mental illness has lacked clear articulation, coherence, and specification of principles guiding practice. Consequently, it has lacked a strong theoretical, research, and evidence base that can raise its profile as a standard for mental health services. A notable exception to this assumption has been the advancement in the mental health field of a particular form of activity and participation – employment, particularly in the form of supported employment (see for example, Drake et al., 2012; Kinoshita et al., 2013).

3. The intervention approach is based on the assumption that the disruptions in activity and participation experienced by people with serious mental illness results from a **complex interplay of influences**. The intervention approach asks service providers to integrate all of these considerations in their efforts.

4. The intervention approach developed in this manual has been developed with a view to promoting a **spirit of interprofessional practice,** *including peer providers and supports*. Although the philosophical, theoretical, and practice elements of the approach come from the field of occupational science and occupational therapy, the magnitude of the issue and the interprofessional nature of mental health and social service delivery speaks to the importance of developing practice structures that will ensure all providers

are in a position to support health promoting activity and participation patterns. Indeed, the nature of practice directed to activity and participation depends on good **cross-sectoral** understanding, communication, and collaborations.

5. The intervention is intended as a guide to promote practice in the area of activity and participation. Effective implementation will depend on the **sensitivity, reasoning, and investment** of service providers. For example, while the manual is organized by chapter in a linear way, the realities of practice require sensitivity to the complexities of people's everyday lives and adaptations to the practice approach to meet the needs of individuals in a timely way.

6. While the intervention approach offered in this book offers a structured foundation, advancements in this area of practice will require **ongoing sharing and dialogue** among service providers and with people with lived experience and their families.

I.4 Conceptual Foundations

The development of this intervention approach was guided by five conceptual models or frameworks: International Classification of Functioning, Disability and Health (ICF); Canadian Model of Occupational Performance and Engagement (CMOP-E); Recovery; Do-Live-Well; and Capabilities Framework. They are described briefly here and introduced again throughout the book. Service providers are encouraged to become more familiar with the focus, purpose, philosophy, and critical elements of these conceptual foundations.

International Classification of Functioning Disability and Health (ICF)

The ICF (WHO, 2001) is the World Health Organization's framework for describing and measuring health and disability at both individual and population levels. The framework identifies a comprehensive range of activity and participation domains that are associated with health and well-being, and encompass a life lived fully with meaning. While the ICF offers no specific guidance related to practice, it is meant to have an international and system-wide influence, including: the development of a common language and agreement about core concepts for human function and standards for practice, measurement and monitoring practices, attention to comprehensive outcomes associated with health, and the advancement of disability policy and law (WHO, 2013). International efforts have seen the development of useful and easily accessed resources for the mental health field, such as the Core Categories for schizophrenia (see www.icf-research-branch.org/icf-core-sets-projects2/mental-health/icf-core-set-for-schizophrenia).

Canadian Model of Occupational Performance and Engagement (CMOP-E)

The CMOP-E (Townsend & Polatajko, 2007) is a conceptual framework that focuses on occupation as fundamental to human health and well-being. The term 'occupation' is used by occupational scientists and therapists to capture the complex interplay between individuals, their activities and participation, their environments, and how they are aligned with human health and well-being. The CMOP-E assigns a spiritual element to occupations in recognition of their capacity to bring meaning in life. It also provides a framework for considering the cognitive, affective, and physical aspects of occupations as well as the cultural, institutional, physical, and social environment components.

A particular strength of the CMOP-E as a guiding framework is its concern with the individual's *experience* of occupation in addition to the *performance* (or 'doing') aspects of occupation. It provides a framework for understanding and addressing the fact that serious mental illness can disrupt an individual's emotional connection to occupation.

Recovery and Serious Mental Illness

Recovery has gained widespread acceptance as a paradigm for service design and delivery in mental health. Distinct from recovery as cure, recovery has been conceptualized as a personal journey whereby the individual comes to live a life of meaning in spite of mental illness. While individuals with mental illness lead their own recovery, service providers, programs, and systems can enable recovery. Activities and participation have been recognized as key elements of the recovery process by people with serious mental illness (Drake & Whitley, 2014).

Do-Live-Well (DLW)

The DLW framework advances the evidence-based links between activities and participation and health and well-being (Gewurtz et al., 2016; Moll et al., 2014; see www.dolivewell.ca). DLW is based on the idea that *what people do* in their day-to-day lives matters to health and well-being. The framework organizes the relationship between daily life activities and a range of health and well-being outcomes as influenced by several dimensions of experience, activity patterns, and personal and social forces.

Capabilities Framework

The capabilities framework developed by Sen (2000) and Nussbaum (2003, 2011) is a theoretical perspective of social justice that focuses on situations where the expression of the full potential of people is compromised.

Capabilities in this framework are defined as 'freedoms' that 'not only make our lives richer and more unfettered, but also allows us to be fuller social persons, exercising our own volitions and interacting with—and influencing—the world in which we live' (Sen, 2000, p. 15). The central concept of *capability* refers to what people are actually able to do and to be. Injustice occurs where human dignity and well-being is compromised and the guarantee of basic human capabilities falls below an acceptable threshold for particular communities and populations. The framework thus highlights the moral imperative of supporting individuals to have the capabilities to live the kinds of lives they value.

Consistent with each of these conceptual models and frameworks is a foundation set of values and principles that guide the practice of the Action Over Inertia intervention approach:

- *Person-centred practice* – The practices are designed to identify and respect the strengths, preferences, interests, needs, and obligations of the individual served. Service providers must remain sensitive to the fact that the choices and alternatives, and an individual's sense of agency with respect to these, may have been seriously undermined in the context of their daily life experiences with mental illness. While the service provider has knowledge and expertise related to activities and participation, activity patterns, and health and well-being, the individual served is respected as the 'expert of his/her own life', and as having the capacity to carve a life of meaning beyond the experience of mental illness.
- *Practice is a partnership* – The intervention approach encourages a partnership between the provider and the individual served. Given that the approach is designed for individuals who have experienced profound disruption or disengagement from meaningful activities and participation, the provider will need to be sensitive to the amount of support and guidance an individual requires, while always respecting the individual's ultimate ownership of the process.
- *Respect for diversity* – The activities and participation that people engage in are reflective of and enriched by their cultural and community connections. The approaches used in this workbook are meant to enable the recovery of meaningful activities and participation in daily life in a manner that respects and celebrates diversity. Practice is also oriented to acknowledging that for individuals served, equity and inclusion are not always fundamental characteristics of the context for their activity and participation.
- *Citizenship, integration, and inclusion* – Initiatives focused on activities and participation for people with serious mental illness have a long history in mental health care and service systems. However, they have

not always been developed and delivered with an understanding that their activity and participation patterns should give them access to social status, voice and influence, and a sense of belonging and mattering in society and their communities. While the activities and participation patterns developed will be highly individual, the service provider needs to remain sensitive to the fact these activities are socially situated. Attending to the broader social meaning of activity and participation patterns and how they are reflective of social justice, full social inclusion, and the rights and responsibilities of full citizenship is considered integral to the process.

I.5 Practices Used to Promote Change

The specific intervention approaches used in this workbook integrate various practices related to supporting health and well-being through activity and participation. Each intervention approach has a growing evidence-base. These practices are described briefly below.

Enabling Engagement

Practices that enable engagement create the conditions for individuals to understand and reflect upon their personal activity and participation patterns and to evolve new and meaningful opportunities and potentials. Enabling skills in the context of profound disengagement focuses on creating the momentum to overcome the inertia and the associated apathy, lethargy, and inactivity. These practice skills can be described as the formation of a relational bond that serves to 'exhort people to action'. For example, skills underlying engagement practices include: building trust, sparking hope, supporting the 'just right' challenge, involving in 'doing', tapping in to potential, identifying and affirming strengths, values, and potentials, supporting new ways of being and doing, sharing in playfulness and celebration, and valuing activity and participation in its many forms (Barris et al., 1988; Krupa, 2016; Townsend & Polatajko, 2007).

Enabling Performance and Experience

Along with focusing on 'what people do' this intervention approach highlights the need for service providers to understand the 'why', 'when', 'where', and 'how' related to what they do. The practice skills central to the intervention are directed to eliciting personal narratives about activity and participation, interpreting activity and participation patterns, and collaborating with individuals to determine the nature of the changes in activity and participation patterns and associated personal/environmental level supports. Beyond the focus on the functional aspects of performing activity and participation, practice attends to the experience that people have when they engage, and

supporting positive experiences associated with health and well-being.

Envisioning and Creating Opportunities

Where the life of an individual or population of people is characterized by activity and participation constraints and deprivation, a critical practice skill is the ability to envision, innovate, create, and expand the benefits of real-world opportunities. This shifts the traditional focus of mental health services on the individuals themselves, to the broad range of life activities, their conditions, and contexts. It is based on an understanding that while health promoting activities and participation are ordinary and every-day, their structure and operation in society are intricate and their potential benefits powerful.

Psychoeducation

Psychoeducation focuses on providing individuals with information so that they are in a better position to understand their illness and health experiences and actively participate in changes that can promote their health and well-being. Psychoeducation is believed to have the potential to build trusting alliances with service providers (Cho et al., 2016). There is much that individuals served can learn about the association between serious mental illness and activity and participation and ultimately health and well-being.

Complementary Intervention Approaches

It may be that the effectiveness of the Action Over Inertia approach can be enhanced by the introduction of complementary interventions. For example, many people with serious mental illness will experience significant cognitive impairments that interfere with their ability to choose, perform, and enjoy activities. Evidence-based cognitive adaptation training (perhaps targeting apathy), could be applied to promote the likelihood of achieving positive changes in activity and participation patterns (Kidd et al., 2014). Likewise, focused interventions such as cognitive behavioural therapy (Kukla et al., 2020; Lecomte et al., 2020) and social cognition training (Bartholomeusz et al., 2013) may be helpful in targeting, respectively, problems associated with thoughts and feeling patterns and functioning in social situations. All have potential to interfere with engagement in activities and participation patterns aligned with health and well-being.

I.6 Action Over Inertia and Evidence-Based Practice

Since the inception of Action Over Inertia, efforts have been directed to advancing the evidence-base related to promoting health through activity and participation in the mental health field. A pilot-test, using a randomized controlled design of the first version of Action Over Inertia, focused on individuals receiving services from Assertive Community Treatment teams. It demonstrated positive changes in the balance of activity patterns with less time spent in sleep and incidental naps, and more time distributed across self-care, leisure, and productivity. The qualitative aspect of this evaluation demonstrated positive experiences with the intervention by both occupational therapists and by recipients of the intervention approach, but also provided important feedback about areas for refinement (Edgelow & Krupa, 2011). A study conducted in Germany demonstrated positive change with an increase in time directed to self-care (Höhl et al., 2017). A qualitative study examined the experiences of individuals receiving community residential services in Australia who received Action Over Inertia in a group format. The findings highlight the extent to which inertia impacted daily routines. The experiences provided findings consistent with the importance of addressing inertia, the nature of the challenges experienced, and the processes inherent to the intervention approach that were beneficial. It also added information about the potential benefits and drawbacks of using a group to implement the approach (Rees et al., in press). Psychometric testing of the main outcome measure in the first version of the approach, the Activity Engagement Measure (see Appendix B), has demonstrated good reliability and validity. In this second version of the intervention, efforts have been made to develop the theoretical foundations of the intervention, to provide a more robust description of the intervention approaches, and to specifically outline key competencies. Changes to the main measure capture more specifically the experience of 'meanings' associated with activity and participation. With these changes, critical components of the intervention are more explicit, as are elements of health and well-being, advancing elements critical to establishing an evidence base.

I.7 Using This Intervention in Practice

This intervention approach has been developed by a group of occupational therapists for occupational therapists and other service providers, including peer supports and providers, who are committed to ensuring that individuals who experience serious mental illness have access to opportunities and supports to enjoy the many health and well-being benefits associated with a range of daily activities and participation. While details related to specific approaches and interventions are provided, they do not capture the depth of knowledge related to activity and participation that has accumulated. The implementation of the practices outlined in this intervention approach will be strengthened when providers possess a foundational knowledge-base related to activity, participation, and health and well-being – or have access to colleagues

or other service providers who can provide consultation, supervision, and share knowledge.

The strategies and tools developed in this intervention book have been designed to have maximum application in the field, but there will be circumstances where they cannot meet the unique needs of particular individuals or populations. In these cases, it is expected that some of the language or tools used will be adapted. For example, where literacy levels are low, adaptation of worksheets will be necessary. Where individuals served are averse to worksheets, alternate strategies to deliver the intervention approach in a collaborative manner will be necessary.

Each of the chapters in this intervention workbook is organized using the same structure.

1. An abstract, which describes the focus of the chapter and itemizes the organization of sections
2. Vignette of Alex and Jamie illustrating the concepts and critical ingredients of the intervention approach covered in the specific chapter
3. The vignette is followed by a few focused questions, to encourage reflection on the content and its relevance to situations encountered in everyday practice
4. A list of worksheets and resources provided in the chapter
5. Description of the intervention approach, with references to the vignettes, and the associated worksheets and resources
6. Each chapter concludes with a summary of key competencies associated with the practices outlined

In addition to the vignette of Alex and Jamie, two other vignettes of Sol and Ananthi are offered in Appendix A. These vignettes offer the opportunity to compare and contrast important factors such as the influence of housing stability, age/developmental stage, family involvement, cultural factors, etc.

I.8 Key Competencies

The key competencies associated with this chapter are primarily related to the attitudes, knowledge, and skills that reflect a readiness to practice the Action Over Inertia intervention approach. They include:

- Openness to including activity and participation as integral components of health and well-being.
- Being curious about 'what people do' in their daily lives, and why and how they do these things.
- Holding a belief that people with serious mental illness have the capacities and the right to experience health and well-being through activity and participation.
- Being sensitive to diverse experiences with activity and participation.

- Holding a belief in the values and principles underlying the intervention approach.
- Accessing and synthesizing information and knowledge about the concepts and conceptual models related to the Action Over Inertia intervention approach.

- Engaging in ongoing self-evaluation and reflection related to the attitudes, knowledge, and practice skills associated with this intervention approach.
- Identifying and collaborating with others who have expert levels of knowledge related to health and well-being through activity and participation.

1 Preparing to Use This Workbook

Initially Alex was uncertain about discussing his daily activities with Jamie. Although he experienced distress and unhappiness with his current activities, he became noticeably anxious at even the thought of making changes to his daily activity and participation patterns.

Jamie reflected on the knowledge gained about Alex that led to interpreting his activity and participation patterns as unlikely to promote health and well-being. Jamie then discussed these concerns with colleagues who also knew Alex and asked for their perspective. Jamie and other service providers agreed that Alex's daily activity and participation patterns were largely passive, and it seemed that he spent large parts of his days without any defined or recurring activities. Overall, they expressed concern that he had few opportunities for meaningful and fulfilling social and community connections.

Jamie supported Alex in a process of self-reflection about his activity and participation patterns. Jamie introduced Alex to the worksheets, presenting them as offering a way to consider what benefits he gets (or might get) from his activities and participation. While completing the worksheets, Jamie briefly described the meaning of some of the items. For example, Alex was unsure about the meaning of 'values' as it related to activities, and Jamie explained that when people are involved in activities and participation that they consider important they can experience a sense of well-being. Although he was tentative and cautious, Alex's own reflections were consistent with what Jamie observed. He agreed that his daily activities were bringing little satisfaction and offered him few opportunities to develop interests. Alex mentioned that his parents would probably like to see him involved in more activities, and participating in more things like other people his own age. Jamie shared information about the connection between activity patterns and health and well-being. Jamie also provided Alex with a bit of information about the link between problems of mental health, like his own, and activity and participation. Jamie assured Alex they would move ahead to address his patterns at a pace he was comfortable with and remain sensitive to his needs and wishes. Jamie told him, 'You know Alex, you are the one in charge of how you live your day-to-day life, but I will try to support you to find satisfaction and meaning in what you do'.

Focused Questions:

1. How familiar are you with an activity and participation-oriented intervention approach?
2. Think of a time, in practice, when you were concerned about the activity and participation patterns of an individual you served? What was concerning about these patterns?
3. At a recent workshop on the Action Over Inertia intervention approach, a mental health service provider reflected, 'You know, I never really thought about what the people I see in my daily practice will do during the day, after our visit'. How does this compare to your own practice experience?

This chapter includes the following worksheets:

Worksheet 1.1: Making appraisals about activity and participation patterns explicit (service provider version)

Worksheet 1.2: Evaluating the benefits experienced through current activity and participation patterns (service provider version)

Worksheet 1.3: My current activity and participation patterns

Worksheet 1.4: Benefits of my current activity and participation patterns

Worksheet 1.5: What do others say about my activity and participation patterns?

DOI: 10.4324/9781003111368-1

1.1 Making Appraisals of Activity and Participation Patterns Explicit

The Action Over Inertia intervention approach was designed specifically to address the needs of those individuals who, in the context of serious mental illness, have been alienated from and/or deprived of meaningful activity and participation opportunities. The approaches and practices in this chapter will encourage both the service provider and the individual served to reflect on activity and participation patterns from a range of perspectives. This chapter focuses on promoting the development of collaborative decisions directed to realizing positive changes in activity and participation patterns.

Worksheet 1.1: Making appraisals about activity and participation patterns explicit (service provider version) and *Worksheet 1.2: Evaluating benefits experienced through current activity and participation patterns (service provider version)* give service providers a framework to consider their perspective on the activity and participation patterns of an individual. The service provider considers each of the dimensions of activity and participation and reflects on whether it provides a good description of the individual's current status. Where specific dimensions are checked, the service provider is encouraged to identify some specific examples to provide clarity to a thought or opinion. A service provider who is clear about their own evaluation, with examples, is in a better position to engage in meaningful discussions with an individual: discussions that may include contrasting understandings and opinions. Jamie, in our opening vignette, was able to use the worksheets to gather information and reflections from other colleagues who know Alex, and also to point out to Alex where they had common concerns.

Service providers who work in an interdisciplinary setting may find it useful to engage other service providers in the reflection process. This allows for a broader picture of the individual's activity and participation patterns and engages other providers in recognizing the importance of activities and participation in the health and well-being of people served. There is no 'correct' pattern that signifies health and well-being, but the reflection worksheets provide the opportunity to clarify assumptions and prepares providers to speak to the individual served in a way that promotes their own personal reflections and discussion, builds trust, and ultimately supports collaborative decision making.

1.2 Supporting Consideration of Current Activity and Participation Patterns

The decision to make changes in activity and participation patterns, and the nature of those changes, depends on the involvement of the individual receiving services. For people living with serious mental illness, this is particularly essential because too often they have not been involved in important decisions and opportunities regarding their own lives and well-being.

Individuals who experience profound disengagement from important and meaningful activities and participation will likely be hesitant. Encouraging the individual to adopt an expanded view of their own activity and participation potential can help alleviate concerns. To encourage an informed decision about involvement, the individual needs to be aware of the potential benefits to be gained and how they relate specifically to their own situation.

Worksheet 1.3: My current activity and participation patterns and *Worksheet 1.4: Benefits of my current activity and participation patterns* exactly mirror the reflection processes described for the service provider earlier in this chapter, providing an opportunity for discussion about differing or similar perspectives. The third and final worksheet in this section, *Worksheet 1.5: What do others say about my activity and participation patterns?* provides an opportunity for individuals to consider their own activity and participation patterns in relation to the perspectives of other important people in their lives.

1.3 Collaborative Evaluation of Activity Patterns

The worksheets provide the service provider and the individual with the opportunity to share their respective perspectives on activity and participation patterns and encourage collaboration in considering if change is desired and what the nature of these changes might be. Reviewing and discussing both the service provider's and individual's personal perceptions of current activity and participation patterns is meant to encourage informed decision-making.

Although the reflection activities in this chapter are meant to be quick and simple, the reflection process itself may be overwhelming for the individual. If, for example, this is the first time the individual has explicitly and directly considered their activity and participation patterns, they may be surprised and demoralized by how constrained and restricted they have become. Good practice skills will motivate and mobilize involvement while allaying personal concerns and reservations. The individual may, like Alex, benefit from some clarification about elements of the worksheets, or help in identifying specific examples that might be entered on the worksheets and assurances that positive changes can take many forms.

1.4 Considering the Activity and Participation Patterns of People Served by the Program or Service

While the practice approaches outlined in this chapter focus primarily on working with *individuals*, reflections about the activity patterns at the population level (i.e., the *group of people* served by a service or program) are also important. The evaluation of how activity and participation patterns are expressed across a range of people served has relevance, as it can actually facilitate the process of enabling change for any individual. For example, if many of the people receiving mental health services from a program experience problematic activity and participation patterns, the service provider might consider how practice approaches with any one individual might be applied more broadly in the program. The service provider might consider how others who were successful in making positive activity changes might be involved as role models, mentors, or personal supports. The mental health field is now replete with examples of peer supports, providers, and mentors engaging with individuals to promote health and well-being (see for example, Mahlke et al., 2014).

1.5 Tips for Introducing the Workbook and Interventions

Service providers who address the activity and participation patterns of individuals with serious mental illness who are profoundly disengaged from activities and participation will always walk a fine line. While they may intend their approaches and practices to be perceived as supportive and collaborative, they run the risk of being experienced as coercive. Sullivan & Carpenter (2010) described how, even with the best of intentions, community mental health services can be delivered with practices that are coercive in manner. Subsequently, intervention approaches need to be delivered in a manner that respects the fine balance between encouraging/facilitating and judging/controlling.

Practice skills that authentically engage individuals are those that are oriented to 'spark visions of possibilities and hope' (Townsend et al., 2007, p. 114) in the individual served.

The following tips are offered. Providers who are sensitive to the status and needs of individuals served will apply these suggestions at critical moments as necessary:

- Explain the background of the change intervention to the individual.
- Describe the evidence that shows a link between living with mental illness and disruption in daily activity and participation patterns. Highlight that these disruptions can be addressed.
- Present activity and participation as a public health issue – something that impacts all community members.

- Reinforce the notion that many people living with serious mental illness report that through involvement in activities and participation they have been able to realize positive changes.
- Introduce individuals to resources developed by people living with serious mental illness (e.g., websites, first person narratives, etc.) that describe the process of moving from inertia to well-being through activity and participation.
- Reassure that any plans to change activity and participation patterns will be designed and carried out with sensitivity to personal needs and to ensure that process is rewarding and fulfilling.
- Remind the individual what *benefits* they may gain.
- Demonstrate a belief in the individual's potential and the possibilities that might be realized through the change process.
- Remind the individual that you will ensure that they receive the support they need and want throughout the change process.
- Orient the individual to this intervention approach and clarify expectations and roles.

1.6 Key Competencies

The key competencies associated with this chapter are primarily related to the attitudes and knowledge and skills that engage the individual served in considering personal activity and participation as an area of life where change could be both possible and beneficial. The goal of the key competencies is to secure a collaborative investment in proceeding with processes to address activity and participation patterns. These key competencies include:

- Making explicit judgements and interpretations about an individual's activity and participation patterns.
- Raising the profile of activity and participation patterns among other service providers.
- Understanding the activity and participation patterns of the people served by the program/service.
- Engaging an individual in personal reflections about their activity and participation patterns.
- Collaborating with an individual served to make decisions related to activity and participation.
- Applying supportive processes to enable an individual's engagement in the change process.

Making appraisals about activity and participation patterns explicit (service provider version)

Name of individual served: _____Date:_____

Service provider's name: _____

Criteria	✓	*Examples*
The person's daily activity and participation demonstrate an imbalance between self-care, productivity, rest, and leisure		
The person spends a large amount of time without defined activity and participation on a day-to-day basis		
Much of the individual's day is spent in passive activities or rest		
The person's daily activities and participation limit their contact with others		
The person's daily activities and participation limit their access to a range of community environments		
The person cannot identify activities and participation that are meaningful or of personal interest		
There is little evidence that the person is involved in daily activities and participation that are of personal interest or meaning		
The person experiences distress, or is easily overwhelmed by activity and participation		
The person's involvement in activity and participation is characterized by a limited experience of enjoyment		

If you have checked off **three or more** of these criteria, this individual may benefit from intervention approaches directed to their activity and participation patterns.

Evaluating the benefits experienced through current activity and participation patterns (service provider version)

Name of individual served: _____ Date: _____

Service provider's name: _____

This Person Engages in Activities and Participation Patterns that Provide the Opportunity for…	✓	*Examples/Comments*
Skill and/or knowledge development		
Making a contribution to society		
Physical activity and bodily movement		
The enjoyment of beautiful things		
Self-expression and creativity		
A range of social interactions		
Meeting personal goals, experiencing accomplishment		
Expressing personal values		
Earning a personal income		
Giving to others, such as family or friends		

Check 7–10: Experiences a full range of well-being and health benefits through activity and participation

Check 4–6: Experiences of well-being and health through activity and participation are compromised

Check 3 or less: Experiences of well-being and health through activity and participation are seriously limited

My current activity and participation patterns

Name: _____ Date: _____

Consider each statement and check all that apply.

Criteria	✓	*Examples*
My days are not balanced with time for fun, work, taking care of myself, and rest		
I have lots of time, but nothing to do		
I do not have a regular routine		
I don't see many other people during my day or week or do many things with other people		
I do not go to many different places to do things during my day or week		
I can't think of things I do that are really enjoyable to me		
I get easily upset or overwhelmed when I do activities		
I wish that I could find some things to do that are really enjoyable to me		
There are things I would like to do, but there are barriers to why I don't do them, such as lack of money, transportation, or a friend to go with		

Are you generally satisfied with your activity and participation opportunities? Add any other thoughts or ideas here:

_____

_____

_____

Benefits of my current activities and participation patterns

Worksheet 1.4

Name: _____   Date: _____

Check all of the items that apply to you.

My daily activities and participation give me the opportunity to…	✓	Examples/Comments
Develop new skills and knowledge		
Feel as though I am making a valuable contribution to society		
Be physically active and move my body		
Enjoy beautiful parts of life, such as nature, music, and art		
Express my thoughts and feelings		
Interact with other people socially		
Feel as though I have accomplished something		
Express values that are personally important to me		
Earn a personal income		
Interact with important people in my life (family, friends, etc.)		

What do others say about my activity and participation patterns?

Name: _____ Date: _____

Circle the most appropriate response to each statement below:

1. People tell me that I should be more active throughout the day

   NEVER   **SOMETIMES**   **OFTEN**

2. People tell me I need to find things to do

   NEVER   **SOMETIMES**   **OFTEN**

3. People sometimes question if I am happy with my activities

   NEVER   **SOMETIMES**   **OFTEN**

4. People have told me I should socialize and interact more with others

   NEVER   **SOMETIMES**   **OFTEN**

5. People worry that I have nothing to look forward to during my typical days

   NEVER   **SOMETIMES**   **OFTEN**

6. People tell me I should get more involved in my community

   NEVER   **SOMETIMES**   **OFTEN**

7. People tell me I should get out to visit different places in my community more often

   NEVER   **SOMETIMES**   **OFTEN**

2 Understanding Personal Activity and Participation Patterns

With Jamie's support, Alex gathered information about his typical daily activities and participation patterns. Jamie explained to Alex how 'time-use logs' could be used to collect information in a structured way. They selected two 'typical' days approximately one week apart. On the first day, Alex felt unsure about completing the log and Jamie met with him the following day to review his activities and they completed the time-use log together. Jamie noticed that with some reminders and prompting, Alex expanded his reporting. For example, he forgot to mention that he helped the owner of his home bring in groceries. Following that first experience with the log, Alex felt sure enough to complete the second day on his own, but Jamie and Alex still met to review and expand upon his daily activities.

Alex and Jamie reserved time to review the two time-use logs together. They considered just how much they actually represented 'typical' days. They noted that even though he lived with several people his activities mostly happened alone. Most of the routine structure in his day happened around self-care activities. Much of his time was spent in sleep or rest. His leisure activities were mostly watching television, although he could not identify any particular television shows that he routinely watched and enjoyed. Most of his activities happened close to his home. He indicated that he preferred to walk in the neighbourhood late at night, when he could not sleep and there were fewer people around, but sometimes being out in the dark made him anxious and increased the symptoms of his mental illness. Alex seemed dismayed by this picture of his activities, and Jamie suggested that they make special note of other activities he sometimes engages in to round out the picture – such as speaking with his sister on the phone, shopping for personal items, and attending his health-related appointments. With Jamie's help, Alex completed ***Worksheet 2.15: A measure of my health and well-being through activity and participation***. Overall, he thought he probably could benefit from more opportunities in all of the areas identified. Alex indicated that he used to be involved in a broader range of things. He could use more physical activity and movement and agreed that he was far more sedentary throughout the day compared to when he was younger. He liked the idea that he might be able to improve his finances. Alex recognized that his social contacts were limited, and while he saw himself as a loner, he did value his connections to his family. He was cautious about the meaning of this information, and Jamie reassured him that they would proceed in way that met his needs and preferences.

Focused Questions:

1. What different methods have you used to collect information about activity and participation patterns? What has been your experience with these methods?
2. What activity and participation patterns do you think are associated with health and well-being?
3. How do you think the activity and participation patterns of people with serious mental illness compare to their age and gender-matched peers in the general population?
4. Complete a time-use log to collect information about your own activity and participation patterns. What was your experience of tracking your activities? What did you learn about your activity and participation patterns?

This chapter includes 15 worksheets:

Worksheet 2.1: Daily time-use log
Worksheet 2.2: Considering the variety in my activities and participation patterns

DOI: 10.4324/9781003111368-2

Worksheet 2.3: Considering the balance in my activity and participation patterns

Worksheet 2.4: Exploring values and beliefs influencing activity and participation patterns

Worksheet 2.5: How do I take care of myself through my activities and participation?

Worksheet 2.6: Do I have opportunities to stimulate my mind and my senses?

Worksheet 2.7: Are my activities and participation giving me enough physical activity and movement?

Worksheet 2.8: Considering how I express my identity through my activities and participation

Worksheet 2.9: Developing knowledge, abilities, and potential through my activities and participation

Worksheet 2.10: How do my activities and participation give me the chance for joy and pleasure?

Worksheet 2.11: How do I connect to others through my activities and participation?

Worksheet 2.12: Do I have the opportunity to contribute to my community and society through my activities and participation?

Worksheet 2.13: Can I build prosperity and security through my activities and participation?

Worksheet 2.14: What community environments do I access in my activities and participation?

Worksheet 2.15: A measure of my health and well-being through activity and participation

This chapter includes the following resource materials:

Resource 2.1: Daily activity codes
Resource 2.2: Levels of engagement in activity and participation

2.1 Collecting Information about Activity and Participation Patterns

The process of collecting information involves individuals in considering their current activity and participation patterns with a view to making informed decisions about possible changes and their associated benefits. There are a variety of tools and resources available to develop a collaborative understanding of activity and participation patterns – social role checklists, interest checklists, and leisure inventories. Occupational therapists have developed a range of tools to collect information about activities and participation patterns from a variety of perspectives. For example, occupational balance questionnaires have been developed to evaluate the nature and variety of activities engaged in, as well as satisfaction experienced (see for example, Wagman & Håkansson, 2014). These approaches and tools are helpful and can be used to complement the Action Over Inertia approach.

In this intervention approach, the method used to collect information about activity and participation patterns is the time-use log or daily time diary. Time-use logs have people track *what they actually do* over the course of a day or more. This approach has the advantage of recognizing that, when asked 'what they do', people may identify activities and participation that they may not currently be engaged in. Alex in the opening vignette, for example, indicated that he was raised in a semi-rural area and that he liked to fish. However, discussions reflecting on his time-use patterns indicated that he had not been fishing for several years. Likewise, the approach has the potential to identify activities that are done with some routine but overlooked. Alex's time-use log was filled with time where he initially indicated that he did 'nothing', but with further discussion it was found that during his 'no activity' times, he would passively watch television, sit out on the house patio for a change of scenery, or take unplanned naps.

The use of time-use logs has an established history in the population health field. Many countries collect time-use data on their populations with a view to social policy development, planning infrastructure, and evaluating change over time. The data from time-use logs can help policy makers with informed planning related to addressing commuting time of workers, gender imbalances in activity and participation patterns, and the patterns of vulnerable and high risk groups (see Statistics Canada, 2019). The study and practical application of time-use diaries has extended to those with disabilities and persistent health conditions where activity and participation patterns are disrupted (see for example, Anand & Ben-Shalom, 2014; Enam et al., 2018; Katz & Morris, 2007; Pentland & McColl, 2007).

In the mental health field, time-use diaries have been applied to support specific psychological interventions such as cognitive behavioural therapy, with the goal of making explicit the association between thought patterns and moods, and activities and situations encountered in daily life (see for example, Tallon et al., 2019). However, distinct from these approaches, time-use logs in this intervention approach are used with the purpose of *informing and understanding what people do, what health and well-being benefits they receive from these activity and participation patterns, and how the patterns might be modified and supported to effect positive change.*

Worksheet 2.1: Daily time-use log is a structured format for the collection of information about activity and participation patterns that occur during 'typical' days. This is relatively undemanding and uncomplicated, designed specifically to reduce the likelihood of overwhelming individuals and facilitating investment in the collection of meaningful information.

Collecting time-use information over two or more 'typical' days (i.e., days representative of activities and participation that are usually carried out) helps to provide a more complete picture of activity and participation patterns. Time-use data can be collected by the individual independently, once they are oriented to the log. Some people prefer to use the time-use log as a guide during the selected days, and then to complete the information collaboratively with a service provider. Others will benefit from completing the time-use log with support and prompting.

Several time-use/activity log applications have been developed and some are free of charge. For individuals with access to smartphone technology, these applications may be a useful as a way to keep track of activities in real time, then coupled with conversations about aspects of engagement including social contacts, location, experience of the activity, etc.

The vignette at the beginning of this section illustrates several strategies used to support Alex's sustained investment in the process: prompting, expanding, exploring, and perhaps most important, conveying a genuine interest in Alex's daily activities and participation. Individuals may need assistance in expanding the log to be an accurate representation of time use and to ensure that it reflects activity and participation strengths.

The time-use log has three columns to be completed:

- The first column is used to record activity and participation at specific time periods. Encourage as many details as possible and expand when necessary. Think of this column as the 'what' of activity.
- The second column is for the location where the activity and participation occurred. Individuals are encouraged to make note of different home and community locations where activities are carried out. Think of this column as the 'where' of activity and participation.
- The third column asks if anyone else was present. The individual reports if anyone else was sharing the environment, even if not actively interacting with the individual. Think of this as the 'with whom' column.

The application of time-use strategies to understand activity and participation patterns needs to be sensitive to the specific needs of individuals served. Service providers may need to consider the cognitive and emotional demands of the task and provide support accordingly. Given that individuals served may not be familiar with the approach, they may benefit from information about the approach and its intended outcomes.

A particularly important consideration is what information are individuals likely *not* to report and share without direct consideration. While 'what did you do with your day' is a common question in social interactions, generally the unspoken rule tends to be that the response will include only activities that are considered socially accepted and legitimate. Yet, for example, people may engage in a range of activities associated with substance use on a regular basis. Supporting individuals in identifying and discussing these is important for not only developing a full understanding of activity and participation

patterns, but also to contribute to planning for change. For example, for some individuals smoking may be the primary activity throughout the day. Although the use of substances and alcohol may pose a risk to health, the activities associated with using may be imbued with considerable positive meanings for the individual that are not otherwise accessed – such as earning an income, access to a social network, moving around in the community, looking after others, developing a knowledge and skill set, etc. The nature of the substance use activities, their expression in daily life activities, and the meanings they hold will be important to consider in planning and support.

2.2 Reflecting on Activity and Participation Patterns

Collecting information about daily activity and participation patterns provides a foundation for reflecting on how these patterns are impacting well-being, quality of life, and health. The guided reflections suggested in this workbook are organized by three broad perspectives. These include reflections about: (1) variety, balance, and structure of activity and participation; (2) alignment of patterns with values, beliefs, family and cultural context; and (3) opportunities to experience the health and well-being dimensions of activity and participation.

Providers need to be sensitive to the fact that individuals who might benefit from this intervention approach may have come to their current activity and participation patterns through complex and interacting factors, many of which were beyond their control and even beyond their conscious awareness. Likewise, the relationship between the service provider and the individual served needs to be understood as one where issues of power, and other dynamics (gender, race, class, ethnicity, etc.) will be at play and influence discussions and reflections. While the process of 'reflection' in the health context is expected to lead to some form of insight or personal knowledge, the focus of this reflection and its meaning to individuals can also be expected to be, at times, difficult, uncomfortable, and overwhelming.

This reflection is focused towards completing *Worksheet 2.15: A measure of my health and well-being through activity and participation*. This measure organizes an overall picture of the individual's perspective on their current time-use patterns and provides a foundation for informed planning and evaluation of change.

2.2.1 Reflecting on Variety, Balance, and Structure of Activities

The range of human activity and participation is, for all practical purposes, limitless. It is exceptionally dynamic and context specific and so itemizing all forms of activity and participation is impossible, and subject to becoming quickly out of date. However, taxonomies that attempt to organize activities by categories can be useful for organizing reflections. One of the simplest categorizations is that commonly used by occupational therapists and organizes human activity and participation patterns in to four broad categories of self-care, productivity, leisure/free time, and rest.

Self-care activities are those that maintain the personal physical and mental condition for functioning. Feeding the self, grooming and hygiene, and related community activities are included in self-care. They can include tasks that maintain physical and mental health, such as self-soothing activities, or attending appointments with health providers. Self-care activities provide a foundation for participating in other activities. For example, grooming and hygiene can be critical to successful productivity.

Productive activities are those which provide the opportunity to contribute to the social and economic fabric of the self, families, community, and broader society. Activities include paid work, volunteer work, parenting, and education.

Categorizations of productivity for the purposes of national data collection can include home management activities, such cooking and washing up after a meal, housekeeping activities, and home-related repairs, etc. They are viewed as a form of 'unpaid work', a type of household production.

Definitions of productivity typically include the notion of obligation. Productivity accounts for a large portion of the daily time spent by adults and provides the opportunity to gain a range of health and well-being benefits including: structure to the day; social contact and integration; social status and identity; the good feelings that come from contributing, personal growth, and development; and payment or receipt of other goods or sources of income. Research has demonstrated that the daily time-use profiles of people with serious mental illness have limited participation in productivity compared to the general population (see for example, Eklund et al., 2009), a not surprising finding given, for example, the high rates of unemployment.

Leisure or free-time activities are those which, given their relative freedom from obligation, are associated with opportunities for meeting personal values, interests, enjoyment, and preferences. Leisure or free time can be classified as active, passive, or social. Active leisure involves activities that require mental or physical energy and effort while passive leisure includes activities that are not characterized by significant mental or physical effort. While both types of leisure are essential, too much passive leisure can be problematic because it contributes to being sedentary, and provide fewer opportunities for social interaction, and involvement in community roles and activities.

For *sleep and rest*, people generally need about six to eight hours of sleep per night in order to rejuvenate. Naps can be used during the day as a way to 'refuel' between activities. People with serious mental illness may find that they require additional rest to provide them with the energy to participate in daily activities. However, sleep can be problematic if it is used as a response to inactivity and boredom, leads to activity and participation patterns that are out of sync with others in the community, or if sleep patterns disturb natural circadian rhythms.

Worksheet 2.2: Considering the variety in my activities and participation provides a framework for reflection based on some of the major domains of the ICF. The ICF is open access, available online at www.who.int/classifications/icf/. It also provides an additional opportunity to provide specific examples of activities and participation from each of the main categories. It can serve as an opportunity to add additional activities and participation, perhaps those that are carried out, but not captured on the 'typical' days. Generally, it is a good idea to be over-inclusive in an effort to get a rich picture of patterns and to capitalize on strengths.

Balance refers to the extent to which there is variety across the major categories in an individual's activity and participation patterns. The idea is not that there needs to be equal distribution of time across self-care, productivity, leisure, and rest activities, but rather that the time spent should be balanced in a way that provides the opportunity for a life of meaning and value that capitalizes on strengths. Occupational therapy scholars have named this as 'occupational integrity', a foundation for evaluating balance (Pentland & McColl, 2008).

In the general population, the idea of balance in time use has typically focused on the balance between time in work and other life activities. This is not always relevant for people with serious mental illness who, as a population, have low rates of employment and other related productivity activities. Alex, the focus of the vignettes in this workbook, illustrates another form of imbalance, often experienced by people with serious mental illness – activity and participation patterns that reflect *alienation* or disconnectedness from activities that could bring fulfilment, enjoyment, and meaning.

Worksheet 2.3: Considering the balance in my activities and participation categorizes activities according to the general domains of self-care, leisure, productivity, and rest. Each domain category is broken down into a variety of different types of activities and participation, and these patterns can be considered with respect to how they are represented in daily time use.

Using *Resource 2.1: Daily activity codes*, the hours spent in each category of self-care, productivity, leisure, and rest can be calculated and included on *Worksheet 2.3: Considering the balance in my activity and participation patterns*.

National statistics related to time use often provide a breakdown of typical activity patterns. For example, information from Statistics Canada (2019), indicates that for adults over the age of 15, the average for Canadians is as follows: hours in productivity – 7.9; hours in leisure – 5.1; hours in personal care – 2.0; and hours in sleep – 8.7. For individuals who have not been actively engaged in productivity activities for some time, the time-use patterns of those who are not working full-time may serve as point of comparison, given that they are also organizing daily activities without the structure provided by paid employment. It needs to be remembered that, in national statistics, this often represents people who are out of work in 'retirement', who may be in a more advantageous position financially, socially, and in their housing situation, compared to those who experience long-term marginalization. Statistics Canada reports the following patterns for retired individuals: productivity – 5.1 hours; leisure – 7.4 hours; personal care – 2.4 hours; and sleep – 9 hours.

In the case of Alex, his time-use patterns suggest that he sleeps or naps more than 10 hours a day, a period of time considerably higher than this comparison group. Through focused conversations, Alex and Jamie found that at least two hours of time in sleep was in the form of incidental naps, happening primarily in the context of unstructured time. While Alex's time logs suggested no participation in productivity activities beyond assisting the landlord, he was receptive to the information that his efforts to help were a type of contribution and that a full day of productivity was not a requirement for health and well-being.

Reflections on balance can also attend to the timing of activities and participation over the course of the day. The 'circadian rhythm' of the 24 hour daily cycle refers to the idea that human function occurs in the context of 'body clocks' that influence activity schedules. For example, humans are most active in day time hours, while night is typically reserved for sleep. Disruptions in these rhythms can be associated with a range of health problems and impact general well-being. For many people with serious mental illness, activity and participation patterns can be negatively impacted by the lack of structure and routine, meaning fewer opportunities to engage in the time structures that organize important opportunities such as work and school, and leading to susceptibility to boredom and incidental naps, etc.

It can be difficult to code activities and participation into specific categories. For example, a meal shared with friends might be 'eating' and therefore 'self-care', but if the activity is more valued as a social time with friends it should be categorized as a social form of 'leisure or free time'. Categorizing active and passive leisure can be particularly difficult, but it is worth attending to, since the activity and participation patterns of people with serious mental illness can be dominated by passive leisure.

It is important to consider an individual's *intent* or level of engagement in classifying activities and participation. For example, watching television or listening to music may reflect a specific interest and involve following a plotline or listening intently for certain characteristics in a piece of music. On the other hand, if these activities require little active engagement they can be considered passive. In community mental health, many individuals without daily structure or activity supports can find themselves sitting in a room with the television on for most of the day, without actually attending to the content or actively selecting what they will watch.

Categorizing activity and participation is best accomplished with some discussion about the actual purpose or meaning of the activity. In the context of serious mental illness, the intent or primary features of activities and participation can often be missed. For example, an individual who is managing daily life with acute psychotic symptoms may spend long periods of time sitting alone in a quiet room. It might appear that this is best categorized as passive leisure, but may in fact reflect focused efforts at self-care or self-soothing.

2.2.2 Reflecting on Alignment with Meaning, Values, Beliefs, Family, Culture, and Social Context

Meaning-making is important in the recovery journey of people with serious mental illness and can take many forms. For example, they are faced with making meaning of the thoughts, emotions, functional changes, and other challenges and impacts related to their experiences of mental illness as well as the opinions and diagnoses offered by health professionals (see, for example, the first person narrative by Colori, 2020).

Meaning-making in this intervention approach refers to a specific type of meaning often referred to as a form of finding 'meaning in life'.

While certain aspects of activity and participation patterns, such as the types of activities engaged in and their sequential unfolding in typical days have been found to be remarkably similar across national boundaries (Vagni & Cornewell, 2018), the meaning and relative importance given to activity and participation patterns can have considerable individual variation. Service providers using the Action Over Inertia approach need to remain sensitive to the fact that although the intervention optimizes self-determination, individual choices to varying degrees will be influenced by values, beliefs, and cultural considerations that are tied to their family networks, upbringing experiences, and other influential life contexts. It is important to remember that all of these influences are themselves fluid and subject to evolve over time. The vignette of Ananthi in the appendix, offers an example of a young woman faced with negotiating the beliefs and values of her parents and culture with both her own aspirations and the impact of her illness experience. Just as her activities and participation patterns and the meaning associated with them will develop and transform over the course of her recovery journey, so too may the perspectives of her family.

Focused questions for reflection about meaning, beliefs, etc. may be particularly difficult to frame and navigate in discussions, both because they can touch on areas that are intangible but also potentially distressing. Alex in our opening vignette, for example, is both distressed by his current activity and participation patterns and by discussions about these patterns that leave him vulnerable to being anxious and overwhelmed. Jamie alleviates this distress by posing simple and clear questions, encouraging examples and storytelling, listening attentively, responding with genuine interest, and connecting with the activity and participation experiences.

Worksheet 2.4: Exploring values and beliefs influencing activity and participation patterns provides guiding questions that can encourage discussion and reflection about how values, beliefs, culture, and family are aligned with activity and participation patterns.

2.2.3 Reflecting on Specific Health and Well-Being Dimensions of Activity and Participation

Understanding activity and participation patterns as linked to health and well-being is foundational to this intervention approach. The conceptual framework used to explicate this link is the Do-Live-Well Framework (see www.dolivewell.ca) described briefly in the introduction. The Do-Live-Well framework identifies dimensions of experience through activities that are linked, through evidence, to physical, mental, social, emotional, and spiritual well-being.

These dimensions can be understood as specific forms of meaning that people attach to their activities and participation. People can attach multiple forms of meaning aligned with these dimensions to any particular form of activity or participation. Alex in our vignette, for example, may experience helping the homeowner with chores as a way to contribute to his own community, to develop a social connection, to get some physical activity, and as the opportunity to express important personal qualities such as helpfulness and generosity.

These dimensions are adapted in this intervention with a view to addressing areas related to equity, inclusion, and citizenship. For example, the dimensions of experience in this intervention includes 'Access to Community Environments', not formally identified as a dimension in the DLW framework, specifically because of the social exclusion of people with serious mental illness. The ten dimensions of focus developed in this intervention are as follows:

2.2.3.1 Taking Care of Myself

This dimension of experience refers to activities and participation patterns that are directed to preserving or improving personal well-being. It encompasses a range of daily life activities. These include activities associated with (1) *personal self-care* such as grooming and eating and the associated activities such as shopping for clothing, food, washing clothes, etc.; (2) *taking care of one's home environment* in a way that supports functioning, acceptance and inclusion, safety, and other forms of health and well-being; (3) *spiritual activities* that nurture a sense of meaning or purpose in life, and contribute to feelings of inner peace and connect people to others with similar beliefs and values, activities directed to rejuvenation or managing daily life stresses; and (4) activities directed to actively *managing health*. These activities of taking care of the self are considered foundational for sustaining life and health. For many people with serious mental illness, these are compromised, not only by the functional consequences of illness, but also by the conditions and context they live in. For example, Sol, who is featured in the vignette in the appendix, has a history of homelessness and experiences the need for adjustments to his activity and participation patterns when he becomes housed. Research into the daily lives of people who are homeless has shown the adjustments that people need to make in their self-care (e.g., Skill development, changes in routine) in their transition to stable housing (Marshall et al., 2018).

Worksheet 2.5: How do I take care of myself through my activities and participation? provides a framework for reflecting on activities and participation related to caring for the self.

2.2.3.2 Activating my Mind and Senses

Impairments in both cognition and sensory processing have been identified as problematic issues for many people with serious mental illness. In an effort to reduce the impact of these on the daily functioning and activity and participation of individuals, specific therapies such as cognitive remediation and sensory modulation therapies have been developed (Lipskaya-Velikovsky et al., 2015; Wykes & Spaulding, 2011). That said, the daily activity and participation patterns of people with serious mental illness can also be understood to be at risk of being devoid of opportunities for challenging and stimulating mental and sensory capacities. Activities and participation that engage mental capacities and the senses, when presented with the 'just right' level of challenge and stimulation, can be both personally meaningful and have added benefits in strengthening cognitive and sensory capacities.

There are a broad range of activities associated with exercising the mind and they include, for example, reading (books, magazines, comics, poetry, etc.), games (cards, puzzles, crosswords, computer games, etc.), writing activities (journal keeping, creative writing, writing emails/letters, etc.), and following instructions to create products or problem solving and imagining to innovate. These activities are often integrated within social participation opportunities and roles, such as training and education, social events, group membership, etc. Challenging and stimulating sensory capacities includes activities and participation that activate hearing, vision, taste, and touch, such as listening to music or podcasts, dancing, opportunities for accessing nature, wildlife, and green spaces, creating and trying different foods, and attending fairs, parades, and related community activities to name a few. ***Worksheet 2.6: Do I have opportunities to stimulate my mind and my senses?*** provides a framework for reflection.

2.2.3.3 Getting Some Physical Activity and Moving My Body

For people with serious mental illness, there has been growing attention to the extent to which restricted physical activity contributes to their risk for diseases such cardiovascular diseases and diabetes and their lower life expectancy compared to the general population (Rosenbaum et al., 2014; Williams et al., 2019). Physical activity can have a positive impact on a broader range of health and well-being factors by, for example, reducing the risk of falls, improving symptoms such as depression, and preparing individuals to engage in the physical demands of other activities that are associated with well-being such as leisure and employment (Perez-Cruzado et al., 2017).

Physical activity is often associated with activities and participation in the forms of exercise and sport. In this intervention approach, service providers are encouraged to engage individuals in reflecting on how a broad range of activities and participation can be associated with being more active physically, moving the body and becoming less sedentary. So, for example, visiting a friend, going shopping, gardening, singing in a choir, or participating in a rally will all promote a physically active day, even where they are not the main meanings attributed to the activity.

Examples of guided reflections related to physical activity are provided in ***Worksheet 2.7: Are my activities and participation giving me enough physical activity and movement?*** While gold standard guidelines for physical activity among the general adult population have been developed (see for example the Canadian 24 hour Movement Guidelines at https://csepguidelines.ca/), the available evidence related specifically to people with serious mental illness is limited, and evidence-informed guidelines are yet to be finalized for practice. That said, guidelines from other populations with disabilities or movement restrictions suggest activity that is of moderate-vigorous intensity at a frequency of two to three times a week for a total of 150 minutes per week, and muscle and bone strengthening activities of major muscle groups two days per week. With evidence suggesting a higher risk for injury related to falls, people with serious mental illness are also encouraged to consider integrating activities that impact balance two to three times a week. Where high levels of sedentary behaviour are common, physical activity guidelines recommend avoidance of prolonged periods of sitting (McGinty et al., 2013).

2.2.3.4 Expressing Identity

This dimension refers to the potential for our activity and participation patterns to align with and express personal interests, personality characteristics, curiosities, preferences, and strengths. Identity is a complex concept that can be understood from at least two distinct but highly interactional perspectives: personal identity and social identity. Personal identity refers to the sense people have of themselves as distinct selves that have some coherence and continuity. Social identity refers to how people identify themselves in relation to others and the broader world. The relationship between identity and health and well-being is a complex one, but includes the idea that well-being is promoted where there is congruence between the person's sense of their identity and their actions, social relations, and conditions of living (McLean & Syed, 2015; Sharma & Sharma, 2010).

For people with serious mental illness, the disruption in the processes underlying personal and social identity development and expression can be enormous. Personal narratives of those with lived experience have illustrated how conceptions of 'who I am' are shaken. Patricia Deegan, for example, refers to how her diagnosis of mental illness, took on the 'master status in terms of her identity' until through her recovery journey she discovered and evolved other aspects of herself (see, Recovery from mental disorders, lecture by Pat Deegan – Recovery Stories 2013, www.recoverystories.info/recovery-from-mental-disorders-lecture-by-pat-deegan).

Contemporary perspectives on recovery and mental illness have highlighted the importance of evolving a sense of personal and social identity beyond that of mental illness. Through activity and participation patterns, individuals with serious mental illness have the potential to develop and express strong self-concepts and engage in social interactions in a way that both acknowledges and helps evolve this self-concept. For many, engaging in activities and participation with others who experience serious mental illness can be an important means to develop positive collective identities and as a way to effect positive change (Quinn et al., 2020). ***Worksheet 2.8: Considering how I express my identity through my activities and participation*** provides the opportunity to reflect on various aspects of identity.

2.2.3.5 Developing Capabilities and Potential

This dimension focuses on the extent to which activity and participation patterns can contribute to the development of skills, knowledge, abilities, aptitudes, and capacities. The development of these capacities impacts health and well-being in a range of ways, for example: helping individuals to negotiate difficult situations, reducing the experience of stress because personal capacities are aligned with demands, and positively impacting social economic status by increasing the match between knowledge, skills, and experiences, and demands in educational and employment situations.

The experience of serious mental illness typically begins and evolves in adolescence and early adulthood – an important time for the development of knowledge and abilities, particularly through formal education. Subsequently educational attainment is considered an important goal to address social marginalization, health, and well-being. Health and well-being can be impacted by a broader range of experiences related to knowledge and skill development. Enabling the development of capacities can be done through a broad range of formal and informal learning opportunities. ***Worksheet 2.9: Developing knowledge, abilities, and potential through my activities and participation*** provides a framework for reflecting on this dimension.

2.2.3.6 Having Pleasure and Enjoyment

This dimension refers to the involvement in activity and participation patterns that allow for moments of joy and positive emotional experiences, such as contentment, exhilaration, or hedonic pleasure. This dimension is believed to connect to human health and well-being in a variety of ways – by providing relief from stress, bringing strong feelings of meaning in life, supporting intimacy and shared experiences. These experiences and enjoyment are many and varied, but they have in common that they are multi-sensory, fun, and light-hearted, and evoke physical and emotional responses that are perceived as pleasurable. These activities can be as simple as preparing and tasting an exotic food, sharing intimacy, getting the 'emotional high' of conquering a physical challenge, playing with a child, enjoying the hilarity of a comic routine, or, for some people, braving a ride on a roller coaster.

For many people with serious mental illness, opportunities for experiences of simple pleasures and joys can be limited and even absent. Activities and participation related to sexual intimacy, risk taking, humour, etc. are, at best, rarely the focus of mental health services, and at worst subject to judgements about suitability and ethical practice (Gelkopf, 2011). For many, the experience of serious mental illness includes a dampening of the emotions that are associated with pleasure and joy. Alex in our vignette, for example, describes a palpable difference in the experience of pleasure he receives in life compared to his earlier years. Yet, studies on recovery from serious mental illness have suggested that experiences of pleasure are possible and can provide important respite from illness, renew hope, provide something to look forward to,

and can help rediscover one's value as a human, to name a few (Davidson et al., 2006).

Worksheet 2.10: How do my activities and participation give me the chance for joy and pleasure? provides a framework for considering this dimension.

2.2.3.7 Connecting to Others

Social interactions and social networks are important for health and well-being as they are a potential resource for material, emotional, and instrumental support. Social connections have the potential to reduce loneliness and engender feelings of belonging and interdependence (Jaremka & Sunami, 2018). Developing and maintaining positive social connections has been viewed as problematic for people with serious mental illness. Yet, despite the many factors that may compromise social relations for people with mental illness, there is ample evidence in the research literature and from personal narratives that social connectedness in its various forms is an integral aspect of recovery processes (see for example, Leamy et al., 2011). Of course, not all social connections are positive, even where they provide individuals with discrete experiences of well-being. For example, relationships that are characterized by problematic activities related to substance use may be experienced as supportive in some ways by the individual, while also contributing to difficulties in other social relations and poor physical health, and legal problems.

Activities and participation provide the opportunity to do things *with* others and *for* others. This opportunity to do things 'for' others may be particularly important for individuals with serious mental illness who can find themselves in sustained social roles as recipients of care. In this situation, their families, others in their networks, and they themselves can lose the ability to see them as people who have the capacity to give. Certainly, the potential benefits of understanding how people with serious mental illness can and do contribute to the well-being of others in shared, reciprocal attention has received only limited attention (see for example, Haselden et al., 2018).

Sharing activities and participation with others can be done in person, or with technology, in online environments. The vast majority of the literature and research in this area has focused on the use of online environments to provide therapy services. There is a growing body of evidence related to online participation of people with serious mental illness for the purposes of social networking and gaming (Highton-Williamson et al., 2014). Certainly, beyond social networking and gaming, online opportunities for education, learning, and sharing related to hobbies, and virtual volunteering, all have potential.

The potential benefits of connecting with animals and pets has been advanced as a type of social connection with potential health and well-being benefits. Research related to companion animals, for example, has demonstrated that the associated activities can promote connecting to others, community integration, structure and routine to the day, and the opportunity to develop knowledge and skills. The relationship with pets itself has been found to be a source of emotional support and a means to contribute to the well-being of a living being (Zimolag & Krupa, 2009).

An important consideration is the range of types of social contacts that people with serious mental illness have. There contacts can tend to be heavily kin dominated or characterized by overrepresentation of formal service relationships, a situation that leaves them vulnerable to restricted opportunities that might be supported through broader social networks (Degnan et al., 2018). For example, Alex's social network is heavily dominated by family and professional contacts. While his family contacts may hold much potential as a way to develop connections associated with health and well-being through shared activities and participation, over time he may look to form a broader range of social contacts that might provide him access to other forms of support.

Worksheet 2.11: How do I connect to others through my activities and participation? provides a framework for reflecting how social interactions are realized and experienced in the context of daily activities and participation.

2.2.3.8 Contributing to Society and My Community

This dimension involves engagement in activities and participation that reflect the interdependence between individuals and society – whether broad society or the local community. Societies are organized in a way that expects and supports contributions from all citizens, with common examples including paid or volunteer work, parenting and caregiving, and involvement in civic activities like advocacy (for a broad range of causes), political activities, etc. Being a student can be understood to be a form of societal contribution, particularly when it is meant to prepare individuals for a broad range of social roles. From a health and well-being perspective, this interdependence expressed through activity has the potential to promote belonging, strengthen social bonds and trust, and position individuals as valued members of their community, with legitimate rights to the resources and opportunities of that community.

For many people with serious mental illness, their social exclusion and marginalization can be viewed as a process by which their contributions to society and community are seriously undermined. Current thinking suggests that assumptions underlying the stigma of mental illness (such as assumptions related to incompetence and dangerousness) are sustained when community members have limited contact with people with mental illness in pro-social roles and contributions (Corrigan et al., 2012). Seeing people with mental illness involved in valued activities and participation such as those offering contributions

to community is a powerful way to reduce stigma and discrimination, including self-stigma (Ashcraft, 2013).

Much of the effort directed to improving the activity and participation in the mental health field has been devoted to employment. This is not surprising given the power of employment to influence social status, economic self-sufficiency, inclusion and acceptance, etc. Many of the practices in this Action Over Inertia intervention approach are well aligned with evidence-based supported employment, but oriented to a broader range of activity and participation opportunities.

Worksheet 2.12: Do I have the opportunity to contribute to my community and society through my activities and participation? provides a framework for reflecting on these contributions to community and society.

2.2.3.9 Building Security/Prosperity

This dimension refers to involvement in activities and participation that contribute to financial and social security and well-being. While most often associated with access to an income and livelihood, this dimension of experience can also relate more broadly to securing access to important material resources and other assets. People with serious mental illness are often living in poverty and experience material deprivation, or a state of economic strain and restrictions that limit access to important resources and opportunities associated with health and well-being (Tøge & Bell, 2016). For example, this material deprivation may impact their access to healthy foods and necessary medicine, to safe living conditions, to education, to recreation with friends, or even to dress for work.

In countries where established social safety nets provide a basic income through a form of disability benefits, these funds typically provide a poverty-level income and can be structured in a way that disincentivizes efforts towards securing an income through employment (Rosenheck et al., 2017). In countries where no such safety net exists, the income and material resources of families can become strained, with the family member with serious mental illness experienced as economically dependent in a family context of financial scarcity. Where economic well-being is restricted, people will often participate in income generating activities that are largely not socially accepted and recognized. Sol, the vignette in the appendix, engages in forms of begging and dealing drugs as a way to access income or material goods.

The experience of poverty has been shown to have a broad impact on the quality of lives of people with serious mental illness (see for example, Wilton, 2004). In such a condition of economic scarcity, even a modest increase in finances or material resources can positively impact aspects of activity and participation.

Activities and participation related to building financial status can include a range of efforts including paid work, bartering activities, producing food, and exploring (or developing) opportunities that are subsidized or otherwise promote access to income through goods or services produced. In addition, investments, and formal or informal savings activities can produce financial benefits that positively impact other activity and participation opportunities. Participation in activism efforts directed to policies focused on economic security and access to specific financial resources as well as access to educational opportunities related to financial literacy are also included. ***Worksheet 2.13: Can I build prosperity and security through my activities and participation?*** provides a framework for reflection in these areas.

2.2.3.10 Accessing Community Environments

Given their history of exclusion from full community participation, and the fact that stigma and discrimination are common, access to community environments is a particularly important area for direct consideration for people with serious mental illness.

Community integration is a complex construct and can be organized into different types of integration: *physical integration*, which refers to the physical location of activities, especially participating in activities outside of the home; *social integration*, which involves interacting with people and activities in the neighbourhood and community; and *psychological integration*, which is a sense of belonging to a community (Aubry & Myner, 1996; Ecker & Aubry, 2017). Physical integration provides benefits for well-being, even if no active socialization occurs. Visiting a number of different public environments is associated with increased social integration, as the opportunity for social interaction increases. On the other hand, people who spend the majority of their time confined to a limited number of isolating environments are likely to experience social detachment and have less opportunity to contribute to society. Accessing community environments without the purpose and direction afforded by activity and participation can compromise the individual in the community (Fitzgerald et al., 2005). For example, people with serious mental illness may be viewed as loitering or walking without direction in a public environment, further increasing the risk of victimization (Hiday et al., 1999; Sells et al., 2003).

Using ***Worksheet 2.14: What community environments do I access in my daily activities and participation?*** considers the extent to which activities are confined to the home environment and the variety of community environments accessed. Given that many people with serious mental illness are living with limited financial means, and may reside in poorer socio-economic neighbourhoods, it will be important to consider the extent to which the immediate environments provide a sense of security and offer access to important resources that support activities, such as transportation.

2.3 Interpreting Activity and Participation Patterns

This chapter has provided a broad framework for reflection on activity and participation patterns and their alignment with health and well-being. It offers a variety of perspectives to guide this reflection: balance, variety, meaning, values, social and cultural context, and dimensions of experience.

Bejerholm, Hansson, & Eklund (2006) looked at the time-use patterns of people living with mental illness by analyzing a 24-hour time-use diary. By integrating information from different dimensions of activity participation they were able to identify three different patterns in their participants: disengagement, partial engagement, and engagement. ***Resource 2.2: Levels of engagement in activity and participation***, applies these levels to dimensions of health and well-being through activity and participation that have been developed in this chapter. These provide qualitative descriptions of patterns that are associated with varying levels of health and well-being.

While this profile of levels of engagement is meant to be helpful as a reflection guide, it does not reflect the range of daily activity and participation patterns that may be experienced in the context of mental illness. For example, individuals who experience periods of mania or hypomania may experience activity patterns that are characterized by over-engagement. This situation compromises the quality of the activity experience and performance, as well as health and well-being.

Worksheet 2.15: A measure of my health and well-being through activity and participation provides the opportunity for an overall picture of the individual's perceptions of their current activity participation. The tool can support choices related to potential areas for change or enhancement while highlighting areas of strength. It can also be used to track changes over time, to monitor the progress made, and to contribute to service evaluation and development. These latter two possibilities are developed further in Chapters 6, 7, and 8.

2.4 Key Competencies

The competencies associated with this chapter are related to the attitudes, knowledge, and skills underlying the ability to engage the individual in reflecting on personal activity and participation patterns from a variety of perspectives. These competencies facilitate the sense of trust, respect, and sensitivity necessary for the individual to consider if and how changes in personal activity and participation patterns may be both personally rewarding and possible. These competencies include:

- Demonstrating knowledge of activities and participation and their relationship to health and well-being.

- Sustaining the interest and commitment of the individual served in reflecting on personal activity and participation patterns.
- Supporting the well-being of people served throughout the process of reflecting on personal activity and participation patterns.
- Encouraging and supporting the use of worksheets and other resources to promote reflection.
- Attending to and remaining sensitive to diversity of values, experiences, beliefs, etc.

- Establishing a shared understanding of activity and participation patterns and issues with the individual served.
- Engaging individuals served to identify values, beliefs, meaning, and contexts that underlie their activity and participation choices and engagement.
- Identifying the strengths and resources within activity and participation patterns.

Daily time-use log

Name: _____ Date: _____

In the chart below, fill in how you have recently spent a typical day.

Time	Activity	Where?	The Activity Was Done: Alone/with Someone Else
12 midnight			
12:30 am			
1:00 am			
1:30 am			
2:00 am			
2:30 am			
3:00 am			
3:30 am			
4:00 am			
4:30 am			
5:00 am			
5:30 am			
6:00 am			
6:30 am			

Time	Activity	Where?	The Activity Was Done: Alone/with Someone Else
7:00 am			
7:30 am			
8:00 am			
8:30 am			
9:00 am			
9:30 am			
10:00 am			
10:30 am			
11:00 am			
11:30 am			
12 noon			
12:30 pm			
1:00 pm			
1:30 pm			
2:00 pm			
2:30 pm			
3:00 pm			
3:30 pm			
4:00 pm			

Worksheet 2.1

Time	Activity	Where?	The Activity Was Done: Alone/with Someone Else
4:30 pm			
5:00 pm			
5:30 pm			
6:00 pm			
6:30 pm			
7:00 pm			
7:30 pm			
8:00 pm			
8:30 pm			
9:00 pm			
9:30 pm			
10:00 pm			
10:30 pm			
11:00 pm			
11:30 pm			

Considering the variety in my activities and participation patterns

Name: _____   Date: _____

For each of the activity/participation examples, check if you are involved in them routinely, and if you would like to see changes in your level of involvement.

Domain of Activity/Participation	This Is Included in My Routine Activity and Participation Patterns (Check Those that Apply)	This Is an Area of My Life I Think Could Use Some Changes in My Level of Involvement (Check All That Apply)
Self-Care and Home Activities		
• Grooming		
• Managing my diet		
• Managing my fitness		
• Taking care of my health and preventing illness		
• Buying or obtaining items for daily living and home		
• Preparing and eating meals		
• Taking care of my living area		
• Caring for my clothes		
• Assisting others with their well-being		
• Taking care of pets		
• Taking care of plants		

Worksheet 2.2

Social Relationships		
• Sharing in activities with family		
• Sharing in activities with friends		
• Developing new relationships		
• Developing or maintaining a romantic relationship		
Major Life Areas		
• Participating in education		
• Participating in paid or unpaid work		
• Taking care of my finances		
Community, Social, and Civic Life		
• Participating in a community clubs or associations		

• Recreation and leisure
  – Playing games
  – Sports
  – Arts and culture
  – Crafts
  – Hobbies
  – Socializing		

• Participating in religious or spiritual activities		
• Activities to support human rights		
• Participating in activities associated with citizenship such as politics and government		

Considering the balance in my activity and participation patterns

Name: _____ Date: _____

Looking at your time-use logs, label each activity you recorded as self-care, productivity, or leisure. Use Resource 2.1: Daily activity codes to help. Total the hours spent in each category for one day. This will give you a visual image of the balance of your activities.

Category	*Hours Spent*
Self-care	
Productivity	
Leisure	
Rest	

My Time Use

Hours Spent

12
11
10
9
8
7
6
5
4
3
2
1
0

Self-Care   Productivity   Leisure   Rest

Worksheet 2.3 (continued)

Self-Care Activities	Examples	Examples of My Activities	Time Spent
Personal care	~ bathing ~ dressing		
Health-related care	~ attending appointments ~ filling prescriptions		

Productive Activities	Examples	Examples of My Activities	Time Spent
Paid work	~ work for an employer for pay ~ self-employment for pay		
Unpaid work	~ work for an employer without pay		
Volunteer and other civic work	~ unpaid work for another or for an organization		
Education and related	~ attending school ~ attending workshops or training ~ Web-based learning		
Day programs	~ attending treatment programs or services		
Parenting	~ taking care of children		
Home management activities	~ cleaning ~ renovating ~ shopping for goods and services		

Leisure Activities	Examples	Examples of My Activities	Time Spent
Active leisure	~ sports ~ clubs ~ attending entertainment events		
Passive leisure	~ reading ~ watching TV ~ listening to music		
Socialization	~sharing a coffee with a friend ~attending a dinner party ~talking with a friend on the telephone ~joining a friend's Facebook site ~Writing a letter to a friend		

Rest Activities	Examples	Examples of My Activities	Time Spent
Night sleep	~ the time of day when you get the bulk of your sleep		
Naps	~ incidental sleep during the day		

Exploring values and beliefs influencing activity and participation patterns

Name: _____ Date: _____

These are some guiding questions that can support the exploration of how your culture, values, beliefs are present in your current activity and participation patterns. They can also start you thinking about how you might incorporate them in to your daily life activity and participation in the future.

1. Thinking of the past week, what activities were your favourite? Why are they your favourite?

_____

_____

_____

_____

2. What were your least favourite activities this past week? Why?

_____

_____

_____

_____

3. What is important to you?
- What activities do you do that are aligned with what you consider important?

- _____

    _____

- What activities do you WISH you could do that are in keeping with what you find important?

- _____

    _____

- Were there activities that you used to do that were important to you, but you are no longer doing?

- _____

    _____

4. **When you think about your family or other important people in your life, what would they say is important? What activities would they see as important?**

_____

_____

_____

_____

5. **Are there activities that are EXPECTED of you by others? Are these activities you would like to have in your life?**

_____

_____

_____

_____

6. **What would you like to be doing in the future if it could become possible?**

_____

_____

_____

_____

Worksheet 2.5

How do I take care of myself through my activities and participation?

Name: _____ **Date:** _____

Taking good care of yourself will influence your personal health and well-being. Think of a typical week. What activities do you do to take care for yourself? Check examples that apply to you.

Personal self-care

Manage illness or the health conditions

Taking care of my home environment

Taking care of myself

Rejuvenate or managing stresses

Spiritual activities

		I Do	*I Need to Do*	*I Would Like to Do*
Self-Care	Grooming – bathing, shaving, wearing clean clothes			
	Grooming – brushing teeth, oral hygiene			
	Grooming – washing and brushing hair			
	Grooming – clipping nails, skin care			
	Healthy eating			
	Shopping for groceries			
	Shopping for clothing or personal items			
	Doing laundry			
	Managing my finances			
	Other:			
Home Care	Cleaning/organizing your home			
	Washing the dishes			
	Decorating my home			
	Caring for a home garden			
	Other:			

Worksheet 2.5

		I Do	I Need to Do	I Would Like to Do
Spiritual Activities	Activities contributing to a sense of meaning or purpose in life			
	Activities contributing to feelings of inner peace			
	Activities connecting to people with similar beliefs and values			
	Other:			
Stress Management	Exercise			
	Going for a walk			
	Practicing relaxation			
	Doing a leisure activity			
	Other:			
Illness Management	Managing medication			
	Participating in a self-help group			
	Participating in psychoeducation			
	Recovery and wellness activities			
	Other:			

Do I have opportunities to stimulate my mind and my senses?

Name: _____ Date: _____

Stimulate the Mind – Some Examples

- *Reading* – books, magazines, newspapers, comics, poetry
- *Writing* – keeping a journal, creative writing, writing emails/letters/blogs, etc.
- *Playing games* – puzzles, crosswords, chess, sudoku, board games, online or computer games
- *Learning something* – a language, playing an instrument, following a new recipe or instructions for a hobby, taking a course, etc.

Stimulate the Senses – Some Examples

- Listening to music, podcasts, audiobooks
- Tasting different flavours and spices
- Visiting an art gallery or museum
- Going swimming
- Going for a walk in nature, feeding the birds
- Attending a parade or community fair
- Gardening

1. In the past week have you done activities that stimulated your senses or mind?

_____

_____

_____

_____

_____

_____

_____

2. What activities that stimulate your mind/senses would you like to do more?

_____

_____

_____

_____

_____

_____

_____

Are my activities and participation giving me enough physical activity and movement?

Name: _____ **Date:** _____

Current guidelines for physical activity and movement recommend activities to improve:

- Aerobic fitness – through increases in breathing and heart rate
- Movement – through reducing long periods of sitting

Some people follow these recommendations through focused exercise, but they can also be achieved through everyday activities built in to the day.

Improving Health and Well-Being Through	*Recommended Guidelines for People with Health Conditions*	*Examples of Everyday Activities*
Aerobic fitness with Moderate intensity activities (you can talk while active even though your breathing and heart rate increases	2–3 times a week aiming for 30 minutes each time	Brisk walking Swimming Dancing Gardening Vigorous cleaning Raking/shovelling Sports
Movement – reducing long periods of sitting	Sit for less than one or two hours at a time	Take a break from sitting every 30 minutes to stand and walk around Build in movement to your typical activities – for example, walk to your activities, take the stairs when possible, stand while reading or online

Did your typical activities have more aerobic intensity and movement in the past?   YES   NO

Consider your activities in your typical days. Are you reaching the recommended guidelines for physical activity and movement?   YES   NO

Are physical activity and movement important to you?   YES   NO

Are there ways you could get more physical activities and movement in your day? If yes what are these ways?

_____

_____

_____

_____

Are there things preventing you from getting more physical activities and movement in your day?

_____

_____

_____

_____

Considering how I express my identity through activities and participation

Name: _____ Date: _____

When we think about our identity there are many things about us that make us the unique person we are and contribute to our well-being.

Each of the petals of the flower are aspects that define who we are and how that influences our choice in activities and participation.

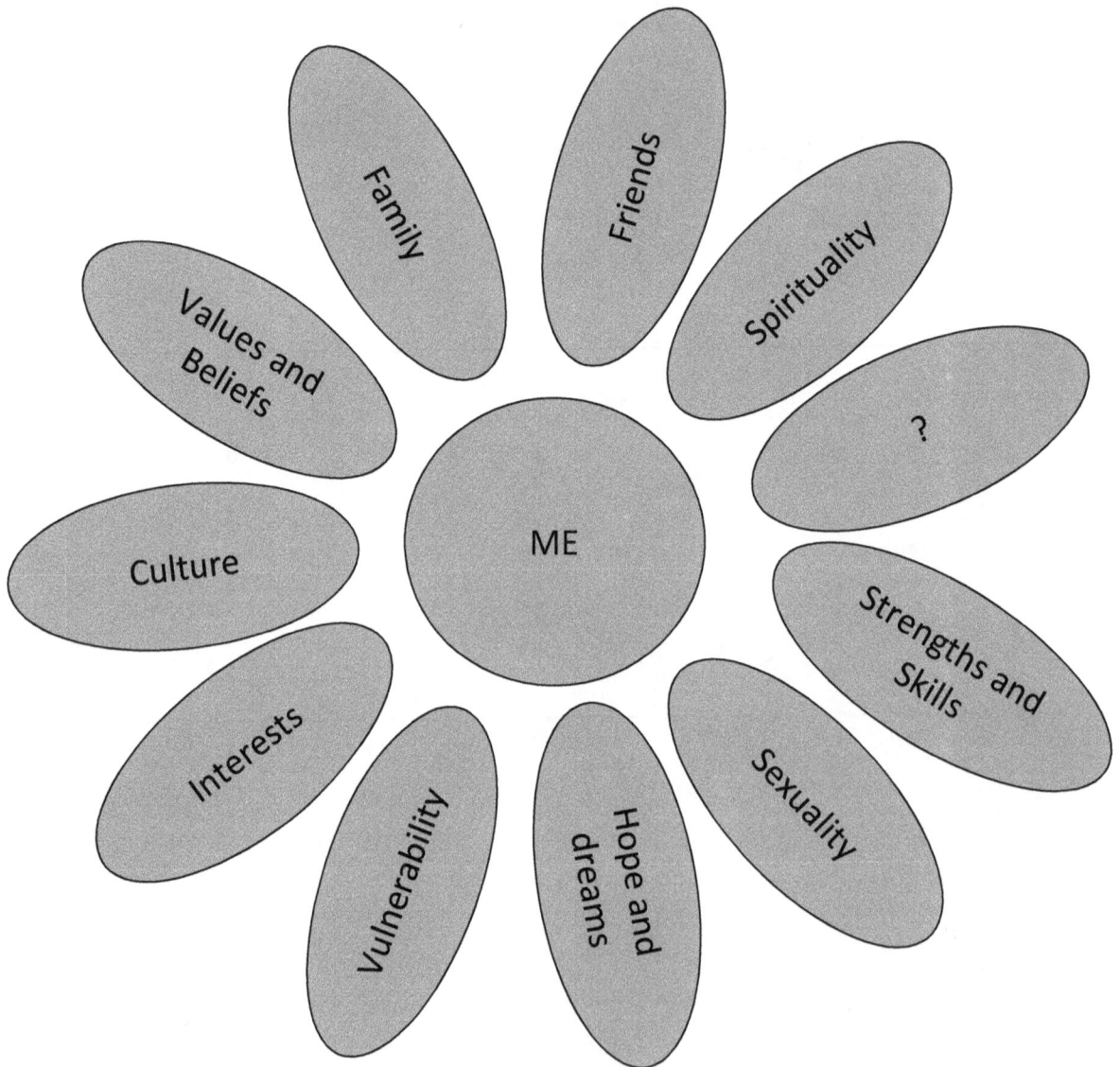

Family

Friends

Spirituality

Values and Beliefs

?

Culture

ME

Strengths and Skills

Interests

Sexuality

Vulnerability

Hope and dreams

Worksheet 2.8

1. **Which petals on the flower influence your activity and participation choices and actions? How do they influence your choices and actions?**

   _____

   _____

   _____

   _____

   _____

2. **When you think about your typical daily activities and participation which of these 'petals of you' is:**

   - Most expressed in what you do?

   _____

   _____

   _____

   _____

   _____

   - Least expressed in what you do?

   _____

   _____

   _____

   _____

   _____

3. **Are there certain petals that are more important to you in making choices about your activities and participation? If so, which ones and why?**

   _____

   _____

   _____

   _____

   _____

   _____

Adapted from Patricia Deegan (2002). Recovery as a Self-Directed Process of Healing and Transformation. *With permission.*

Worksheet 2.9

Developing knowledge, abilities, and potential through my activities and participation

Name: _____ **Date:** _____

The questions here are meant to get you thinking about how your daily life activities and participation might be constructed to give you more opportunities to develop your personal qualities, capacities, and strengths.

I. *Knowledge*
I have the opportunity in my daily life to learn about new things I think are interesting or valuable
Yes   No
Examples _____

_____

_____

_____

_____

_____

II. *Education/Training*
I have the education/training that I need to help me to do the things I want to do in my daily life
Yes   No
Examples:_____

_____

_____

_____

_____

_____

III. *Interests*
Does my daily life include opportunities to participate in activities that are of interest to me?
Yes   No
Examples:_____

_____

_____

_____

_____

_____

IV. *Skills/expertise*

Here are a few things I am pretty good at.

_____

_____

_____

_____

_____

I think that my daily life activities give me a chance to practice these skills.
Yes   No
Examples:_____

_____

_____

_____

_____

_____

V. *Strengths*

These are a few things I consider my strengths.

_____

_____

_____

_____

_____

_____

I have the opportunity to do things that highlight my strengths in my day-to-day activities
Yes   No
Examples:_____

_____

_____

_____

_____

_____

How do my activities and participation give me the chance for joy and pleasure?

Name: _____ Date: _____

Consider the activities you identified as part of your typical daily activities and participation.

1. **Which activities brought you feelings of joy and pleasure?**

   _____
   _____
   _____

2. **Which of these activities brought you the least amount of joy and pleasure?**

   _____
   _____
   _____

3. **Do any of the activities cause you stress and feelings of discomfort?**

   _____
   _____
   _____

4. **Are there particular times of day when you experience more joy and pleasure in your activities?**

   _____
   _____
   _____

5. **What activities have you done in the past that brought you joy and pleasure? Have you been able to participate in these activities lately?**

   _____
   _____
   _____

6. **Thinking of your overall activity and participation patterns – do they bring you joy and pleasure?**

   _____
   _____
   _____

7. **What changes in your activity and participation patterns might bring you more joy and pleasure?**

   _____
   _____
   _____

How do I connect to others through my activity and participation?

Name: _____ **Date:** _____

The activities we participate in can involve developing social connections. These connections contribute to our health and well-being. The chart below lists possible social connections as part of your typical daily activities and participation. Add any people/social connections that you see often and connect with.

Types of Social Connections	*My Current Social Connections Include*	*Activities We Do Together*
Family		
Friends		
Co-workers		
Neighbours		
Service workers		
Peers		
Pets/companion animals		
Social media connections		
Group members i.e., religious, support groups, sports teams		
Other		

1. **Are there people or social connections currently in your life that are problematic, that you might like to change?**

_____

_____

_____

_____

2. **Are there are certain types of social connections you would like to make or experience more of?**

_____

_____

_____

_____

3. **Are there things preventing you from doing the things you would like to with others?**

_____

_____

_____

_____

4. **Are there ways to connect with these other people/social connections to do the things you would like to do?**

_____

_____

_____

_____

5. **Would you like the opportunity to have more interactions with animals? If so, what types of interactions?**

_____

_____

_____

_____

Worksheet 2.12

Do I have the opportunity to contribute to my community and society through my activities and participation?

Name:_____ **Date:**_____

The chart below lists some possible ways that you may use your time to contribute to society and your community. Think back on what you learned about your typical time use to complete the chart below and learn about your contributions.

Activities/Participation	I Do Right Now	I Might Like to Do
Working for pay		
Volunteer work		
Caregiving i.e., parenting, taking care of friend or relative		
Education pursuits		
Helping others in the community		
Participating in advocacy groups on issues of importance to me		
Taking care of animals		
Recycling, or other environmental protection activities		
Participating in elections (i.e., voting, helping a candidate, working at a voting station)		
Joining a community group or sports team		
Participating in peer support activities		
Mentoring others		
Other		

Worksheet 2.12

1. **Are there current activities that you engage in that contribute to your community you would like to do more?**

   _____

   _____

   _____

   _____

   _____

   _____

2. **Are there things that prevent you from engaging in activities that contribute to society and your community?**

   _____

   _____

   _____

   _____

   _____

   _____

Can I build prosperity and security through my activities and participation?

Name: _____ **Date:** _____

This worksheet asks about your thoughts on how your activities and participation can influence your financial and economic well-being now and in the future.

What is your current source of income? What is the income you receive?

_____

_____

_____

Respond to these questions thinking about your current income source and financial situation

1. **Sometimes my finances don't cover the costs of my basic needs (for example, rent, food, hygiene products).**
   YES   NO   MAYBE

   _____

   _____

   _____

   _____

2. **There are things I would like to be able to buy for myself or others, but I can't afford them.**
   YES   NO   MAYBE

   _____

   _____

   _____

   _____

3. **I would like to be able to contribute more financially to the well-being of others.**
   YES   NO   MAYBE

   _____

   _____

   _____

   _____

4. **There are activities I would like to do, but can't because of my current financial situation.**
   YES   NO   MAYBE

   _____

   _____

   _____

   _____

5. **My current source of income comes with rules related to my ability to engage in activities that might increase my funds.**
   YES   NO   MAYBE

   _____

   _____

   _____

   _____

6. **My daily activities and participation give me the opportunity to enrich my social and financial situation.**
   YES   NO   MAYBE

   _____

   _____

   _____

   _____

7. **Having the opportunity to improve my social and financial situation through my daily activities and participation is important to me.**
   YES   NO   MAYBE

   _____

   _____

   _____

   _____

8. **I would like to explore how I might improve my finances through my activities and participation.**
   YES   NO   MAYBE

   _____

   _____

   _____

   _____

What community environments do I access in my activities and participation?

Name: _____ Date: _____

Looking back over your daily activities and participation:

1. **List all the different community environments you visited.**

   _____   _____
   _____   _____
   _____   _____

2. **How much time did you spend out in the community, away from your home?**

   _____
   _____

3. **What time of day are you usually at home? What time of day are you usually out?**

   _____
   _____

4. **Where do you spend the majority of your time when not at home? What activities do you do there?**

   _____
   _____
   _____

5. **Do you feel safe in your neighbourhood? If not, what aspects make you feel unsafe?**

   _____
   _____
   _____

6. **What types of interactions do you have with your neighbours? For example, do you greet them, speak with them, etc.? How comfortable are you with your neighbours?**

   _____
   _____
   _____

7. **Are there places you used to visit in the community that you don't anymore? If yes, why don't you visit them anymore?**

   _____
   _____
   _____

8. **Are they certain places that you would like to visit in your community but don't?**

   _____
   _____
   _____

9. **Would you like to know more about your community and places that might interest you?**

   _____
   _____
   _____

A measure of my health and well-being through activity and participation

Name: _____ Date: _____

1. ***Balance in my life***: I could benefit from more balance between my self-care, leisure, productivity, and rest activities.

Rate how true this statement is for you.

1	2	3	4	5	6	7	8	9	10
Very True				Somewhat True				Not True	

2. ***Living my values and beliefs***: I could benefit from activities and participation that I find important and meaningful.

Rate how true this statement is for you.

1	2	3	4	5	6	7	8	9	10
Very True				Somewhat True				Not True	

3. ***Taking care of myself***: I could benefit from activities and participation that improve my personal care

Rate how true this statement is for you.

1	2	3	4	5	6	7	8	9	10
Very True				Somewhat True				Not True	

4. ***Activating mind and senses***: I could benefit from activities and participation that use my mind or stimulate my senses.

Rate how true this statement is for you.

1	2	3	4	5	6	7	8	9	10
Very True				Somewhat True				Not True	

5. ***Physical Activity and movement***: I could benefit from activities and participation that improve my fitness and make me less inactive.

Rate how true this statement is for you.

1	2	3	4	5	6	7	8	9	10
Very True				Somewhat True				Not True	

6. ***Expressing identity***: I could benefit from activities and participation that are connected to my personal interests and qualities.

Rate how true this statement is for you.

1	2	3	4	5	6	7	8	9	10
Very True				Somewhat True					Not True

7. ***Developing knowledge, capacities, and potential***: I could benefit from activities and participation that give me the opportunity to learn new things and build my strengths.

Rate how true this statement is for you.

1	2	3	4	5	6	7	8	9	10
Very True				Somewhat True					Not True

8. ***Experiencing pleasure and joy***: I could benefit from activities and participation that bring me moments of enjoyment and make me happy.

Rate how true this statement is for you.

1	2	3	4	5	6	7	8	9	10
Very True				Somewhat True					Not True

9. ***Connecting with others***: I could benefit from having more social connections through my daily activities and participation.

Rate how true this statement is for you.

1	2	3	4	5	6	7	8	9	10
Very True				Somewhat True					Not True

10. ***Contributing to society and my community***: I could benefit from activities and participation that give me the opportunity to give back to the community.

Rate how true this statement is for you.

1	2	3	4	5	6	7	8	9	10
Very True				Somewhat True					Not True

11. ***Building security and prosperity***: I could benefit from activity and participation that gives me the opportunity to impact my financial situation and provide me with more money or resources.

Rate how true this statement is for you.

1	2	3	4	5	6	7	8	9	10
Very True				Somewhat True				Not True	

12. ***Accessing community environments***: I could benefit from activities and participation that take me out into a range of community environments.

Rate how true this statement is for you.

1	2	3	4	5	6	7	8	9	10
Very True				Somewhat True				Not True	

Summary of Ratings:

Fill in the scores that you assigned to each area above. A lower score in any area suggests that the area could benefit from direct attention and perhaps be given a higher priority for change.

Area of Activity Engagement	*Rating*
1. Having balance in my day	
2. Living values and beliefs	
3. Taking care of myself	
4. Activating my mind and senses	
5. Physical activity and movement	
6. Expressing identity	
7. Developing knowledge, capacities, potential	
8. Experiencing pleasure and joy	
9. Connecting with others	
10. Contributing to community	
11. Building security and prosperity	
12. Accessing community environments	

Daily activity codes

Self-Care Activities

PERSONAL CARE	HEALTH-RELATED CARE
• Personal hygiene and grooming • Religious services/prayer/bible readings • Spiritual activity • Travel to religious services • Meals, snacks, and coffee • Relaxing, thinking, resting • Sexual activities • Other personal care activities	• Medical/health care at home • Medical/health appointments • Filling prescriptions • Travel to medical/health appointments • Other health related care

Productive Activities

PAID WORK	UNPAID WORK
• Work for pay • Activities related to work • Hobbies or crafts done for sale or exchange • Looking for work • Travel to/from work **VOLUNTEER AND OTHER CIVIC WORK** • Including travel to volunteer work	• Work for an employer without pay • Travel to unpaid work site • Household work and related activities • Garden or property care • Vehicle care • Shopping for goods and services • Parenting • Caregiving • Travel associated with unpaid work
EDUCATION AND RELATED • Attending full-time or part-time classes in person or online • Doing homework • Taking a course for career or self-development • Other activities related to education • Travel related to educational activities	MENTAL HEALTH PROGRAM ACTIVITIES Examples: • Work at program site for pay • Prepare/eat meal at site • Attend community trip • Attend presentation/meeting/class • Attend support group, activity • Attend social club • Socialize at the site • Travel to program activities

Resource 2.1

Leisure/Free-Time Activities

ACTIVE LEISURE	PASSIVE LEISURE	SOCIALIZING
• Active sports • Active events • Other active leisure • Activities • travel related to active leisure	• Watching TV/online programming • Reading • Listening to music, podcasts, audiobooks, etc. • Passing time without activity • Entertainment events • Other passive leisure • Travel to passive leisure	• Communicating with others to socialize in person or using technology • Restaurant meals with others • Socializing at a home • Other socializing • Travel to social activities

Rest Activities

NIGHT SLEEP	NAPS
• Night sleep/essential sleep	• Incidental sleep, naps

Adapted from Statistics Canada: Statistics Canada (2019). Activity Group: Classification structure. Retrieved from: https://www23.statcan.gc.ca/imdb/p3VD.pl?Function=getVD&TVD=1230353

Levels of engagement in activity and participation

Use this table to consider how typical daily activity and participation patterns are aligned with health and well-being.

Disengagement	Some Engagement	Engaged
• Imbalance between self-care, leisure and productivity • No identifiable structure and routine organizing activity • A very limited range of activities and participation • Daily activities largely organized around basic needs and sleep • Day/night reversal of activities • Activities and participation almost exclusively in home or program environments • Largely sedentary activity • Few opportunities to engage in activities with other people • Difficult to identify strengths and capacities through daily activities and participation • There are few expectations from others with respect to activities and participation • Little evidence of engagement in personally meaningful activities • Little to look forward to with respect to activities and participation	• Some involvement in self-care, leisure, productivity, and rest activities • Some routines and structure • A limited variety of activity and participation involvements • Large periods of passive activity • Naps and early bedtime • Accesses some community environments for activity and participation • 30–60 minutes of movement in activities daily • Some social interactions regularly • Some interests and strengths expressed in daily activities • Some obligations and expectations present in activity routines • Engages in some meaningful activity • Future perspectives on activity and participation for the immediate future	• Days/weeks with balance between self-care, leisure, productivity, and rest • Daily time use organized around different activities • A range of activity and participation involvements • Night sleep and rest organized to meet needs for meaningful activities • Accesses a range of community environments for activity and participation • More than 60 minutes of movement in daily activities • Regular social connections with a social network that extends beyond family and mental health service providers • Time-use patterns include engagement in activities that are wanted, needed, and expected. • Ongoing meaning derived from daily activity and participation • Looks forward to and plans future activity and participation

3   A First Step

Making Rapid Changes in Activity and Participation

Jamie was pleased to see Alex's interest (cautious as it was) in working together to directly address his activity and participation patterns. However, Jamie was concerned that an intervention process that was lengthy, without any immediate experience of positive change, would prove discouraging for Alex. Jamie suggested to Alex that they consider one or two changes that could be rapidly introduced – activities that had the potential to encourage motivation and give opportunities to experience some of the benefits – sooner rather than later.

Jamie referred to these proposed changes as 'activity experiments' to highlight that they were efforts to try things out. Any activity would need to hold some meaning and interest for Alex. It would not be overwhelming given his experiences of anxiety about participating in new things. At that moment Alex had few contacts with friends and family, and overall a limited network of supports that might encourage his participation or actually participate in the activities with him. He also had limited funds and so any activity changes could not further stress his resources.

During a meeting, Jamie suggested to Alex that they walk to the local park. They took some seed to feed the birds while they talked. Jamie drew Alex's attention to features in the park (a local soccer game, a commemorative statue), and they used an application on Jamie's phone to identify a particular bird. In conversation, Alex reminded Jamie that he was raised in a semi-rural area with easy access to nature. They considered the idea of two activities Alex could try over the next week. Using knowledge of Alex's past and present activities, Jamie raised some possible examples. After some focused conversation, Alex agreed that he would try and add a short mid-day walk and to help the owner of his residence out with one or two activities around the house. Alex welcomed Jamie's offer to approach the home owner together to see what chores or activities he might participate in.

A week later, Alex reported that he had walked through the park on two separate days, and on one of the days he was accompanied by one of his housemates. He found that his shoes became too wet to wear after one of the walks – a problem since he had only one pair. Jamie and Alex discussed options to take care of this problem. Alex had also helped the home owner with preparing the garden for the colder weather, and they joked that the weeds would be back in no time. Jamie shared in the joke, commenting that weeds can always be counted on.

Focused Questions:

1. How does Jamie prompt Alex's interest in his local environment and link these to activity and participation? What other strategies or approaches might you use?
2. Think of a time when you intended to participate in an activity but didn't follow through. What stood in your way?
3. What specific elements of proposed activity and participation changes should be considered to support the chances for successful activity experiments?

This chapter includes the following worksheets:

Worksheet 3.1: Facilitating activity experiments (service provider version)
Worksheet 3.2: Mapping activity and participation opportunities in the local community
Worksheet 3.3: Record of activity experiments

This chapter includes the following resource:

Resource 3.1: Looking for ideas for small activity and participation changes?

DOI: 10.4324/9781003111368-3

3.1 The Potential of Making Rapid Changes

The essence of health and well-being through activity and participation depends on actually engaging in *doing*. Coaching, education, goal setting, and planning are all important practices to support change. However, they cannot replace actions directed to creating opportunities for actual engagement in meaningful activities, supporting the transition from intentions to engagement in these opportunities, receiving feedback about this effort, and gaining experience by doing.

Introducing activity and participation in the way of small changes and efforts can be considered on an ongoing basis throughout the change process. These efforts, named 'activity experiments', are small, rapidly introduced changes that can have a particularly powerful impact early in the process of change because they can:

- Set in motion the 'action of doing', breaking the self-perpetuating force of 'inertia'.
- Introduce the individual to the beginning steps of defining desired changes.
- Create opportunities that counteract experiences of activity deprivation or the lack of opportunities and conditions that support involvement in activities and participation.
- Signal a belief in the potential for positive change.
- Provide the opportunity to experience the health and well-being properties of meaningful activities and participation.
- Provide the opportunity to anticipate and prepare for challenges associated with changing activity and participation patterns.

This idea of 'rapid' introduction to activity changes is well aligned with the principles and practices of evidence-based supported employment which capitalizes on the interest in work without lengthy assessment or preparation processes (Drake et al., 2012). Likewise, the Action Over Inertia approach highlights the importance of informed approaches to supporting rapid introduction to real opportunities for activities and participation. This orientation to engaging people in a way that exhorts them to action in a timely manner is critical, particularly because it is not ingrained in the routine delivery of mental health services. For example, Slade et al. (2014), in their review of misuses of the recovery practices, identified how service providers and systems can be structured to undermine the view that individuals served will be able to live a meaningful life beyond the limitations of illness.

3.2 Considerations for Enabling Rapid Changes in Activity and Participation

Even small changes in activity and participation patterns require consideration. For individuals living with mental illness, their experiences of activity disengagement and marginalization in social participation are sustained by powerful forces. These forces need to be considered.

Of course the activity needs to hold some meaning and well-being properties for the individual –a challenge if an individual's daily life is marked by disconnections from important people, community structures, and routines established with a greater purpose. The individual may experience sustained levels of anxiety and distress, and so any new activities, no matter how small and apparently simple, will need to be considered with regards to their potential for being overwhelming. A life situation characterized by isolation and poverty will, of course, need to be considered in choices. Activities may appear to be 'simple', but to be an effective component of the process of positive change they need to be:

- Personally meaningful.
- Manageable with limited support.
- Sensitive to the individual's living conditions and contexts.
- Require few resources.
- Provide at least one element associated with activity health and well-being as identified in the reflection process.

For example, Jamie considered 'taking a walk' with a view to supporting Alex's efforts and identified several aspects of the activity as developed in Table 3.1.

Table 3.1 Supporting Alex's efforts to engage in walking.

What meaning might taking a walk hold for Alex?	• Aligns with his interest in increasing physical activity • Appeared to connect with the green environment and nature
What features of this activity change are likely to support his engagement?	• Has the physical ability needed • Has past experience with the activity • Easy access to local park and safe walking areas
What factors may interfere with his engagement in this activity experiment?	• Lengthy period of being 'stuck' in current activity pattern • Bad weather • Suitable clothes and shoes
Ideas to facilitate likelihood of engagement in selected activity change.	• Consider family or friends to accompany (sister? housemate?) • Enable access to suitable clothing (visit to local thrift shop?) • Consider ways to increase experience of meaning of activity (digital app to track physical activity?) • Link walks to other activities – give some 'destinations'

Worksheet 3.1: Facilitating activity experiments (service provider version) offers the opportunity for service providers to explicitly recognize challenges inherent in even small changes in activity and participation patterns and consider strategies and approaches that might support activity experiments. These reflections can be helpful in considering why activity experiments were positive or less then successful experiences.

3.3 Enabling the Selection of Activities and Participation

The skilled service provider will use a broader base of knowledge about the individual to identify and expand upon possible choices, to raise possibilities in a supported manner, and to help the individual identify with the positive experiences that specific activities might hold. For example, Jamie had opportunities to observe how Alex's living context might influence his activity and participation patterns and this sparked ideas about possible activities and support needs. Within those opportunities, Jamie purposely made efforts to engage Alex's interest in the surrounding environment, and the activities within those contexts.

Identifying potential activities that can be added rapidly to the individual's life can evolve from:

- Knowledge about past interests and activity involvement.
- Understanding the significance of personal possessions.
- Eliciting narratives or memorable stories about valued activities.
- Observing the individual's interactions with immediate surroundings.
- Knowing about important people and events in the person's life.
- Understanding how the individual's cultural connections might influence activities.
- Knowing the times of day/week that are 'best' and 'worst' for the person.

Knowing the activity and participation offerings in the individual's local neighbourhood can provide useful information. Co-creating a neighbourhood 'activity resource map' can serve to give a concrete picture of local opportunities. Such activity and participation resource maps emerged from the asset mapping approaches developed in well-established community development and capacity building approaches (see for example, McKnight & Kretzman, 2012). For service providers whose work is primarily with individuals, this type of mapping provides a relatively simple way to know community and to consider how community opportunities and associations might be constructed to provide real opportunities for activity and participation. *Worksheet 3.2: Mapping activity and participation opportunities in the local community* provides a simple template for the service provider and the individual served to collaboratively consider potential local opportunities for activity and participation. A wide range of examples of community mappings and examples are now available on the internet.

Resource 3.1: Looking for ideas for small activity and participation changes? identifies a broad range of relatively simple and brief activities and participation that may spur ideas. Other tools are available or could be adapted for a similar use. For example, the Temple University Collaborative on Community Inclusion offers a wide range of examples and tools that can assist with the selection of and engagement in meaningful activities and participation (see www.tucollaborative.org/).

3.4 Supporting the Rapid Engagement in Activities and Participation

The rapid involvement in even very small activities requires attention to the factors and challenges that may interfere. For example, in our opening vignette Alex's efforts to walk in his community were challenged by a lack of footwear, while Sol in the appendix finds his activity selection challenged by breathing issues related to smoking. The skill is for the service provider to balance efforts to exhort the individual to engage in activity, while attending to issues and their potential solutions. For example, support practices could include:

- Spending time during conversations to review the plans for the activity experiments, planning when and where it will occur.
- Balancing the anticipation of potential challenges with the identification of strengths, strategies, or preparatory steps that will be useful in the face of challenges.
- Reflecting on the actual experience of the activity experiment.

Reflection questions for consideration might include, for example:

- How did your experience compare with what you thought would happen when we first talked about this activity experiment?
- Were there unexpected things that occurred? What did these things mean for your involvement in the activity?
- What did you learn from this activity experiment?
- What did you enjoy about the new activity? Is this the first time you have experienced that? What other activities have you done that provide this benefit?
- What was the best part about the change?
- What was the most challenging part?
- Did any other changes occur to your routine as a result of making the change?

- Does this lead you to think of other things you might like to try?
- Is there anything that would have made it a better experience for you?

If the individual found the efforts to engage in activity and participation difficult or overwhelming, or was unable to be involved despite intentions to do so, work together to consider how plans for this quick change could be refined. Encourage the individual to either keep up the new activity or to incorporate another activity in order to maintain momentum towards change.

A record of these activity experiments can be kept on *Worksheet 3.3: Record of activity experiments*. Individuals can also benefit from revising their daily activity logs to reflect on how the addition of even a few small activities can alter their activity patterns. The goal is to build momentum and confidence and to use experimentation to enable learning and motivation for longer term change.

3.5 Key Competencies

The competencies associated with this chapter are the attitudes, knowledge, and skills directed to engaging in 'doing', and prompting supported action in activity and participation. These competencies are particularly necessary when individuals have a history of persistent and significant disengagement from activity and participation. These competencies include:

- Collaborating to conceive of possibilities for rapid activity and participation changes aligned with personal meanings, values, and choices.
- Anticipating potential challenges to rapid activity and participation changes and identifying approaches to facilitate action.
- Supporting individuals in the process of evaluation of personal experiences in activity and participation.

Facilitating activity experiments (service provider version)

Name: _____ **Date:** _____

Activity experiment: _____

Reflection Questions

1. What meaning might this activity experiment hold for the individual?	
2. What features of this activity change are likely to support engagement?	
3. What factors may interfere with engagement in this activity experiment?	
4. Ideas to facilitate likelihood of engagement in selected activity change	

Mapping activity and participation opportunities in the local community

Name: _____ Date: _____

This worksheet provides a template for thinking about potential opportunities located in the local community or neighbourhood. Select a community boundary that can be easily accessed, whether on foot or easy forms of transport. Identify places, associations, organizations, etc. that could be connected to each item. Remember, that this map will provide general information. More information may be necessary to understand more specific opportunities and their potential within each identified option. For example, libraries may be identified as educational/learning facilities, but actually host a wide range of cultural, artistic, and advocacy activities.

Type of Asset	Description	Local Community Examples
Outdoor spaces	Greenspaces, gardens, parks, natural settings for gathering, outdoor sites for sports and exercise	
Community places that centre on activities	Recreational centres, community centres, game rooms and clubs, social clubs	
Educational/ knowledge facilities	Schools (primary, secondary, college, university, etc.), libraries, literacy centres, community information centres	
Artistic/creative places	Art galleries, studios or centres, theatre, cinemas, music or dance facilities	

Public amenities	Shops/malls, groceries, restaurants/eateries/cafés, public markets, community fairs or festivals	
Special interests	Advocacy groups, neighbourhood associations, service clubs, club house, volunteer opportunities, charitable and community assistance services	
Spiritual/religious	Churches, places for spiritual worship and practice, spiritual sites	
Cultural places	Museums, cultural/ethnic meeting sites, heritage sites	
Productivity/work	Employment centres, business associations, partnership/ placement, opportunities, social enterprises	
Sports and fitness	Sports teams and associations, fitness facilities	
Other		

Record of activity experiments

Name: _____ Date: _____

List your selected activity experiments, the date and brief comments about the experiment:

Activity Experiment	Date	Comments about the Experience and Progress

Looking for ideas for small activity and participation changes?

Here is a list of activities that are relatively simple and require little preparation. Consider any that sound interesting to you. Then, try one, two, or a few – you may be surprised how good you feel when you're finished!

A. Examples of Small 'Activity Experiments' in the Area of Self-Care:

PERSONAL CARE

Dressing:
- Wear a shirt you haven't worn lately
- Try to mix/match a top and bottom differently
- Try a new hair style
- Tie dye some clothes
- Explore different styles and layering clothing
- Try different accessories

Bathing:
- Try a new body wash or shampoo
- Play some new music while you bathe/shower
- Take a bubble bath or use a bath bomb
- Sing in the shower

Eating:
- Have breakfast
- Try a new fruit or vegetable
- Try a new restaurant
- Try a new ethnic food – maybe one that a friend enjoys
- Have a meal in a new setting – maybe outdoors
- Take vitamins
- Have a warm drink
- Enjoy an early morning coffee and newspaper

Hygiene:
- Shave
- Get a haircut or try a different hairstyle
- Try a different toothbrushing routine
- Have or give a manicure/pedicure
- Try a new colour of nail polish
- Explore new grooming products
- Use a face mask
- Massage cream into your hands
- Put moisturizing cream on your face/body
- Put on perfume or cologne
- Combing or brushing your hair
- Use dental floss
- Exfoliate your face and body

Resource 3.1

Health:
- Get a flu shot
- Drink more water in your day
- Book an appointment for a medical check-up
- Dispose of your expired medicines
- Read the nutrition facts label on packaged foods

COMMUNITY MANAGEMENT

Transportation:
- Try taking a bus to a new location
- Go for a bike ride
- Walk a short distance
- Ask a friend or family member for a ride

Shopping:
- Try a different store for grocery shopping
- Go shopping with a friend
- Combine a drugstore visit with a rest at the local coffee shop
- Go window shopping in a different area of town
- Support small businesses
- Visit a local farmers market
- Buy music
- Browse at a second-hand book shop
- Go to a flea market

Finances:
- Record what you are spending each day for a week
- Check out a thrift or second-hand shop
- Look at the flyers for sales
- Do up a monthly budget plan

B. Examples of Small 'Activity Experiments' in the Area of Productivity:

PAID/UNPAID WORK
- Look online at the volunteer positions posted
- Dig out your old resume
- Visit the local employment agency
- Do an interest inventory to determine what you like to do
- Visit a volunteer coordinator
- Develop a list of potential jobs

HOUSEHOLD MANAGEMENT

Cleaning:
- Clean off a counter or table surface
- Spend 30 minutes per day on one room
- Organize one drawer or one shelf in your storage closet
- Recycle your newspapers and cans
- Give your old clothes to a local charity

- Vacuum/sweep the floor
- Light scented candles, oils, or incense
- Put up a framed picture or artwork
- Organize and manage your email inbox
- Decorate your living room
- Open the curtains and blinds to let light in
- Do the dishes
- Make your bed with fresh sheets
- Rearrange the furniture in your house

Laundry:
- Do one load of washing and drying
- Shine your shoes

Cooking:
Plan and prepare your favourite food
Try a new recipe
Watch a cooking show
Eat by candlelight
Cook some meals to freeze for later
Make jams or preserves
Make a pot of tea
Make some cookies for a friend

C. Examples of Small 'Activity Experiments' in the Area of Leisure:

QUIET RECREATION:
Pleasurable activities/hobbies/crafts:
- Find an unfinished project
- Make something useful out of recyclable materials
- Look through magazines or on the internet to see if there are any hobbies that interest you
- Look through the local college or city parks and recreation catalogue to see if there is a class of interest
- Play a musical instrument
- Listen to your favourite music
- Listen to a symphony
- Watch a sunset
- Repot a plant
- Listen to a comedian or take in a funny movie
- Cook a vegetarian dinner
- Try a new type of tea
- Write a poem
- Sing in the shower
- Try a new flavour of ice cream
- Reduce your time in front of the TV by a half hour
- Take a nap
- Visit a new website on the computer

- Play a new computer game, video, or board game
- Listen to a podcast
- Create a doodle journal
- Draw or paint
- Try sewing, crocheting, knitting, or embroidery
- Research a topic of interest
- Listen to a podcast or radio show
- Go to a free public lecture
- Re-watch a favourite movie
- Do crossword puzzles
- Flip through old photo albums
- Write down a list of things you are grateful for
- Watch funny videos on YouTube
- Do five minutes of deep breathing
- Make a playlist of upbeat songs
- Make a to-do list of tasks
- Get an adult colouring book
- Try journaling about your day
- Gaze at the stars
- Learn about your family tree
- Write a positive comment on a website/blog

Reading:

- Try finding a short story book and reading one story
- Read a magazine or online article
- Borrow an audio book from the library
- Try a different newspaper
- Read some comics
- Read some poetry
- Read a new type of book or a new online site

ACTIVE RECREATION

Sports:

- Stretch after a warm shower
- Rent a yoga, Pilates, or Tai Chi DVD from the library or store
- Dance around the living room
- Walk along the waterfront
- Make a list of all the sports you have tried and ones you are interested in
- Watch a new sports show on TV
- Read a story about an inspiring athlete
- Take a free yoga class
- Take the stairs instead of the elevator
- Follow a workout video
- Go for a bike ride
- Go for a run

Outings:

- Visit an art gallery, museum, or facility that you have not tried before
- Try a new food from a different culture (e.g., Indian, Vietnamese, Greek, Japanese, Chinese)
- Go to a local event
- Go the local library and borrow a CD, DVD, or book
- Use the internet at your local library
- Visit your seniors' centre
- Paddle or row a boat
- Fly a kite
- Find an activity partner; it is more fun with a friend
- Go on a picnic
- Try hiking
- Visit the local animal shelter
- Spend time in nature
- Go birdwatching or feed the birds
- Walk around the neighbourhood
- Walk around the town and notice the architecture of buildings
- Follow a river path

Gardening:

- Plant, dig, prune, rake, or weed
- Get a new plant
- Put a vase of fresh flowers in your house
- Care for indoor plants/flowers
- Learn about plants that will grow in your region

Travel:

- Take a bus to a new area
- Rent a movie or watch a YouTube video about a travel destination
- Go to a new community in your area with a friend

SOCIALIZATION
Visiting/phone calls/parties/correspondence:

- Invite a friend for a cup of tea at your home or a local shop
- Call an old friend
- Call your favourite relative
- Send a card to someone
- Send an e-mail
- Set up a Facebook account
- Send someone your favourite YouTube video
- Play a boardgame or online game with friends
- Have a movie night
- Video group call with friends or family
- Send a text
- Create a group chat

- Journal the dates of important birthdays
- Picnic with friends
- Do a favour for someone
- Talk to an older relative and ask them questions about their life
- Plan a nice surprise for someone else
- Write an 'I love you' card to a family member or friend
- Talk to or introduce yourself to your neighbours
- Make a gift for someone
- Give someone a hug

4 Providing Education about Activity and Participation, Mental Illness, and Recovery

Alex continued in his collaboration with Jamie to make changes to his activity and participation patterns but remained cautious and tentative. His anxiety about making changes was somewhat relieved with assurances that he was ultimately in control. Jamie also assured Alex that he would be provided the support he required.

Jamie knew that providing information can be an important enabler of the recovery process and shared information on an ongoing basis. Jamie considered what type of information would be most useful to Alex to support his sustained investment in the process of change. Particular attention was paid to presenting information in an accessible manner that would meet Alex's need for knowledge without overwhelming him. Jamie tried to capitalize on those moments where providing information would be likely to be taken up by Alex, and perhaps help him in learning to live beyond some of the limitations of mental illness. For example, when Alex said that he didn't experience pleasure in activity the way that he used to, Jamie provided him with some evidence-based information about why that might be, while also providing evidence-based information about recovery that was meant to induce hope.

Jamie was also sensitive to Alex's perception that he was held to blame for his situation. He once commented, 'I might have had an easier time of learning to live with my mental health problem, if it was ever said that other people contributed [to these problems]'. For example, in discussing mental illness with Alex, Jamie made sure to highlight the growing knowledge and evidence related to social factors.

Over the course of their work together, Jamie and Alex discussed how involvement in activities and participation is believed to influence well-being, and how experiences with mental illness can influence activity and participation. Alex stated that he certainly 'recognized himself' in some of the information. Jamie asked Alex if perhaps his family might benefit from this information; with more awareness and understanding they might be in a better position to be supportive.

Focused Questions:

1. Why do you think people with serious mental illness often have difficulties with engaging fully in activity and participation that could contribute to their health and well-being?
2. The problems experienced by Alex related to his emotional connections to activity and participation are often referred to as 'negative symptoms'. What ideas and language would you use to talk to Alex about his emotional disconnection from activity and participation? What factors did you consider when developing your response?
3. What social factors do you think have a significant influence on Alex's activity and participation patterns?

This chapter includes the following three worksheets:

Worksheet 4.1: The health and well-being benefits of my current activities
Worksheet 4.2: Managing stress in activity and participation
Worksheet 4.3: Understanding how substance use impacts my activities and participation

This chapter includes the following eight resources:

Resource 4.1: The multiple 'well-being' benefits of activity and participation
Resource 4.2: One activity, many benefits
Resource 4.3: Making clear the benefits of activities and participation

DOI: 10.4324/9781003111368-4

Resource 4.4: The recovery benefits of activity and participation

Resource 4.5: How is mental illness connected to activity and participation?

Resource 4.6: Overcoming potential barriers to activity and participation

Resource 4.7: Moving beyond stress in activity and participation

Resource 4.8: Substance use, activity and participation, and well-being

4.1 Information and Knowledge about Activities and Participation and Recovery in Serious Mental Illness

Providing information and education is a common evidence-based strategy to promote recovery in serious mental illness (World Health Organization, 2016; Xia et al., 2011). Psychoeducation is a specific form of education and has been used extensively with people with mental illness to foster their understanding of the illness, develop coping skills, and change problematic lifestyle behaviours. Developing an individual's foundation of knowledge about the mental illness they experience and its influence on their daily lives can enable recovery in several ways. First, it can help develop truly collaborative relationships between individuals and their mental health service providers. Second, it can facilitate the development of the individual's mastery over the illness experience, providing possibilities to move beyond the constraints posed by the illness experience in daily life (Mueser et al., 2002).

Focused education is frequently used as a strategy in public health and community development, as a means to change population-based behaviours that have been linked to poor health. Common public health campaigns have focused on reducing smoking, increasing physical activity, and practicing good nutrition among the general population. Presenting the link between activity, participation, and health as a 'population' issue may serve to increase awareness and commitment by demonstrating that it is an issue with broad applicability, while highlighting issues and information of particular relevance for people who experience mental illness.

Contemporary perspectives on health-related education highlight the importance of grounding initiatives in an 'ecological' framework that recognizes that human health behaviours emerge in the context of complex inter-relationships with social and environmental conditions (Golden & Earp, 2012; Ory et al., 2002). Delivering an educational program about activity and participation, health, and mental illness without due consideration for the complex social and environmental conditions that people with serious mental illness can find themselves in is potentially harmful by creating a situation where people with mental illness are further disempowered, by presenting them as the source of their own problems.

Tips for providing information/education:

- Consider the best 'timing' for providing information. Education can be provided at any point in the helping process where it will have a positive impact.
- The educational materials provided in this section can be offered in either a formal psychoeducational format, or informally as part of ongoing dialogue.
- The resources provided in this section can be adapted for use with groups.
- Include information about activity and participation and mental illness in work with the individual's family and social network.
- Not all the information provided in this section will be relevant to each individual. Use knowledge of the individual to highlight information that may be particularly applicable, present information in accessible language and engage the individual in discussions about its relevance.
- Use personal stories, widely available in the literature or through peer-support connections, to 'bring to life' the information provided through education. For example, the work of Patricia Deegan and others (1988, 1996, or online – Recovery Stories) provides a powerful example of how the activity patterns of an individual with serious mental illness are transformed from deprivation and marginalization to meaning and active civic engagement. A wide range of stories are now available online in written and audio forms.

Tips for increasing understanding about the link between activities, participation, and mental health across the mental health system:

- Display information materials linking activity, participation, and mental health and well-being prominently in your agency or organization.
- Ensure that education about activity and participation patterns and mental health is included in formal psychoeducation interventions.
- Encourage open discussions about the link between activity participation and mental illness among the members of your service. For example, issues related to stress-induced relapse of mental illness can make service providers cautious in promoting activities and participation. Yet, recovery depends on enabling individuals to take on meaningful activities beyond those self-care activities associated with managing illness. This is a 'service tension' that will require ongoing dialogue.
- Contemporary innovations in psychoeducation have advanced the development options to involve peers (Rummel-Kluge & Kissling, 2008). Develop working partnerships between professionals and peer providers who have an interest in and commitment to promoting health through activity and participation.

4.2 The Connection between Activity, Participation, and Health and Well-Being

Public health education related to activity has traditionally focused on physical activity – and specifically on activities that involve physical endurance, flexibility, and strength to maintain body health. Human health and well-being, however, is a multi-dimensional construct that requires consideration of the multiple dimensions, including social, cultural, emotional, psychological, economic, spiritual, intellectual, and occupational dimensions. These eight dimensions have been developed by Dr. Peggy Swarbrick and others in the model of wellness for personal and professional practice (see Collaborative Support Programs of New Jersey, www.cspnj.org) and further defined with information, tools, and resources.

Resource 4.1: The multiple 'well-being' benefits of activity and participation identifies a range of benefits. For example, some of the potential *social* benefits of activity and participation include interactions with other people in the local environment or community, impacting on the well-being of others, and decreasing dependence on others. Potential *spiritual* benefits include contributing to a sense of purpose and meaning in life. *Psychological* and *cognitive* benefits can include the ongoing development of one's knowledge, skills, and abilities, and doing things that build and express self-identity. *Emotional* benefits include the ability to have beautiful, powerful or poignant experiences. Of course, activity has multiple benefits for *physical health.*

Participation in any one activity can bring multiple benefits. ***Resource 4.2: One activity, many benefits*** provides an example of how one activity (working part-time in the public library) has the potential to offer a wide range of personal benefits that can be shared and discussed. This resource can be used to encourage discussion that personalizes the multiple benefits of activity. Similarly, ***Resource 4.3: Making clear the benefits of activity and participation*** provides information about how particular activities that are common to daily routines can influence overall health and well-being.

Understanding the benefits and how they are experienced depends on our understanding of the individual's own unique experience and situation, and the steps they are taking in their recovery journey. For example, an individual living with mental illness who cuts back on activities and participation for a time period, might be doing so in an effort to manage an acute trigger of their illness, a purposeful effort directed to self-care; a process that has been described as 'woodshedding' (Shiers et al., 2009). ***Worksheet 4.1: The health and well-being benefits of my current activities*** provides a collaborative exercise to examine how a range of benefits associated with activity and participation are currently being realized in an individual's daily life.

Working with people who have experience marginalization in their communities, it can be difficult to envision that the first few steps towards activity and participation can lead to major changes in self-understanding, opportunities, social position, civic engagement, and voice. But the potential is indeed there. Personal stories about people living with serious mental illness who found their lives transformed provide poignant and memorable examples.

4.3 Activity, Participation, and Recovery in Serious Mental Illness

Involvement in meaningful activities and participation has consistently been identified as an important element of the process of recovery in serious mental illness (Jaiswal et al., 2020). Enabling activity and participation that is highly individualized, self-directed, and strengths-based is both an important recovery outcome and an integral aspect of the recovery process. The development of both recovery competencies (Russinova et al., 2013), along with focused recovery interventions, such as those offered through *The Recovery Workbook* (Barbic & Krupa, 2009; Spaniol et al., 2009) are good examples of advancements in engaging individuals with serious mental illness in increasing awareness and understanding of recovery and in securing sustained investment to the process. The approach is meant to compliment these important recovery-focused interventions by directing attention to the powerful role of activity and participation in the recovery process.

Resource 4.4: The recovery benefits of activity and participation can be used on its own, or as a complement to other recovery-focused interventions to support understanding about this powerful link between activity, participation, and recovery. The resource offers examples of how engagement in activity and participation characterized by critical features (i.e., personally meaningful, individualized, self-directed, and strengths-based) can serve as a foundation for realizing elements critical to recovery (Jaiswal et al., 2020).

4.4 How Does Mental Illness Impact Health and Well-Being through Activity and Participation?

The relationship between mental illness, activity, and participation is complex and is influenced by interactions across a range of factors. A central goal of this intervention is to provide individuals with information about this relationship, with a view to influencing their ability to positively influence their own well-being through activity and participation. This intervention offers simplified and 'user-friendly' versions of related information. However, service providers who have a sound understanding of the knowledge base related to activity, participation, and health will be in the best position to address any individual's information needs. In addition, a good understanding of the learning needs of an individual will enhance the likelihood that the materials provided will be delivered in a relevant manner.

People with serious mental illness often describe tremendous changes in the way they experience their daily activities. These descriptions have typically included difficulties with feeling motivated and sustaining interest in activity; a weakened sense of enjoyment and pleasure from activities; unpleasant emotions such as anxiety associated with activity and participation; few opportunities for activity and participation that hold meaning and value; difficulty in activities and participation with particular types of social interactions; difficulty in planning and following through with activities and participation; cognitive changes or changes in thinking such as reduced attention, working memory (i.e., holding information in your mind), and flexibility in thinking processes; and sensory overload or under stimulation in activity and participation. Often these changes begin occurring well before the onset of an identified mental illness, and in many cases many years before (see for example, Velthorst et al., 2017).

The reasons for these changes are complex and not completely understood. In the Action Over Inertia approach, explanations of how mental illness and activity and participation are connected are organized according to three broad categories: *biomedical*, *psychological*, and *social*. **Resource 4.5: How is mental illness connected to activity and participation?** provides a summary of the main points for sharing and discussion. The information provided here is brief, and service providers are encouraged to both familiarize themselves, and keep current with the knowledge and growing evidence-based fundamental to each. While information is meant to be empowering, a danger is that the issues raised can seem overwhelming and insurmountable. Frequent reinforcements about the potential for positive change are integral. **Resource 4.6: Overcoming potential barriers to activity participation** is meant to encourage consideration of how some common reasons for limited activity and participation might be addressed.

4.4.1 Bio-Medical Perspectives

Biomedical explanations focus on the structures, physiology, and functions of the human body that could account for disruptions experienced in activity and activity patterns. Although the information here presents distinct central nervous system structures and functions, they actually operate as an integrated whole.

4.4.1.1 Brain Structure

The brain is divided into two halves – the left and right hemispheres. Each hemisphere contains four lobes: frontal, parietal, occipital, and temporal. One area that has been found to play a role in activity and participation in people with mental illness is the frontal lobe. The frontal lobes are responsible for complex thought processes, such as planning activities, making decisions, interacting with others, controlling behaviour, processing emotions, and personality.

An impact on the frontal lobes through illness or injury can lead to changes in personality and behaviour. This can interfere with motivation to do things that were once enjoyable and the sense that the thinking and planning involved is overwhelming.

The frontal lobes are adjacent to the temporal lobes, and their functions overlap. The temporal lobes contain the limbic system, which is known as the 'reward centre' of the brain, and important for motivation and pleasure. Changes in the limbic system associated with mental illness may be another reason why activities are experienced as less rewarding.

Some forms of mental illness have also been associated with enlarged lateral ventricles. Ventricles are cavities within the brain that hold *cerebrospinal fluid*, which acts to cushion the brain and protect it from injury. The ventricles are adjacent to many important brain structures. Enlarged lateral ventricles have been associated with lower energy and motivation, less social interaction, lack of enjoyment, and decreased ability to sustain attention – all likely to impact the experience of engaging in activities.

4.4.1.2 Neurophysiology

Neurotransmitters are the chemical messengers that *neurons* or nerve cells use to communicate with each other. Neurons carry information from the body to the brain and vice versa. There are billions of neurons in the brain. Impulses from other neurons are received by the dendrites and sent to the cell body of the neuron. The cell body receives all impulses and keeps track of all of the inputs. If enough inputs are received, the cell body reaches its threshold and transmits the impulse down the *axon*. When information travels along the axon, it is called an action potential. The axon is covered with myelin, which is a fatty layer that acts as an insulator and speeds up the rate at which information travels along the neuron.

At this point, the impulse has travelled the full length of the neuron. For the impulse to be transmitted, it has to be passed on to another adjoining neuron. Passing impulses between two neurons is called synaptic transmission. A synapse is the space between the synaptic terminal of one neuron and the dendrites of the receiving neuron.

How is the impulse transmitted across the synapse? It is passed along by chemicals called neurotransmitters. When the action potential reaches the end of the axon, it signals to the release of neurotransmitters which then spill into the synaptic cleft, and land on receptors on the postsynaptic membrane of the receiving neuron, where the whole process begins again. What do neurotransmitters have to do with the experience of enjoying occupation? Changes in neurotransmitters appear to be involved in the way people with mental illness experience activities. Dopamine, serotonin, and glutamate (among others) are neurotransmitters that have been associated with a wide range of mental illnesses. Disruptions in neurotransmitters in the context of mental illness might affect the experience of activities, by impacting motivation rewards, mood, impulsivity, enjoyment, attention, energy, etc.

4.4.1.3 The Impact of Medications on Activity

Medications taken to treat mental illness and their side effects may also change the experience of activities and participation. While medications can be very effective in reducing symptoms and avoiding relapse of acute mental illness, the ongoing use of medications can bring many challenges. Deegan's (2020) personal narrative of using medications to support recovery details a range of challenges that individuals may need to deal with, from learning to become active participants in the treatment process, to integrating the use of medicines into one's self identity. Medications meant to contribute to health may also come with unwanted side effects related to activity and participation that require the development of coping strategies to deal with the impact on activity. Common side effects of medications that impact activity participation include: feeling tired, lack of motivation and/or energy, sexual dysfunction, difficulty concentrating or feeling 'foggy', weight gain, and changes in body movements.

4.4.2 Psychological Perspectives

The psychological elements of particular relevance are those functions that lie at the heart of human potential for growth and change. These are the psychological processes that influence how humans think about themselves in relation to activities and participation and how this influences their engagement.

Humans are inherently motivated for activities and participation – this motivation is fundamental to survival. Motivation is a complex psychological process that includes initiating human activity, giving direction and purpose to action and sustaining involvement. Motivation can be quickly and profoundly disturbed by experiences with mental illness. The following are a few ways this disruption in motivation for activity and participation can be expressed:

4.4.2.1 Hopefulness vs. Hopelessness

Ongoing symptoms of mental illness, personal limitations experienced in the wake of mental illness, and the disruption of important life plans and activities can interfere with an individual's ability to imagine a future with meaningful possibilities and potential. Hopefulness is considered a foundational element of the recovery process in serious mental illness.

4.4.2.2 Active Involvement or Agency vs. Passivity or Powerlessness

Individuals experiencing mental illness can feel that they have lost control of their health and well-being and of their present and future lives. Deegan (1988) described how her inertia in daily life was a type of strategy in response to overwhelming sense of hopelessness and powerlessness.

4.4.2.3 Activity-Promoting Self-Evaluations vs. Activity-Inhibiting Self-Evaluations

Negative experiences with mental illness can impact self-confidence and self-esteem and belief in one's own abilities. This self-doubt can lead to caution and even avoidance of activities. The experience of serious mental illness, with its impact on thinking and feeling, and even physical appearance, can disturb an individual's sense of their own identity and this can impact the choices they make (or do not make) related to activity and participation. Seeman (2017) in an interesting review argues that people with serious mental illness, with a specific focus on the diagnosis of schizophrenia, should be supported in their efforts towards self-redefinition.

4.4.2.4 Affect/Mood that Promotes or Inhibits Activity and Participation

There are a broad range of human emotions connected to activity and participation. While pleasant emotions are easily understood to be enabling of activity and participation, unpleasant emotions can also play an important part in promoting function and action. However, where people with serious mental illness experience high levels of anxiety, distress, worry, fear, etc., they may find some activities and participation opportunities uncomfortable or threatening, even when the desire to engage in a particular activity or participation option is present. Knowledge about the emotional states experienced in serious mental illness is advancing with new understandings being proposed. For example, anhedonia, or the inability to experience pleasure, has long been identified as prevalent among individuals with some forms of serious mental illness. However, recently studies have suggested that the idea of anhedonia may need to be reconsidered, and that perhaps individuals can experience pleasure, but other processes, such as issues related to seeking out and engaging in activities may be at the core (see for example, Strauss et al., 2018).

4.4.2.5 Interpersonal Processes that Enable
or Inhibit Activity and Participation

Engagement in activity and participation will place a range of demands on an individual to interact with others, in a variety of ways, for a variety of purposes, and within the bounds of varied social norms. In serious mental illness, the psychological processes underlying social interaction can be impacted by, for example, compromising trust in others, understanding and responding to complex social situations, dealing with conflict, and enacting social behaviours. Certainly, individuals can find themselves having to manage particularly difficult social situations, for example, dealing with disclosure, and making up for previous breaking of social norms (see for example, Lester & Tritter, 2005).

4.4.2.6 Coping and Adaptation

Participation in valued activities and participation requires ongoing coping and adaptation. Engagement in valued activities while living with a serious mental illness requires the development of new coping strategies and the resilience to bounce back and learn from successes and problems. Coping strategies used will be influenced by a range of factors, such as personal aptitudes and resources, social-environmental factors, and often in the case of serious mental illness judgements about the appropriateness of particular types of strategies. For example, using religion and spirituality is a recognized coping strategy, and yet may be subject to negative judgements in mental health service delivery (Gearing et al., 2011).

4.4.3 Social Perspectives

Social explanations focus on factors 'external' to the individual that can impact activity patterns. They can occur in an individual's immediate environment, reflect social and cultural expectations, or emerge from the structure or organization of important resources in the community.

4.4.3.1 Impact on 'Typical'
Developmental Milestones

For many individuals, mental illness is first experienced in youth or young adulthood, at a critical time period for the creation of activity opportunities, learning important skills, and establishing the social networks that will support activity engagement. For example, engaging in education is a typical activity of youth, but when it is disrupted by mental illness it can have far reaching implications for the individual as they age – impacting career opportunities, influencing the ability to secure good references, and constraining the ability to develop a good support network that will enable intimacy and romance, family life, work, and career and leisure possibilities. In many cases, the disruption of these important activity and participation opportunities occurs well before the mental illness is formally recognized. With this in mind, efforts have been directed to identifying individuals early in the course of mental illness, in the context of their natural community environments, with a view to providing early treatment and reducing the impact on personal and social development (see for example, Li et al., 2010).

4.4.3.2 Spending Time in Hospital or Other
Settings Removed from Daily Routines,
Activities, and Participation

Receiving treatment is an important resource for individuals who experience mental illness. For some people that treatment might be delivered in a hospital setting. If the hospital stays are relatively brief and infrequent, they may pose only a minor disruption to activity participation and patterns. For some people, hospital stays, or other time away from the community where daily activities occur, can have a significant impact on activity experiences and participation. While in hospital, daily routines and activities may be curtailed and offer few choices. Hospital rules or procedures may limit access to certain types of activity opportunities. Following a hospital stay, some people report the need for a period of recuperation, overwhelmed by their absence from daily activities and unsure how to reengage. The development and implementation of recovery-oriented practice is now being extended to acute care settings, including examples of intervention approaches designed to enable the person's connection to community activities and participation (Chen et al., 2014; Lipskaya-Velikovsky et al., 2020).

4.4.3.3 Stigma and Discrimination

Societal stigma and discrimination have been described as particularly powerful forces constraining the opportunities for individuals with mental illness to engage fully in personally and socially valued activities. Members of the public can hold powerful assumptions that people with mental illness do not have the abilities needed for community activity and participation, and even that their involvement can be threatening to others. The inclusion of these assumptions into policies, standards, and other social structures surrounding important activities is a type of structural stigma. For example, hiring procedures for paid or volunteer work might be designed in a way that discriminates (even inadvertently) against people with mental illness.

Stigma is a particularly powerful force when it is accepted by the person – a process referred to as 'internalized stigma'. Of particular relevance to the Action Over Inertia approach, is the evidence that supports the potential of personal contact between people with mental illness engaged in pro-social activities and participation and the general public as an effective means to reduce stigma. In addition to providing support for the importance of attending to activity and participation, this finding has led to the innovation of important social roles for people living with mental illness as 'educators with lived experience' (Chen et al., 2016).

4.4.3.4 Racial/Ethnic/Sexual Orientation Disparities

The issues related to equitable access to important opportunities and resources based on race, ethnicity, and sexual orientation that are present in society can be expected to be present in the lives of people with serious mental illness. These disparities in access will cut across important social opportunities like education and employment, to the delivery of services meant to address these areas, and access to quality mental health care. In practice, little direct attention has been paid to understanding the nature of these disparities, how they emerge, are expressed and sustained within service delivery meant to address activity and participation, but examples of research in this area is increasing (see for example, Holley et al., 2016; Lukyanova et al., 2014).

4.4.3.5 Limited Resources and Opportunities

Full participation in meaningful activities depends on access to resources: things, people, and opportunities. People who experience mental illness can find themselves with constrained financial means that limits their access to the 'things' required to participate. For example, students may have limited access to the money required for tuition, working may be constrained by limited access to easy transportation or suitable clothing, and leisure may be impacted by limited funds for equipment or entrance fees. Doing activities is supported by social networks, and to the extent that people with mental illness find themselves experiencing reduced social contacts, this situation will decrease their opportunities for participation.

Activity and participation have not been a primary area of concern of service provision in the mental health system. Indeed mental health service providers may not see the active support for activity and participation as a primary area for attention and they may hold faulty assumptions about the relationship between activity, participation, and mental health. Overall the mental health system has been slow to take up interventions and practices shown to support activity and participation.

4.4.3.6 Stress, Serious Mental Illness, Activity, and Participation

Concern is often expressed about the relationship between stress, activity and participation, and mental illnesses. In this workbook, stress is defined as an experience of emotional distress that emerges in response to conditions/situations perceived as personally threatening and capable of overwhelming personal adaptation and coping. Individuals with serious mental illness are considered to be vulnerable to stress (Mueser & Roe, 2016). Current renditions of the stress-vulnerability model highlight that protective factors can be developed to reduce this vulnerability. However, the risk continues that service providers who are not well informed of these factors will express an attitude of caution or even encourage avoidance of activity and participation. All activities and participation bring demands and expectations for adaptation, and avoiding these demands presents a situation where the potential for developing adaptive capacities (a hallmark of recovery) is unlikely. In addition, lack of activity and participation is itself a stressful experience, associated with a range of unpleasant experiences from boredom and loneliness to sustained poverty and community marginalization (see for example, Marrone & Golowka, 1999).

The educational resources provided in this section highlight the importance of managing stress through thoughtful strategies to develop personal adaptive capacities. The focus is on collaboratively and actively creating a good 'match' between the individual and selected activities and participation. This 'match' includes sustaining commitment, adaptation, and well-being by: highlighting the personal meaningfulness of activity and participation; capitalizing on the strengths and abilities; creating learning opportunities and support strategies; engaging resources that will support performance; applying strategies to personally control the experience of stress; and modifying or refining the activity and participation to facilitate the individual's performance and to decrease stressful elements.

Resource 4.7: Moving beyond stress in activity and participation provides a framework for understanding how vulnerability to stress may be reduced in the context of activity and participation. The accompanying ***Worksheet 4.2: Managing stress in activity and participation*** provides an opportunity to apply these ideas to the individual's own circumstances.

4.5 Activities and Participation, Well-Being, and Substance Use

In some jurisdictions, the rates of substance use among people with serious mental illness are remarkably high, yet substance use and its impacts often go unrecognized and poorly addressed by mental health services. Without direct attention, the relationship between substance use and activity and participation patterns can remain 'invisible' and therefore unaddressed in intervention approaches. Individuals are unlikely to spontaneously report substance use in their daily activity logs; substance-using behaviours are more likely to be embedded within other activities and therefore easily missed. Indeed the actions and experiences associated with substance use have features associated with meaningful activity and participation; they can bring an income, develop social connections, activate the senses, etc. For this reason, occupational therapy scholars have proposed understanding these as 'using' occupations, or 'non-sanctioned' occupations, with a view to highlighting the complexity of human activity and participation relative to social norms and values (Kiepek et al., 2019).

While reducing harmful substance use is not the primary outcome of this intervention approach, it may be useful as a complement to other interventions that directly target the reduction of harmful substance use. For example, as a match to the functional analysis of substance use, the time-use log described in Chapter 2 can provide an opportunity for reflection on the actual patterns of substance use in the context of daily activities and participation. It can help to create a more thorough picture of: conditions/context that enable substance use; substance-free activities that can perhaps serve as a foundation for reducing substance use; valued activities or circumstances that are at risk because of substance use and can thus be used to motivate behaviour change; and support needs associated with decreasing substance use in activity and participation.

While there has been a lesser focus on other high-risk addiction behaviours among people living with serious mental illness, service providers are encouraged to remain sensitive to the presence of these behaviours and to direct attention to how they might be influencing activity health and well-being. For example, gambling at casinos may not be typical of individuals with serious mental illness who are highly marginalized from community roles and locations, but gambling behaviours such as purchasing 'instant-wins' or 'scratch-cards' may be more common and place an individual at financial risk.

Resource 4.8: Substance use, activity and participation, and well-being provides information about substance abuse, activities and participation with particular focus on potential negative impacts on achieving health and well-being. *Worksheet 4.3: Understanding how substance use impacts my activities and participation* provides the opportunity for collaborative reflection on how substance use may be constraining activity and participation, as a means to encourage motivation and planning for change.

4.6 Key Competencies

The competencies associated with this chapter are aligned with the role of service provider as educator in support of recovery, health, and well-being through activity and participation. These competencies include:

- Providing evidence-based information relevant to activities and participation, and mental illness to individuals served and their families.
- Providing information in a timely manner, adapted to meet the specific needs of individuals served.
- Engaging individuals served to clarify their understanding, beliefs, and assumptions related to activity and participation and serious mental illness.
- Clearly communicating the relationship between recovery in serious mental illness and activity and participation.
- Providing information in a way that is both hope inducing and builds on strengths.

The health and well-being benefits of my current activities and participation

Name:_____ Date: _____

	Health and Well-Being Benefits
Self-care activities:	
Leisure activities:	
Productivity activities:	

Managing stress in activity and participation

Name: _____ Date: _____

Strategies to Reduce or Manage Stress	I Use this Strategy and It Works for Me	I Would Like to Use This Strategy or Improve the Way I Use This Strategy
Be clear about what is stressing me		
Build in breaks		
Make sure expectations are clear		
Learn from my past experiences with managing stress		
Modify activities so that stress is reduced		
Practice meditation or exercise to help me manage stress		
Take care of myself – e.g., watch my diet and sleep		
Avoid arguments or confrontations		
Make sure I give myself credit and see my strengths		
Watch my thinking patterns so that I don't make the situation worse		
Talk to someone I trust or depend on; use good social relationships for support		
Practice relaxation techniques		
Work on the skills that I need to meet the demands of the activity		
Practice spiritual or religious beliefs		
Use journal writing, art, or other creative activities to help me cope		
Use positive self-talk		
Learn about the things that trigger my stress and specific ways to manage these triggers		
Other		

Understanding how substance use impacts my activities and participation

Name: _____ **Date:** _____

Use these questions to consider how substance use might be impacting your activity participation and well-being.

	Yes/No	*Comments/Thoughts*
Substance use is a part of my daily routine		
I regularly use substances over the course of a typical week		
My use of substances tends to be linked to certain activities		
Using substances helps me deal with bad feelings or moods		
I regularly participate in a range of activities that do not involve substance use		
My use of substances could put activities I value at risk		
My use of substances has been a source of conflict with important people in my life		
The money I spend on using substances limits my ability to participate in other valued activities		
Using substances helps me cope with the anxiety or stress I sometimes feel in activities		

The multiple 'well-being' benefits of activity and participation

Every person needs to have the opportunity to experience a variety of activities in order to enhance their health and well-being and satisfaction in their life.

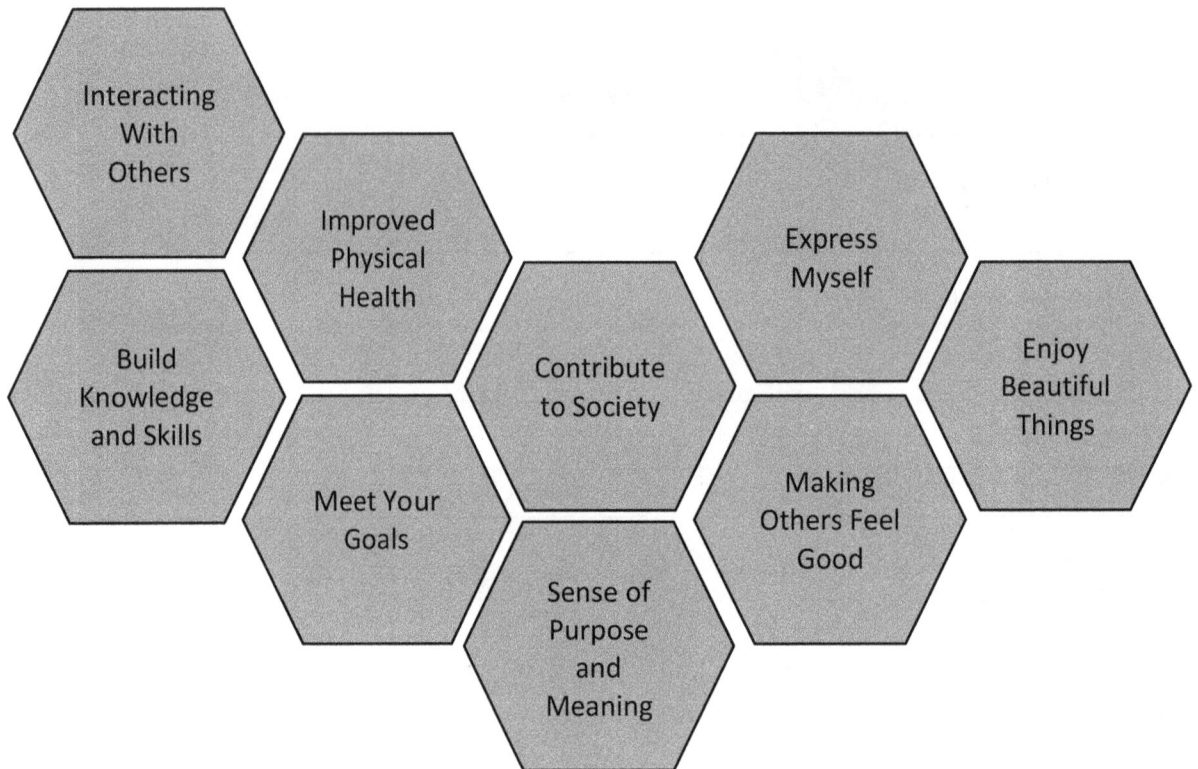

Interacting With Others

Improved Physical Health

Build Knowledge and Skills

Contribute to Society

Express Myself

Enjoy Beautiful Things

Meet Your Goals

Making Others Feel Good

Sense of Purpose and Meaning

Through activity and participation, you have the potential to experience all these benefits!

Resource 4.2

One activity, many benefits!

Any one activity may provide several benefits. For example, a person who works part-time at the public library could experience all of the following personal benefits:

Developing knowledge and skills:
Part-time work can help to develop important work skills, particularly when an individual has experienced a lengthy period out of the workforce. It also requires the development of skills to complete the job (for example, learning how books are catalogued or how to use technology for library searches). This work would also give access to reading and other resources for personal interest.

Interacting with others:
Working at the library could allow for social contacts with both the staff and the patrons. It also provides an experience that can be shared with family and friends.

Personal income:
Part-time work will provide an income that might be small but could provide extra funds to meet expenses or to save for an important purchase. It could also supplement pocket money and be used for social opportunities such as going to the movies with a friend, or buying a gift for a family member.

Contributing to society:
The library is a public resource that depends on community members to keep it going.

Try to choose activities that provide more than one benefit. For example, if you are going for a walk, invite a friend along, challenge yourself to go a longer distance, go to a new location, stop to watch a soccer game in the park, and so on. This will help to get the most from activities.

Making clear the benefits of activities and participation

Here are some benefits of a few common activities. Think about your own activity patterns – what benefits do you get?

Activity/Participation	Possible Benefits
Going for walks	• Improved mood • Maintain a healthy body weight • Decrease risk of diseases such as cancer, diabetes, heart disease • Better endurance and stamina for other desired activities • Enjoy nature
Preparing and enjoying meals	• Good nutrition and maintaining a healthy weight; lowers risk for many diseases such as Type II diabetes • Proper nutrition can give energy to participate in activities • An activity that can be enjoyed with others • Learn about the habits and routines of other cultures and develop skills in the kitchen that will be appreciated by others
Socializing	• Social supports can help in time of crisis and sadness • A social network can offer practical help • Social contacts can encourage and support participation in a range of activities • Social contacts appear to protect people against some forms of illness • It feels good to give support to others • Social interactions can lead to laughter, intimacy, feeling understood, and other positive feelings
Work and Volunteering	• Having a job or volunteer position can give a sense of purpose and importance • Personal aptitudes and interests can be used in work and volunteer activities • New skills can be learned • Social skills can be practiced in the work place and new friends can be made • Working can provide financial benefits
Grooming Routines	• Can improve self-esteem and increase comfort in public situations • Can be an important form of self-soothing that helps to reduce anxiety or distress • Can reduce the costs associated with costly health/dental care
Relaxation	• An antidote to stress • Can improve mood and reduce frustration • Can sharpen thinking skills • Reduces physiological effects that can lead to poor health

The recovery benefits of activity and participation

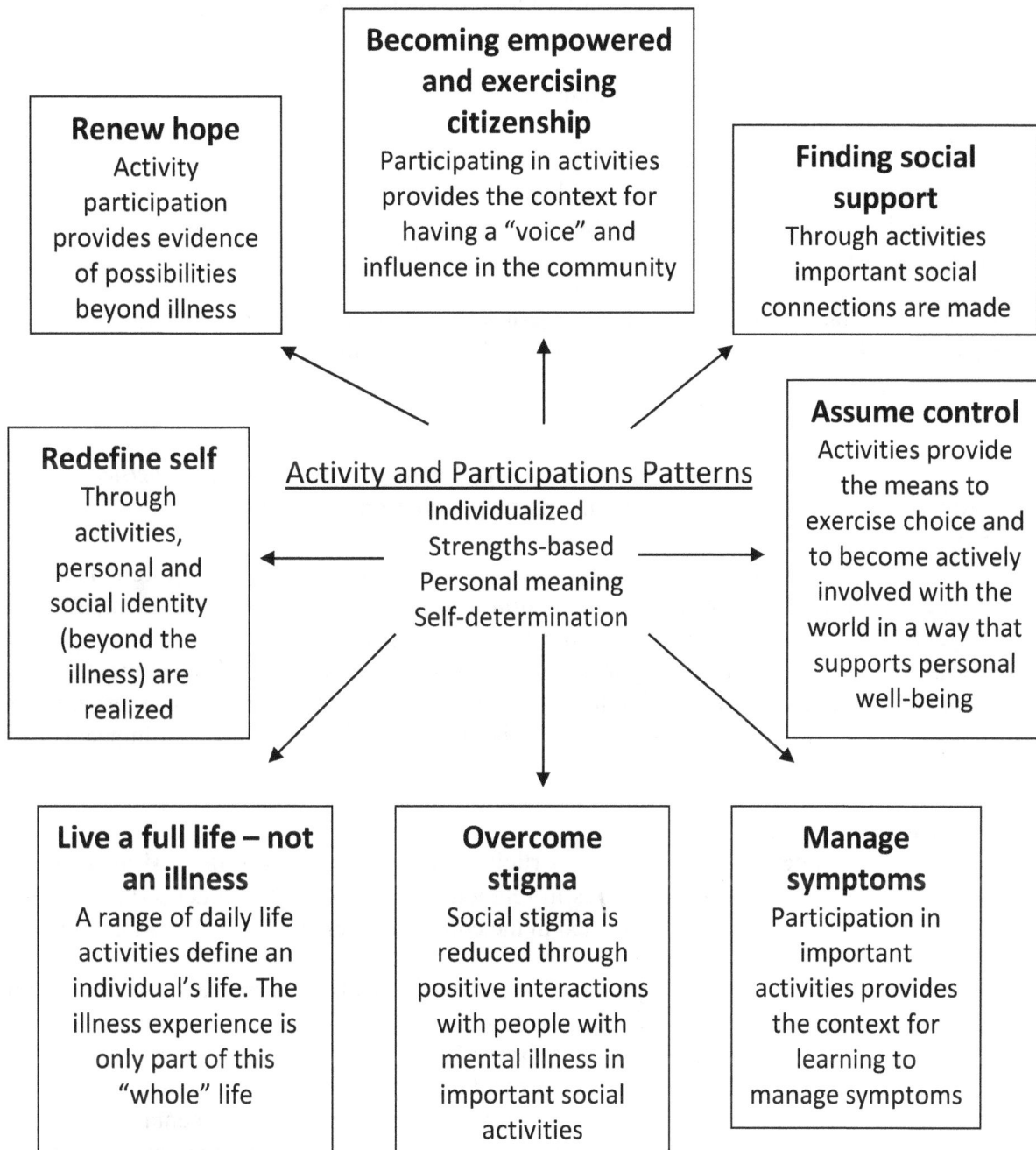

Renew hope
Activity participation provides evidence of possibilities beyond illness

Becoming empowered and exercising citizenship
Participating in activities provides the context for having a "voice" and influence in the community

Finding social support
Through activities important social connections are made

Redefine self
Through activities, personal and social identity (beyond the illness) are realized

Activity and Participations Patterns
Individualized
Strengths-based
Personal meaning
Self-determination

Assume control
Activities provide the means to exercise choice and to become actively involved with the world in a way that supports personal well-being

Live a full life – not an illness
A range of daily life activities define an individual's life. The illness experience is only part of this "whole" life

Overcome stigma
Social stigma is reduced through positive interactions with people with mental illness in important social activities

Manage symptoms
Participation in important activities provides the context for learning to manage symptoms

How is mental illness connected to activity and participation?

People with mental illness often describe troubling changes in the ways **they experience daily activities and participation,** including:

- Difficulties feeling motivated and sustaining interest
- Weakened sense of enjoyment
- Unpleasant emotions, such as anxiety
- Fewer opportunities that hold meaning and value
- Difficulties in performing valued activities
- Sensory overload or under stimulation

There are three broad explanations for the factors that underlie these changes in activity and participation. Talk to your health provider about how these might apply to you.

Biomedical Explanations:

- Some forms of mental illness have been associated with changes in ***brain structures*** that are linked to important aspects of activity and participation such as planning activities, motivation and energy, emotions, the control of behaviour.
- Changes in ***neurotransmitters***, the chemical messengers that carry information through the nervous system to the body can occur. The disruptions can impact motivation, enjoyment, attention, energy, and other important aspects of activity and participation.
- ***Medications*** used to treat mental illness and their side effects will help control mental illness but can contribute to experiences like feeling tired, reduction in motivation and energy, feeling mentally 'foggy', weight gain, and changes in body movements, all which can impact activity and participation.

Psychological Explanations:

While humans are instinctively motivated to participate in activities, **psychological processes**, or the ways that people think about themselves in relation to activities, will influence their involvement. These mental processes can be impacted in the context of mental illness. For example:

- ***Hope vs hopelessness*** – With disruptions in important life plans and activities it can be hard for people to imagine a future with valued possibilities.
- ***Active involvement and agency vs inactivity/passivity*** – Individuals can feel they have lost control of their health and well-being and their present and future lives.
- ***Self-evaluations that promote vs inhibit activity*** – When experiences of mental illness negatively impact self-confidence and esteem, this can lead to self-doubt, caution, and even avoidance of valued activities and participation.
- ***Feeling pleasure vs distress*** – Mental illness can be a pleasure and motivation thief that leads to inactivity and more negative emotions. Engaging in activities that elicit a sense of mastery or pleasure can help reduce the chances of feeling distressed.

- *Interpersonal interactions* – Activities and participation can bring demands on social abilities that are difficult, such as dealing with conflict and disclosure,
- *Coping and adaptation vs feeling defeated* – Participation in valued activities while living with a mental illness requires ongoing coping and adaptation. The development of new coping strategies and the resilience to bounce back and learn from successes and problems can prevent feeling defeated.

Social Explanations:

There are factors that are 'external' to an individual that can impact activity and participation. They can occur in an individual's immediate environment, reflect social and cultural expectations, or emerge from the community structure of resources.

- *Impact on 'typical' developmental milestones* – Mental illness first experienced in young adulthood can disrupt the creation of activity opportunities, learning of important skills, and establishment of the social networks.
- *Spending time in hospital away from daily routines and activities* – Receiving treatment in a hospital setting can be important, however frequent hospital stays or time away from the community can significantly disrupt activity and participation.
- *Stigma and discrimination* – Societal stigma and its related discrimination are powerful forces constraining the opportunities for individuals with mental illness to engage fully in activities and participation in the community. Stigma can include negative assumptions that people hold, but also the inclusion of negative assumptions in to policies, standards, and other social structures. Stigma is a particularly powerful force when it is accepted by the person themselves – a process referred to as 'internalized stigma'.
- **Limited resources and opportunities** – Individuals who experience mental illness can find themselves with constrained financial means that limit their access to important resources (for example, transportation, equipment, access to opportunities because of cost) required for activity and participation.
- **Issues of equity** – people with mental illnesses can experience the same forms of inequity and disadvantage common among the general public – including disadvantage relative to race, ethnicity, age, sexual orientation, disability level, gender, etc.

Understanding the factors that might be involved in supporting or limiting activity participation can be helpful in taking steps to move forward.

Overcoming potential barriers to activity and participation

Factors constraining activity participation may be present but are not necessarily insurmountable. Here are just a few examples to get you thinking:

Stigma	Overcoming Stigma
Some people who have not experienced mental illness hold misguided attitudes about mental illness. These attitudes may make it difficult for people with mental illness to maintain healthy self-esteem or to be included in important community activities/opportunities.	Being active in the community can help to change people's attitudes about mental illness. Through such positive interactions stigma and discrimination is lessened.

Anxiety	Overcoming Anxiety
Feelings of anxiety and worry, whether due to mental illness or because of stigma and negative experiences, can make it difficult to engage in new activities or return to activities once enjoyed.	Being bored can also create feelings of anxiety and depression. When people are inactive, they tend to spend a lot of time alone, which also increases anxiety. Being active is an effective distraction from worry, and learning relaxation and anxiety management techniques can help.

Stress	Overcoming Stress
The fear that stress could prompt a relapse is often a barrier to participating in activity.	Engaging in valued activities is important in learning to manage illness and experience recovery. Best practice in mental health matches activity participation with supports to enhance coping, manage expectations and demands, and ensure much needed supports are in place.

Resource 4.6

Changes to Social Networks	Developing New Social Networks
Social contacts can change or be lost during the course of mental illness. Confidence to socialize can be shaken. Changes in activity patterns can also affect the opportunity to meet new people.	Friends provide social support that can help to enjoy and manage day-to-day activities. By participating in new activities, opportunities to meet new people and develop new friendships can present.

Financial Barriers	Dealing with Financial Barriers
People with mental illness on a limited income may find their activity options limited. Activities can be costly, which may be a barrier to participation. Disability income may impact work opportunities.	Activities do not have to be costly. Low cost (or no cost) activities exist. Funds may be available to cover some costs of working. Familiarity with the policies related to income can ensure that all opportunities for activity participation are pursued.

Moving beyond stress in activity and participation

Consider these strategies to actively manage stress experienced in activity and participation:

I. **CHOOSING ACTIVITIES**
   Choose activities that hold personal meaning and value
   Choose activities that are a good match for your strengths, skills, abilities, and past experiences
   Learn more about your own experience of stress

II. **MANAGING STRESS IN ACTIVITY**
   Learn new skills necessary to participate in the activity
   Take stock of your coping style and skills and learn new skills to help you adapt
   Learn to identify signs/symptoms of your mental illness in activity
   Develop supports and resources to assist you with your activity participation

III. **REDUCING THE EXPERIENCE OF STRESS IN ACTIVITY**
   Consider how the activity might be changed to support your participation and reduce stress

Substance use, activity and participation, and well-being

While the use of street drugs and overuse of alcohol has been shown to increase symptoms and community living problems associated with mental illness, it can also interfere with the ability to experience the benefits of important activities and participation.

Here are a few examples:

- Substances can be *expensive*, taking away from money that could be spent doing valued or potentially rewarding activities.

- Getting street drugs and other non-prescription drugs may be *difficult and dangerous*. Getting these drugs may deplete energy – energy that could be put into other rewarding and valued activities.

- Abusing substances can cause *isolation* from important family and friends. Activities that do not depend on substance use are more likely to provide opportunities for positive social connections.

- The effects of using drugs or alcohol may make it *unsafe, difficult, or even impossible* to do other activities.

- Frequent substance use can *reduce the opportunity to experience the pleasure* and good feelings that can be associated with activity.

- While using substances might reduce anxiety or other distress associated with participating in valued activities, in the long run it can seriously *limit opportunities* for learning healthy ways of participating.

Consider reducing your use of substances. Services and resources are available to help.
Ask your mental health service providers for more information!

5 Making Longer-Term Changes

Alex and Jamie considered possible longer-term activity and participation changes. Jamie encouraged Alex to consider one or two activity changes at a time. In this way, they could plan for the supports he might need, and make changes as needed to ensure that the activities met his expectations and needs. Jamie reminded Alex that the planned changes could build on the progress already made and focus on areas of that held personal meaning and capitalize on strengths.

Together they reviewed the completed worksheets and considered possibilities. Alex decided to focus changes in two areas. First, he was interested in expanding his opportunities to participate in activities with family members. Second, he was interested in securing an opportunity to earn some money. Looking back on areas identified in *Worksheet 2.15*, Alex and Jamie noted that these planned changes had potential to solidify his social connections, improve his physical activity levels and financial well-being, and learn and practice new skills.

Looking at his family network, Alex identified his parents, his sister, and a cousin who lived locally as people with whom he would like a stronger connection. Alex noted that although he is generally cautious and uncomfortable in social contacts, his family is important to him. He recalled times (particularly early during his journey living with mental illness) when his relationship with his family was strained. Alex and Jamie discussed the possibility of rebuilding these relationships through shared activities starting with one activity with a family member each week. Alex thought that this would not overwhelm him or his family. The nature of these shared activities would need to be decided upon with his family members, but Alex noted some possibilities. For example, he hoped to be included in a family dinner at least once a month, and maybe go fishing with his father, an activity they previously enjoyed.

The second goal was initially less clear. Alex had a long history of being without work and no well-defined work interests. His main interest was in working to earn some additional income. Building on his past efforts to help out around his house, Alex and Jamie considered how these types of activities could translate into paid activities in his local community. They discussed how doing these activities for pay might compare to doing them to help out around his home. For example, working for pay would likely come with some time demands and expectations related to the quality of his work, and the need for some clothing suitable for the job. Together they learned about people or organizations in his community that might offer casual work opportunities. They also spoke to his family members and to the homeowner to see if they had any ideas about paid work opportunities that might come from these ideas.

Focused Questions:

1. How did Jamie support the selection of activity and participation changes that would be meaningful to Alex? What other strategies or approaches might you use?
2. What do you think are some of the biggest challenges to making longer term activity and participation changes for people with serious mental illness? How do these challenges compare to those experienced by people in general, when they seek to make changes in their activity and participation patterns?
3. What accessibility issues might Alex and Jamie encounter in using community organizations such as those directed to casual employment?
4. Are there any examples of activity and participation that you think are not suitable for people with serious mental illness? What are these examples? How

DOI: 10.4324/9781003111368-5

would you explain your rationale to the people you serve?

This chapter contains the following eight worksheets:

Worksheet 5.1: Mapping activity and participation to optimize health and well-being
Worksheet 5.2: Advancing inclusion, citizenship, and empowerment through activities and participation
Worksheet 5.3: Preparing for changes in activity and participation
Worksheet 5.4: Prioritizing plans for activity and participation changes
Worksheet 5.5: Accessibility checklist
Worksheet 5.6: Planning for activity and participation changes
Worksheet 5.7: Giving shape to plans for activity and participation changes

This chapter contains the following two resources:

Resource 5.1: Managing challenges to activity and participation changes
Resource 5.2: Road bumps on the path from inertia to action

5.1 Types of Changes

Enabling sustained changes in activity and participation patterns requires careful consideration and sustained and focused supports. The final aim is less about 'finding something to do' and more about ensuring that individuals with serious mental illness are able to enjoy the well-being and health benefits associated with activity and participation.

There are at least four types of changes to activity and participation patterns that can be considered. These are identified in Table 5.1 and each is described briefly in the following section.

5.1.1 Adding New Activities and Social Participation

This type of change comes readily to mind when daily life routines have a limited range of activities, when important activity and participation opportunities are no longer available, or when activity and participation patterns are characterized by deprivation. Consider the vignette of Alex. Despite the fact that Alex has used walking as a

form of mobility for his entire life, the addition of walking as a purposeful activity meant to contribute to a range of well-being benefits is essentially a new activity. Walking as a new form of activity will require considerations such as: what kinds of environments do I want to walk in? How long/far should I walk? What resources do I need to walk? What benefits can I get from walking? Are there any particular challenges that need to be considered to start and sustain walking as an activity?

5.1.2 Building on Previous Activities and Participation

Changes in activity and participation patterns can be directed to reintroducing activities and participation that held (and hold) meaning for the individual. This form of change has the benefit of building on established knowledge and experience. Alex, for example, identifies fishing with his father, an activity from his younger days, and accessible from his family home. Ananthi, the vignette in the Appendix identifies a return to college courses, a form of participation consistent with her values and expectations for her future. Despite familiarity, reintroducing activity and participation can bring new issues or challenges for consideration. Ananthi's return to college may lead to study in an entirely new field, require her to manage social situations damaged during earlier experience of mental illness and form new social relationships, bring new financial demands, etc.

5.1.3 Constructing Activity and Participation Patterns to Meet a Broad Range of Health and Well-Being Benefits

Chapter 2 in this text provided an overview of various perspectives on health and well-being through activity and participation patterns that need to be considered in planning for change. For example, consideration of balance, the extent to which there is variety across the major activity and participation categories of self-care, leisure, productivity, and rest, can guide choices and planning. Similarly, attention to circadian rhythms, the sleep-wake cycle, can be very relevant for individuals with serious mental illness, who may find their sleep cycles disturbed or out of sync with society.

A particular focus of the Action Over Inertia approach is the development of opportunities to experience a range of health and well-being benefits. Categorizing any form of activity or participation as an exemplar of one health

Table 5.1 Types of changes in activity and participation patterns

1. Adding new activity and participation opportunities
2. Building on previous activity and participation
3. Constructing activities and participation opportunities to meet a broad range of health and well-being benefits
4. Modifying activity and participation patterns to positively impact inclusion, citizenship, and empowerment

and well-being benefit is problematic; they can all be constructed to allow for a range of health and well-being experiences. For example, sport-related activities are often classified as 'leisure' activities with physical health benefits. Yet, depending on how they are constructed and experienced, sport-related activities can also be productive or work activities, associated with parenting or other forms of caregiving, self-care, making social connections, and contributing to the community. In the opening vignette, Alex is interested in translating his experience with chores to activities that might bring an income.

Activity mapping is a useful technique to evolve ideas for how specific activities and participation could provide access to a range of health and well-being experiences. The exercise of mapping involves considering specific forms of activity and participation in relation to how they might be intentionally constructed to provide specific health and well-being benefits. For example, using Alex's examples of 'walking' and helping with gardening, the mapping exercise might look like Figure 5.1:

Worksheet 5.1 Mapping activity and participation to optimize health and well-being provides a structured opportunity for collaborative planning related to identifying the potential health and well-being benefits of specific activities and participation.

5.1.4 Modifying Patterns to Positively Impact Inclusion, Citizenship, and Empowerment

As highlighted in the introduction, the Action Over Inertia approach is purposely aligned with principles of equity, inclusion, citizenship, and empowerment. Marginalization from the activity and participation opportunities afforded a society's citizens often characterizes the lives of people with serious mental illness and so direct attention to this issue is essential in preparing for longer term changes.

For service providers working in a mental health system, too often the default expectation is that activities and participation opportunities will occur within that system, with people with serious mental illness involved as 'clients' or 'patients' of 'programs'. This expectation can emerge for a range of reasons: stigma about the capacities of individuals, limitations in knowledge about supporting activity and participation, constraints related to time and resources, and operating within service systems that do not prioritize the rights of people with serious mental illness to lives characterized by meaningful activity and participation, etc. Research and scholarship detailing the philosophies, structures, and processes that sustain the constraints on citizenship and inclusion perspectives have contributed to the call for mental health systems to address these issues (see for example, Nelson et al., 2001; Ponce et al., 2016)

This intervention approach highlights the importance of collaborating with the individual around how activity and participation patterns could evolve to provide opportunities for social inclusion, for exercising citizenship

and supporting personal confidence and authority. While these might seem to be lofty ideals, they can be advanced through relatively simple strategies in day to day practice. Continuing with the example of 'walking', some of these strategies are offered as examples in Table 5.2. As noted in other parts of this book, the options provided through peer support need to be considered as distinct; they may have significant potential for bringing positive impact to personal and collective empowerment. In this way, they are not necessarily viewed as 'stepping stones' on the road to natural contexts, but rather options that add value through their unique contributions.

Worksheet 5.2 Advancing inclusion, citizenship, and empowerment through activities and participation provides an opportunity to consider how inclusivity and citizenship can be integrated into choices and related planning.

5.2 Identifying and Prioritizing Plans for Change

The reflection exercises from earlier chapters have been developed to serve as guide to focus directions for changes in activity and participation patterns. Supported planning and implementation of changes in activity and participation patterns should be directed to ensuring that they are perceived by the individual as:

- Manageable
- Within a reasonable timeframe
- Having the potential to be rewarding to the individual
- A learning experience
- Meeting personal support and resource needs

These are consistent with evidence-based principles underlying goal setting for a broad range of collaboratively planned changes in health service delivery (see for example, Wade, 2009; Clarke et al., 2009). Distinct from traditional goal setting approaches that press for clear definition of behaviourally defined goals, time frames, and conditions, this approach encourages a focus on the experiences of planned changes, and maintaining an experimental perspective that allows for rapid modifications in response to new learning. The process of planning changes is therefore a type of dynamic and negotiated practice. In essence, the focus of goal setting is on directing efforts towards intended changes. In the Action Over Inertia approach, the intended outcome is experiencing personally identified health and well-being benefits and this is best achieved by sensitivity to and flexibility in response to ongoing feedback.

5.2.1 Making It Manageable and Within a Reasonable Time Frame

Prioritizing a limited number of changes – perhaps two or three – can be a good way to start. Reasonable plans

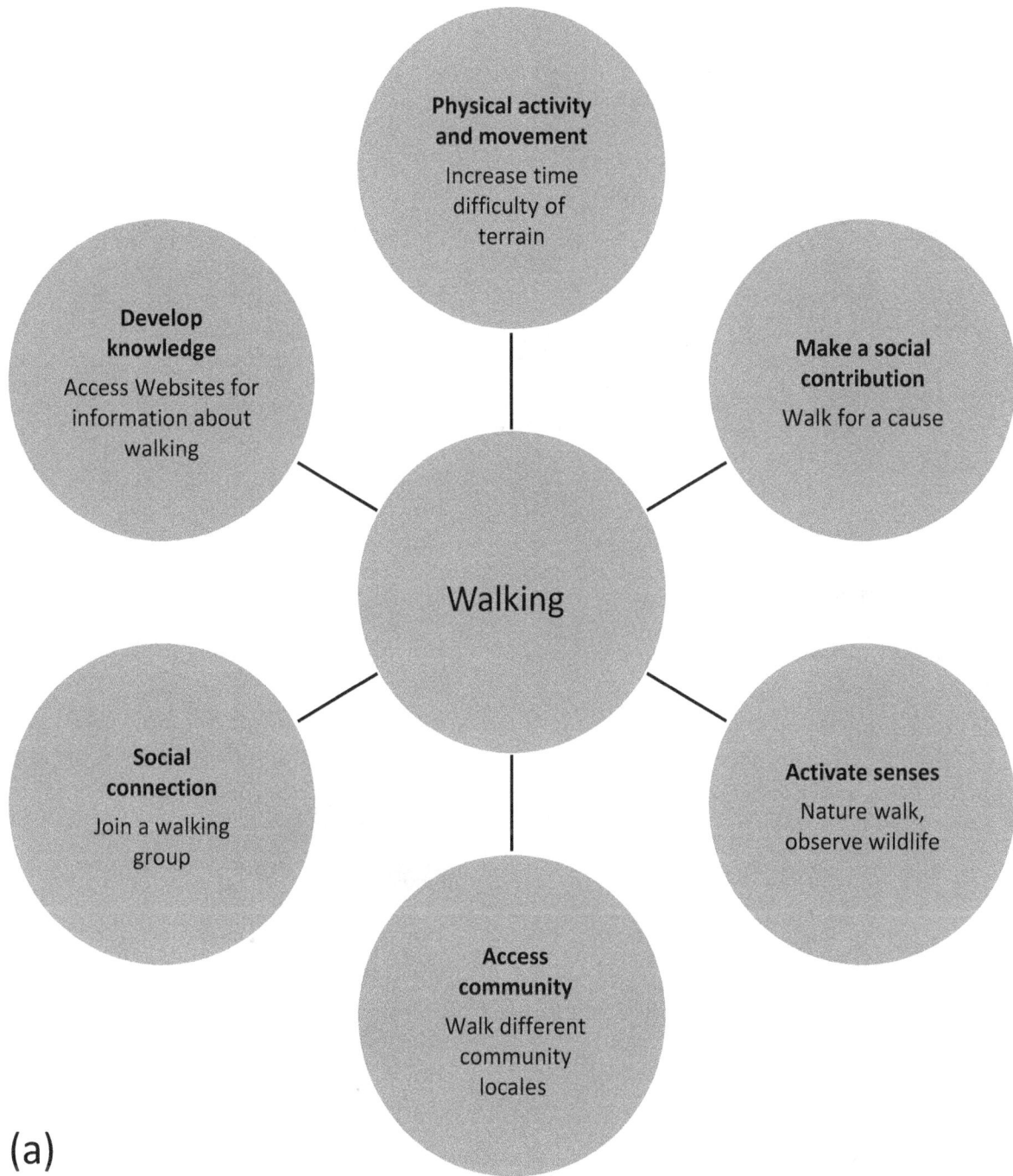

Physical activity and movement
Increase time difficulty of terrain

Develop knowledge
Access Websites for information about walking

Make a social contribution
Walk for a cause

Walking

Social connection
Join a walking group

Activate senses
Nature walk, observe wildlife

Access community
Walk different community locales

(a)

Figure 5.1 Activity mapping – examples for walking and gardening.

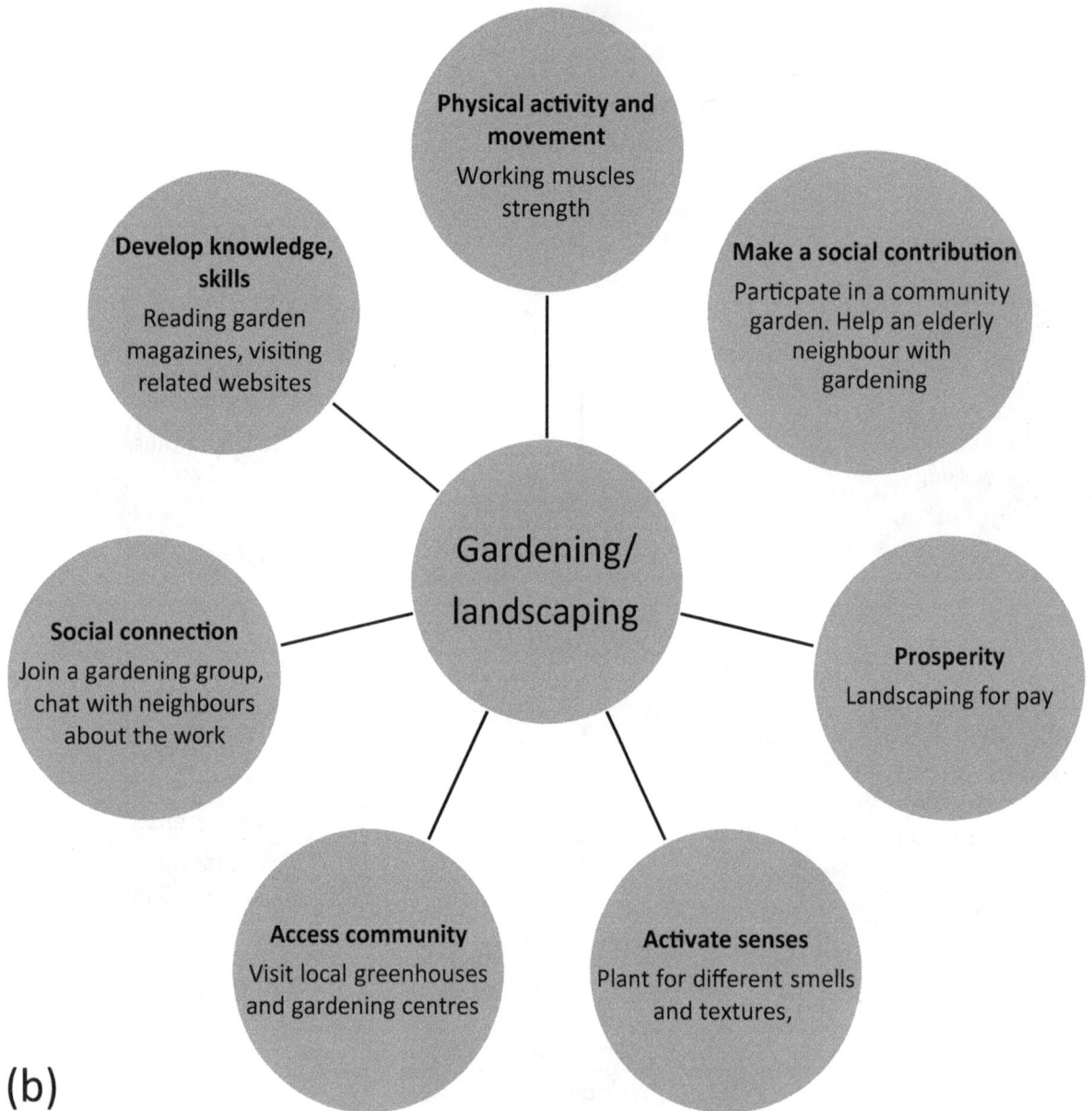

Physical activity and movement

Working muscles strength

Develop knowledge, skills

Reading garden magazines, visiting related websites

Make a social contribution

Particpate in a community garden. Help an elderly neighbour with gardening

Gardening/ landscaping

Social connection

Join a gardening group, chat with neighbours about the work

Prosperity

Landscaping for pay

Access community

Visit local greenhouses and gardening centres

Activate senses

Plant for different smells and textures,

(b)

Figure 5.1 Continued

Table 5.2 Advancing inclusion and citizenship through activities and participation: using the example of 'walking'

Walking as a 'patient' or a 'client'	Walking as part of an out-patient walking group
Walking through engaging with the support and collective power of peers	• Joining a walking group organized through a local peer support organization • Participating in organized walks to raise awareness and advocacy related to mental illness
Walking: participating in natural community options	• Joining a walking group run by the local community recreation centre • Walking regularly with friends and family

for changes are those that can be achieved within a two-to-three month time frame, or less. Consider breaking down identified changes that are longer term into discrete activities that shorten the time frame for achievement. For example, Ananthi's goal of returning to college, might begin with taking an interest course online, or brushing up on needed computer applications, both to prepare her for re-entry into post-secondary studies, but also in recognition of the fact that there may be a considerable waiting period before college courses begin.

5.2.2 Having the Potential to be Rewarding

The earlier reflection exercises were meant to personalize the health and well-being benefits of activity. Planning efforts should build on these reflections by making clear the connection between selected activities and participation and expected rewards and outcomes. These benefits can also be used in the process of monitoring outcomes. So, for example, if activity and participation selection is guided by a desire to increase access to a range of community environments, monitoring progress should include attention to the extent to which this is happening, challenges and barriers, and if it is in fact meeting the individual's needs. This monitoring can lead to changes in plans and supports, with even minor changes having the potential for positive impact.

5.2.3 A Learning Experience

The process of activity planning and implementation is a dynamic process that involves some trial and error, a bit of adventure, and a lot of personal learning and growth. Lapses to inactivity or activity avoidance can happen for a range of reasons and can be viewed as opportunities for personal learning and regrouping. An open attitude to learning is as important for the service provider as it is for the individual served. Moving forward with possible changes is likely to take the service provider into new and 'unchartered territory'. This is simultaneously the challenge and the joy of offering services that focus on activity and participation. For example, Alex's interest in earning some money, perhaps by translating his activities related to home management into a type of paid work, is likely to reveal a range of challenges for both Alex and Jamie, and require that they maintain an attitude of learning and possibility.

5.2.4 Meeting Personal Support and Resource Needs

Enabling changes in activity participation and patterns will require direct attention to the many challenges that an individual may face. The lack of commitment or interest that some individuals with serious mental illness demonstrate toward potential activities and participation can be a reflection of a deeply internalized perspective that these will present with overwhelming challenges and threaten well-being. This is why the ideal of personal 'choice' is a complex issue, requiring careful consideration of underlying factors.

In addition to prioritizing changes in activity and participation patterns based on those identified as most important by the individual, other considerations can be discussed. Other considerations for setting priorities can also include balancing changes with respect to different features, such as changes

• Likely to occur in a very short time frame with those that will take longer.

• That will likely require intensive support with those requiring less intensive support.

• That are perceived as 'needed' or 'expected' by the individual balanced with those that are experienced as purely 'wanted'.

• That meet different health and well-being needs.

Worksheet 5.3: Preparing for changes in activity and participation provides the opportunity to consider potential types of activity changes. ***Worksheet 5.4: Prioritizing plans for activity and participation changes*** provides a structured opportunity to prioritize the types of rewards or benefits expected of any change and leads to the identification of more specific direction or goals.

The skills used to help individuals identify potential activity and social participation possibilities are closely aligned with those of 'coaching', specifically with an emphasis on assisting individuals to recover a sense of direction and purpose and to be active in constructing meaningful daily lives (Kessler & Graham, 2015). These coaching processes are highly collaborative, and strengths-based. In the Action Over Inertia approach, the reflective exercises outlined in Chapter 2, and the experiences of rapid involvement in activities and participation, can provide important information to move ahead to give shape to potential opportunities. The service provider in this context stays sensitive to the needs of the individual in reflective conversations, encourages possibilities without overwhelming, and can provide feedback, information, and other forms of support.

Fossey et al. (2016) provide several examples of practice approaches that can advance the identification of potential activities and participation that hold meaning for individuals:

- Be open to the idea that your ideas about activities and social participation are different than those held by other people.
- Don't assume that identified activities or participation options are 'unrealistic' – be prepared to challenge your own assumptions and look at each option with 'fresh eyes'.
- Encourage exploration of activities and participation in real-life contexts – part of the everyday world and not therapeutically controlled.
- Attend to what an individual knows about activities and participation and their strategies for engaging.
- Consider that challenges can be overcome, rather than unreconcilable.
- Explore the use of tools that have been developed to identify activities and participation that may hold meaning and well-being benefits.

Service providers who are serious about developing their expertise in enabling meaningful and health promoting activities and participation will learn from the people they serve, stay attuned to possibilities, collect stories and examples, and develop related networks and resources that can be used in practice.

5.3 Building Opportunities, Inclusivity, and Community Capacity for Engagement

The Action Over Inertia approach is based on the assumption that the ways that activity and participation opportunities are organized, structured, and maintained have not, historically, enabled or accommodated easy access by people with serious mental illness. Subsequently, intervention approaches that are directed only to supporting change *by the individual* being served are likely to be met with resistance, and continue to unjustly identify the individual as being the source of the 'problem' that accounts for challenges and marginalization.

Developing opportunities and addressing community capacity and inclusivity can seem like a tall order – one that is typically associated with broader advocacy and social change efforts. Yet service providers can have considerable impact on enabling social level changes in their day to day practices addressing activity and social participation. In fact, the impact can be quite profound, particularly when conditions that marginalize people from full participation are revealed and local solutions and potentials are developed. Here we identify three specific strategies and use our vignettes to offer examples in practice:

5.3.1 Identifying Opportunities throughout the Community

Building opportunities within society requires service providers to think of individuals they serve as citizens of their communities, with rights to access the opportunities for activities and participation available to the public. It requires service providers to think 'outside the box' of the mental health system to identify potential opportunities. Identifying opportunities requires service providers to continually build their knowledge about 'what people do' in their communities, 'how they do these things', and 'what they get' from these involvements. It also requires building an understanding of how communities are developed to provide these opportunities – both for the well-being of their individual citizens and for the well-being of the community as a whole. It requires understanding of the strengths and potential capacities of the individual served and how these align with community opportunities.

Here again, we note the unique and important role played by peer led organizations in promoting access to health and well-being through activities and participation. Unlike mental health services that are organized and run by professionals, peer organizations are developed and run by people with lived experience of mental illness. They can, for example, play an important role in reducing dependency on traditional mental health services, foster supportive relationships, build on the strengths and demonstrate these strengths publicly, provide access to a range of activities and roles that promote health and well-being, and promote individual and collective pride and empowerment (see for example, Brown, 2012). They are important community assets and partners in improving the activity and participation opportunities for individuals with serious mental illness, both as individuals and as a collective. In our vignette of Alex, for example, peer organizations have developed opportunities to access casual work in the community, aligned with his own interests, and they may present an option that is personally acceptable.

5.3.2 Collaborating to Create Conditions for Inclusive Activity and Social Participation

The ways that activity and participation opportunities are structured can be organized in such a way that they unintentionally reduce access by particular people and groups. Service providers working collaboratively with an individual experiencing serious mental illness are in a good position to identify structures and processes that stand in the way of inclusive participation and to work with the entity, group, organization, agency, etc. to see if conditions for accessibility could be improved. The conditions might include, for example, the costs associated with attendance, supports to enable active involvement and a sense of belonging, education or training processes, and structures to support personal safety, including freedom from stigma and discrimination. In the vignette of Sol (see Appendix), service providers attended to both physical and social conditions that will enhance both involvement and satisfaction with his return to basketball. Similarly, the service provider working with Ananthi (Appendix) considered how the resources at an educational setting might be utilized to improve her access and experience.

The approaches used by service providers to increase accessibility are meant to be aligned with equity values of community groups. The conversation with community groups and organizations is not focused on the question of 'how can you serve people with mental illnesses who have been socially disadvantaged and marginalized', but rather 'how can you ensure your initiatives are accessible to all community members'. *Worksheet 5. 5: Accessibility checklist* identifies accessibility issues that can be considered when exploring the potential of community groups or organizations.

5.4 Anticipating Challenges and Implementing Supported Change

Human behaviour change is complex, presenting with many challenges. Implementing selected changes requires direct attention to these challenges and to the nature of the supports required to implement and sustain commitment. Some of these challenges can be anticipated, but some will inevitably emerge in the context of 'doing'.

There is a growing understanding of challenges that can reasonably be expected. Below are a few frequently encountered challenges and related support needs.

- *Personal learning*: Taking on activity and participation changes will make new demands on an individual. These can be related to the performance of specific tasks, the underlying procedures or processes (such as the organization, or the steps of involvement) and the social or interpersonal demands. Changes may require opportunities for new learning or skill development. For example, attention to social demands is a common area of concern for people with serious mental illness. In our vignette, Alex's social discomfort will certainly be triggered by activities and participation efforts that are linked to social interactions.

  The idea that people with serious mental illness may benefit from direct attention to skill development is well established in the mental health system, and a range of approaches to skill have been developed to increase the efficacy of skill development relevant to natural community settings (see for example, Gibson

et al., 2011). Certainly, these skill development technologies may be a useful and relevant complement to planned activity and participation changes.

- *Illness management*: Recovery theory highlights that individuals can become effective in daily activities and participation while they manage features of their illness. For example, there might be a need to build in structured times for rest in response to the addition of employment or volunteer activities, or the individual might need to learn to manage particular symptoms that emerge in the context of activities. There are a range of illness management and recovery tools available that can support activity and participation changes. For example, Wellness Recovery Action Planning (WRAP) (Cook et al., 2010) is an evidence-based approach to self-designed prevention and wellness that could complement the Action Over Inertia processes for change.

- *Affective and emotional well-being*: Activity and participation changes are meant to increase the individual's experience of well-being. Identifying and addressing unpleasant affective issues such as anxiety, anger, insecurity, or anhedonia will be important if they interfere with well-being in activity and participation. Individuals who experience anxiety might benefit from learning anxiety management techniques. Those with anhedonia might benefit from support that helps them recognize and connect to a range of positive emotions associated with the activity; so for example they might not have a pure experience of joy or pleasure in the activity, but still appreciate the value of contributing to the well-being of others.

  Material resources: Doing any activity requires material resources in the form of finances, transportation, equipment, technology, etc. These are particular concerns for people with serious mental illness who can find themselves living in poverty conditions or highly dependent on others for their material well-being. For example, local recreation centres may offer reduced rates for individuals on social financial assistance, but individuals are still faced with securing the fitness clothing and equipment that will help them to 'fit in'.

- *Managing social judgment*: It needs to be remembered that the social interactional demands on individuals with serious mental illness engaging in community activity and participation are likely to be complicated by a range of factors. For example, for Ananthi (see Appendix), developing new friendships at college or interacting with instructors might involve social skills that require her to negotiate issues of disclosure, the physical manifestations of side-effects of medications including changes in her body image if weight gain has occurred (see for example, Krupa et al., 2010).

Stigma and discrimination have been identified as profound barriers to full participation in important community activities. In recognition of this, interventions focused on helping individuals to manage such complicated social situations have been developed, and these may complement activity and participation change efforts. For example, an intervention program designed to reduce self-stigma has been developed and demonstrated some positive outcomes related to recovery (Lucksted et al., 2011).

- *Activity modifications/accommodations*: While activities may bring particular demands and expectations, these can frequently be modified to meet individual needs without losing the overall purpose of the activity. For some activities attached to public or private social structures (i.e., employment or housing), making reasonable accommodations is the law in some jurisdictions. For example, modifications related to work schedules or environments with decreased distractions are commonly requested employment accommodations for people with mental illness.

  Analysis of the Alex vignette may suggest that translating helping out with chores around the house to working for income may require attention to possible modifications. It may be that consideration will need to be given to expected hours of work, if for example, the effects of his medications, lengthy periods of inactivity, and the set routines of his housing are such that early morning involvement is impacted.

- *Social supports*: Human activity participation is enabled by social supports that offer practical assistance, information, and emotional support. For people with serious mental illness whose social networks have been eroded, developing these social supports may be essential for enabling activity participation. An individual might have access to ongoing professional supports but benefit more from the support of people in their natural environments where activities occur. Ananthi's vignette (see Appendix) illustrates how even supportive relations, within particular social and cultural contexts, may be strained in their capacity to provide support for particular activity and participation choices.

- *Negotiating environmental challenges*: The environmental context within which activity and participation occurs will bring demands and challenges. People with serious mental illness may live in neighbourhoods where access to basic resources and opportunities are unavailable, or at least difficult to access. For example, the idea of 'food deserts' refers to low income geographical areas, which become devoid of a range of retail resources, and in particular full service grocery stores, because of market forces (Wolf-Powers, 2017). This situation would both constrain access to an important range of community environments and also threaten the basic nutritional resource to take care of oneself. Similarly, many individuals live in community environments where they may be subject to victimization, assault, and other forms of harm.

While intervention approaches designed to address the activity and participation of individuals cannot directly change fundamental elements of neighbourhoods and communities, intervention approaches can be directed to helping an individual negotiate these issues. For example, focused-intervention programs have been developed to improve 'street smarts' of individuals to reduce personal vulnerability to these issues, and subsequently increase freedom to engage in meaningful activities and participation (De Waal et al., 2019; Holmes et al., 1997).

Worksheet 5.3: Preparing for changes in activity and participation along with *Resource 5.1: Managing challenges to activity and participation changes* provide an opportunity to identify and address challenges in both the planning stages, but also in the context of actual activity participation as issues emerge. *Resource 5.2: Road bumps on the path from inertia to action* provides a comprehensive framework for the change process that accounts for the many forces that facilitate and block change and offers an example of how the framework was used to understand the change process related to the addition of one participation example.

5.5 Building on the Momentum of Activity Change

Making changes to activity and participation may be enabled by formalizing processes for achieving these desired changes. As mentioned earlier in this chapter formalizing the process of change towards identified goals for any activity participation goal might include attention to:

- *Making specific plan statements* – what is the specific activity/participation plan or goal? What is the purpose?
- *Identifying who will be involved in supporting this plan.* How will they be involved?
- *Identifying expected timelines for change.*
- *Identifying how successful change will be measured* – identifying outcome indicators and how they will be evaluated. Will it reflect a change in time use patterns? Will it demonstrate particular health and well-being benefits? Will narratives and examples be gathered?

Worksheet 5.7: Giving shape to plans for activity and participation changes provides the opportunity to consider some of these features of changing activity participation.

5.6 Attending to Assumptions, Judgements, and Biases about Activity and Participation.

Choices related to activity and participation in daily life are highly personal, even though situated in and influenced by factors within the community and society. At the societal level, concepts such as full citizenship and inclusion propose equitable access to opportunities for the full spectrum of activity and participation options. However, communities and societies also value activity and participation options differently and they can also place judgements on the relative value of activities and participation for people, like those with serious mental illness, who can require resources and supports to enable their engagement (Wasserman, 2006).

It is important to recognize that this extends to the values, beliefs, and assumptions held by service providers, and the service organizations within which they work, and that this will influence the nature of the support offered to people with serious mental illness with respect to activity and participation. Without direct attention, the response of service providers to the activities and participation patterns of the individuals they serve has the potential to be charged with negativity, ranging from a vague sense of discomfort to avoidance of topics and issues, neglect, and all the way to denial of support.

What form might these difficult activity and participation issues take? The following are just a few activity and participation related examples gathered from practice that stirred ethical questions about the role of and responses by service providers:

1. Monies received from monthly government disability benefits are used to
   - Buy a big screen television.
   - Go to the horse races and place bets on races.
   - Invest in the stock market.
   - Enjoy a meal at a restaurant once a month and then visit a foodbank when finances are insufficient to cover basic needs.
   - Visit a local convenience store regularly to buy scratch and win lottery tickets.
2. Productivity and income-related activities and participation including:
   - Plans to volunteer in a day-care and offer babysitting services for a small income.
   - Becoming a regular paid plasma donor to increase income.
   - Exchanging sexual favours for income or to barter.
   - Dealing drugs.
   - Brewing and selling alcohol.
   - Parenting, or the desire to become a parent.
3. Making social connections such as:
   - Engaging in intimate relations with a romantic partner, who also has lived experience of mental illness.

- Joining a pool league at the local pub.
- Using internet dating sites to look for a romantic partner.

Each of these examples sparks discomfort and some distress among service providers. At the core, the examples led to questions for service providers such as:

- To what extent do I respect the autonomy of individuals related to their activity and participation? Are there examples where I don't think autonomy is the ideal? Why?
- What am I willing to do as a service provider to support health and well-being through activity and participation?
- What do I see as my role in supporting health and well-being through activity and participation? Are there examples where I cannot see myself involved in supporting an individual? Why?
- What activities and participation examples do I judge as problematic or inappropriate? Why? Do I hold the same judgements when I think about members of the general public, my friends, and acquaintances engaging in these opportunities?
- How does my concept of my duties, practice standards, and responsibilities influence my response to activity and participation decisions?

The ability of service providers (and their service organizations and systems) to support health and well-being through activity and participation patterns will be strengthened when uncertainty, conflicts in values, and underlying assumptions and judgements are addressed explicitly through conversations, openness to learning and reflection on values, and a solution focused response that considers and respects the needs and perspectives of all stakeholders.

5.7 Key Competencies

The competencies associated with this chapter are the attitudes, knowledge, and skills directed to helping individuals to shape and invest in dynamic plans for activity and participation changes aligned with values of personal choice, inclusion, empowerment, and citizenship. These competencies include:

- Integrating reflections and experiences to enable personal choices for longer term activity and participation changes.
- Using coaching skills to collaboratively develop plans for longer term activity and participation.
- Applying skills in activity and participation analysis.
- Demonstrating an understanding of the individual's strengths and vulnerabilities matched to specific activity and participation opportunities.

- Demonstrating a working knowledge of the activity and participation related assets, resources, and opportunities in the individual's community environment.
- Applying knowledge and skills related to community capacity assessment and development.
- Working collaboratively to construct activity and participation opportunities to both address individual needs and expand health and well-being benefits.
- Anticipating potential challenges to activity and participation and advancing approaches to address these challenges.

- Supporting individuals in the process of ongoing evaluation of personal experiences in activity and participation.
- Supporting individual investment in the planning process and adaptation of plans as appropriate.
- Demonstrating openness to regular reflection on attitudes, judgements, and personal values and beliefs influencing practice related to activity and participation.

Mapping activity and participation to optimize health and well-being

Name: _____ Date: _____

Selected activity or participation option: _____

Worksheet 5.1

For the selected activity or participation option, consider how it might be constructed to optimize a range of health and well-being benefits.

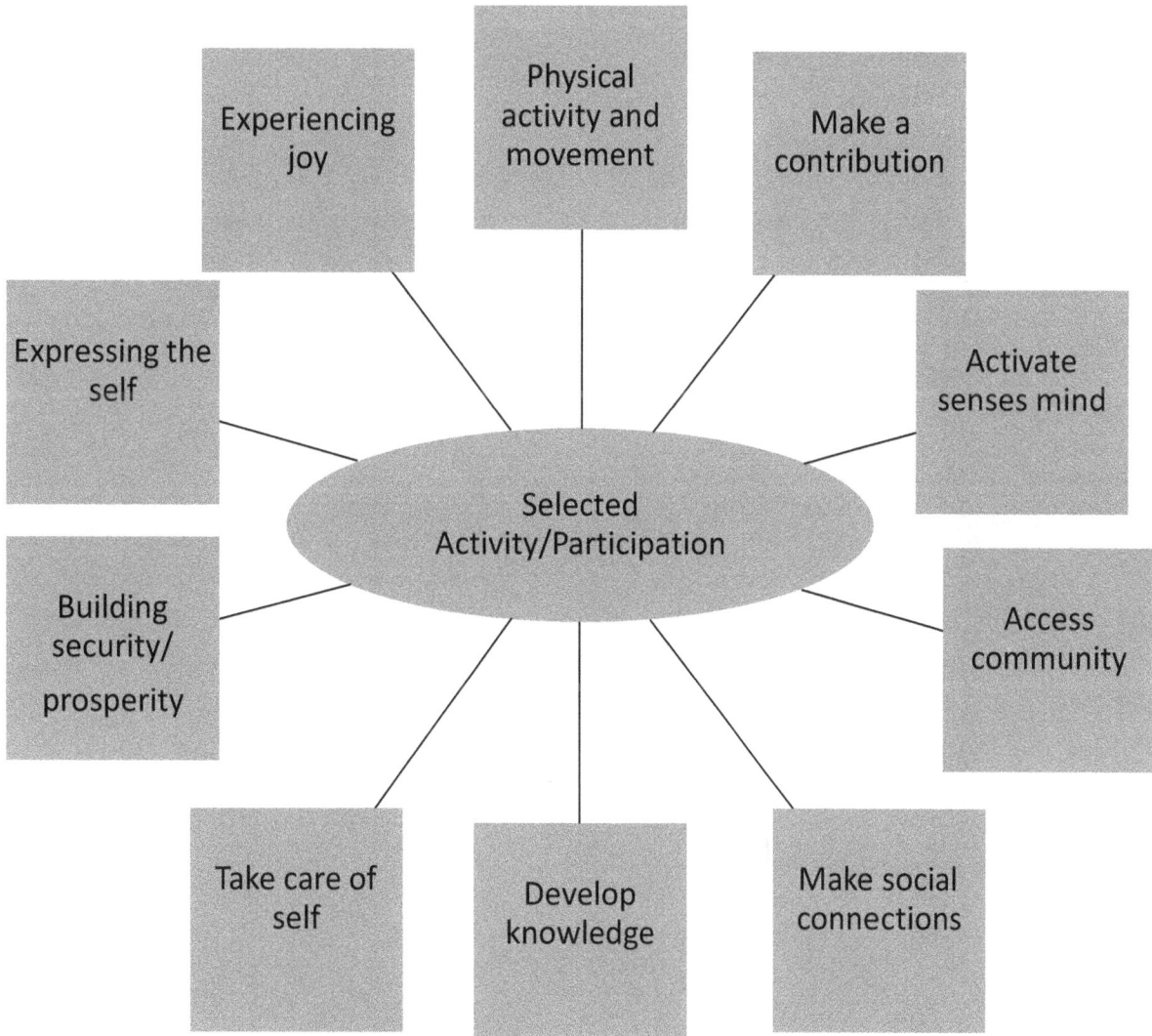

Experiencing joy

Physical activity and movement

Make a contribution

Expressing the self

Activate senses mind

Building security/ prosperity

Selected Activity/Participation

Access community

Take care of self

Develop knowledge

Make social connections

Advancing inclusion, citizenship, and empowerment through activities and participation

Name: _____ Date: _____

Identified activity or participation option: _____

Consider what options for this activity or participation option could potentially be available in each of these contexts

Contexts for Activity and Participation	Potential Examples of Opportunities
Options offered to patients or clients of the mental health system	
Options offered through peer organizations	
Options offered in natural community contexts	

Worksheet 5.3

Preparing for changes in activity and participation patterns

Name: _____ Date: _____

1. The activities that I enjoy doing now are:

_____

_____

_____

2. Activities that provide structure and order to my days are:

_____

_____

_____

3. The most meaningful activities I now do are:

_____

_____

_____

4. Thinking about the way I now spend my time, the things I don't want to change are:

_____

_____

_____

5. The activities I do now that I don't enjoy are:

_____

_____

_____

6. If I could change one thing about the way I spend my time, it would be:

_____

_____

_____

7. My ideal day would include these activities:

_____

_____

_____

Worksheet 5.4

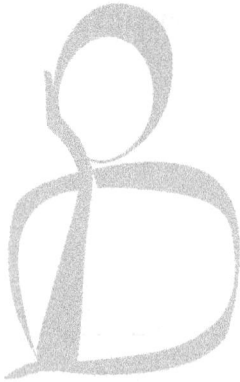

Prioritizing plans for activity and participation changes

Name: _____ Date: _____

A look back at Worksheet 2.15: A measure of my health and well-being through activity and participation. What rating score did you assign to each of the twelve categories? Remember that a higher rating indicates that you thought you could benefit more from this dimension in your activity patterns. Fill in the chart below, using your ratings.

Area of Activity Engagement	*Rating (Out of 10)*
Having balance and a range of activities and participation	
Living my values and beliefs	
Taking care of myself	
Activating mind and senses	
Physical activity and moving my body	
Expressing identity	
Developing knowledge, abilities, and potential	
Having pleasure and enjoyment	
Connecting with others	
Contributing to society and community	
Building security and prosperity	
Accessing community environments	

Based on these scores, what three areas would you rate as the most important to improve?

1. _____

2. _____

3. _____

B. Look back on all of the worksheets and reflections. What activities or activity patterns have you identified as perhaps requiring change? Write them down here.
Add other new activities or activity pattern changes that you have been thinking of:

_____ _____

_____ _____

_____ _____

_____ _____

_____ _____

_____ _____

C. What changes to your activities or activity patterns would you most like to make?

1. _____

2. _____

3. _____

Accessibility checklist

Name: _____   **Date:** _____

This worksheet can be completed collaboratively to identify the structures and processes that can stand in the way of inclusion in activities and participation. Identification of barriers can inform problem solving approaches to increase accessibility for all community members.

Accessibility Issue	*Yes or No*	*Comments/Plan*
Transportation required		
Costs of transportation		
Costs to access opportunity		
Public stigma/discrimination		
Self-stigma		
Need for technologies i.e., internet, smart phone, computer		
Processes used to provide training/education		
Geographic location		
Environment meets needs i.e., level of stimulation, noise, distractions		
Schedule/timing of opportunity		
Protection of personal safety		
Other		

Worksheet 5.5

In thinking of the above accessibility issues, below are some potential accommodations to support inclusion. They are common accommodations used to support inclusion for all.

Accommodations	Yes or No	Comments/Plan
Flexibility of scheduling		
Modification of the environmental context		
Modify processes for support		
Personalized training/education		
Modified duties/tasks		
Subsidised costs		
Other		

Worksheet 5.6

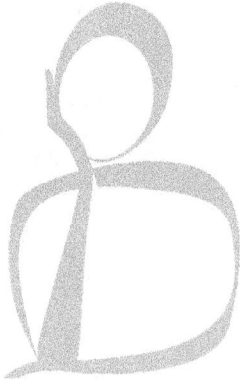

Planning for activity and participation changes

Name: _____ Date: _____

1. List ONE desired activity change: _____
2. What challenges or issues do you expect might arise in making this activity change? Use Resource 5.1 and Resource 5.2 to help guide you in this exercise.

✓	*Challenges*	*Examples*
	Personal learning	
	Material resources	
	Illness management	
	Emotional needs	
	Managing social judgments	
	Activity modifications or accommodations	
	Social supports	
	Other	

3. Consider each of the challenges listed in the previous section.

How might these issues or challenges be managed to help you participate successfully in this activity? What supports might you need to address these challenges?

Challenge	How Can this Challenge be Reduced or Managed?

Giving shape to plans for activity and participation changes

Name: _____ Date: _____

1. I would like to make the following change to my activity participation:

_____

_____

_____

_____

_____

2. In order to make this change I will: (outline the steps to be taken)

_____

_____

_____

_____

_____

3. The following people will be involved in helping me achieve this plan for change: (identify the person and explain how they will be involved)

_____

_____

_____

_____

_____

4. The changes I expect as a result of this change are:

_____

_____

_____

_____

_____

5. I will begin working on this plan (when) _____

I hope to achieve this change in activity participation by _____

Managing challenges to activity and participation changes

Changing routine activities always presents challenges. Identifying and addressing these challenges along the way can be helpful. Here are some examples of the types of challenges that might present and a few examples of how they might be addressed.

Challenges	*Examples*
Personal learning New activities might require new information/knowledge or skills or 'tuning up' old skills	• *Practice asking co-workers for assistance or asking a supervisor for clarification* • *Learn about a new area of town or transportation services* • *Learn how to use a new or updated computer program*
Material resources Every activity will require access to things such as transportation, new clothing, equipment, etc.	• *Secure employment supports available through government financial assistance* • *Gain access to a computer to use social networking programs* • *Update clothing for a job interview*
Illness management Understanding how features of your illness present in new activities and learning how to manage is important	• *Speak with the doctor about a medication schedule that reduces morning fatigue* • *Identify symptom 'triggers' in the activity and learn to avoid or manage these triggers* • *Build rest times into my day to give me the energy to manage symptoms*
Emotional needs Keeping up involvement in any new activity depends on experiencing positive emotions and a sense of well-being	• *Learn relaxation techniques to help deal with feelings of anxiety* • *Identify negative thought patterns that are affecting the experience* • *Remember the positive experiences of activity to counterbalance any negative emotional aspects*
Managing social judgments Addressing misguided attitudes about mental illness that other people hold can help make activity participation more pleasurable and rewarding	• *Decide what to 'disclose' about mental illness and practice how to disclose* • *Connect with supportive people while participating in activity* • *Become familiar with legal rights protecting involvement in community activities*
Activity modifications or accommodations There are aspects of activities that can be changed or modified when activity participation is difficult.	• *Work schedules can be flexible to accommodate the need for a later start because of early morning fatigue* • *Training time can be increased to give more opportunities to meet learning needs* • *Private space can reduce distractions*
Social supports Activity participation is enhanced when practical, emotional, or information support is available from other people	• *Identify a friend who is willing to participate with you* • *Find a confidante who will give another perspective or help with problem solving* • *Organize your time to be with other people just for fun – to offset other activities that are challenging.*

Road bumps on the path from inertia to action (with an example of 'joining an art class')

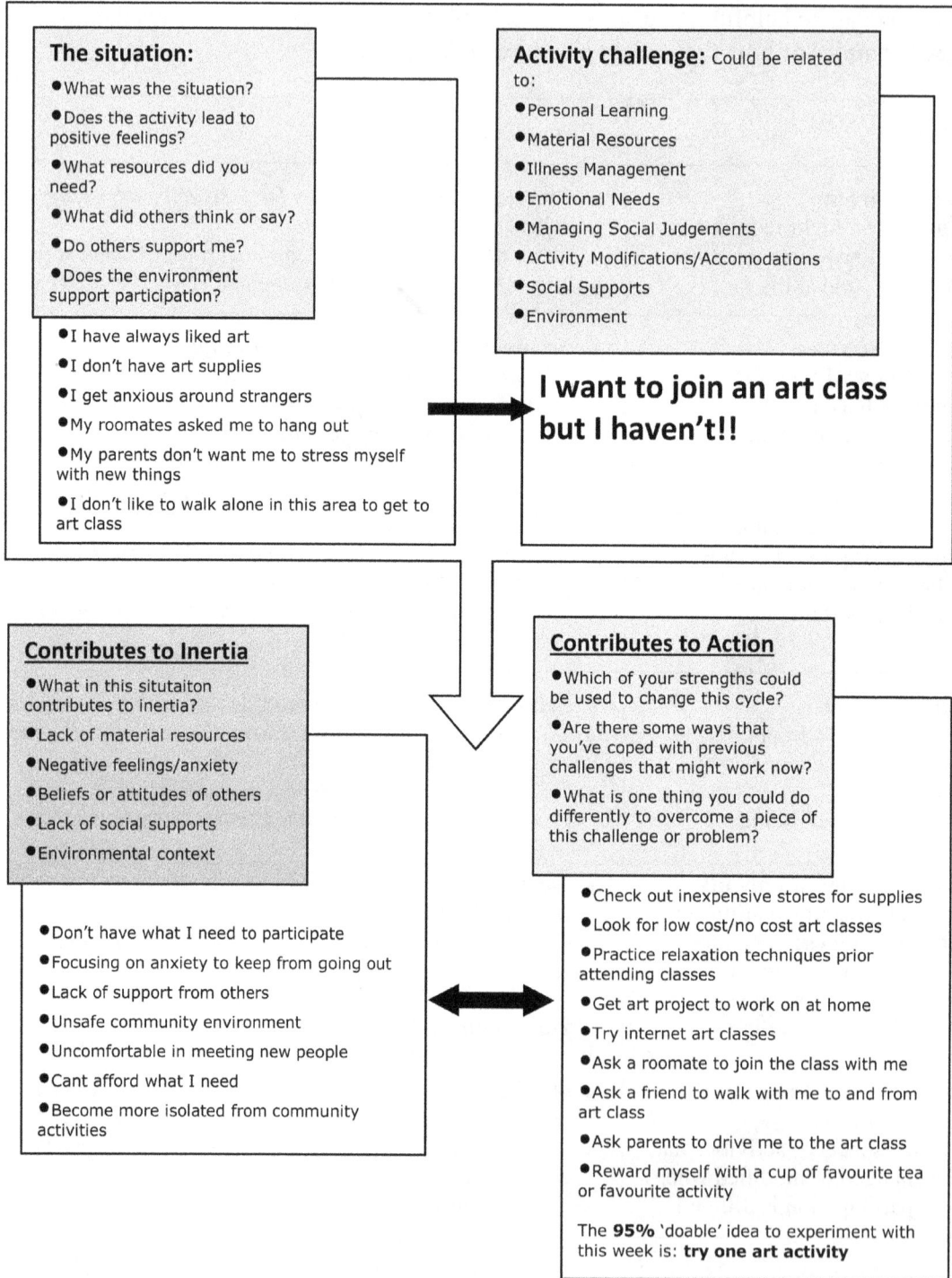

The situation:
- What was the situation?
- Does the activity lead to positive feelings?
- What resources did you need?
- What did others think or say?
- Do others support me?
- Does the environment support participation?

- I have always liked art
- I don't have art supplies
- I get anxious around strangers
- My roomates asked me to hang out
- My parents don't want me to stress myself with new things
- I don't like to walk alone in this area to get to art class

Activity challenge: Could be related to:
- Personal Learning
- Material Resources
- Illness Management
- Emotional Needs
- Managing Social Judgements
- Activity Modifications/Accomodations
- Social Supports
- Environment

I want to join an art class but I haven't!!

Contributes to Inertia
- What in this situtaiton contributes to inertia?
- Lack of material resources
- Negative feelings/anxiety
- Beliefs or attitudes of others
- Lack of social supports
- Environmental context

- Don't have what I need to participate
- Focusing on anxiety to keep from going out
- Lack of support from others
- Unsafe community environment
- Uncomfortable in meeting new people
- Cant afford what I need
- Become more isolated from community activities

Contributes to Action
- Which of your strengths could be used to change this cycle?
- Are there some ways that you've coped with previous challenges that might work now?
- What is one thing you could do differently to overcome a piece of this challenge or problem?

- Check out inexpensive stores for supplies
- Look for low cost/no cost art classes
- Practice relaxation techniques prior attending classes
- Get art project to work on at home
- Try internet art classes
- Ask a roomate to join the class with me
- Ask a friend to walk with me to and from art class
- Ask parents to drive me to the art class
- Reward myself with a cup of favourite tea or favourite activity

The **95%** 'doable' idea to experiment with this week is: **try one art activity**

6 Supporting Sustained Changes in Activity and Participation Patterns

Alex and Jamie noted the considerable changes in his activity and participation patterns. He engaged in one planned activity with a family member each week, including a family dinner at his sister's home, shopping with his mom, and a day of fishing with his father. Jamie, who had no experience with fishing, asked if it was true that good fishing depended on being able to 'read' the water. Alex's cousin was away on extended travels but they agreed to stay in touch by e-mail. His cousin helped him to set up an e-mail account and to use the internet provided at the local library. Alex and Jamie shared many laughs over his cousin's travel stories.

Organizing activities to earn an income required a bit more planning. Initially they considered which local residents or community organizations might have casual paying jobs. Alex found the level of personal contact required to secure these jobs on his own too interpersonally demanding. With more research they found a local peer-support group had organized a business around casual work in the community. This allowed Alex to focus on doing the work, rather than selling his services. Alex said that he might make use of intervention approaches to help him become more confident socially.

Alex felt tired and sluggish in the morning and he was concerned that this would interfere with his ability to work for pay. Alex agreed that Jamie could speak to his doctor about this to see if his medical treatments might be reviewed to see if they were contributing to his fatigue and Alex agreed to follow up with his doctor at their next appointment.

Jamie encouraged Alex to consider the changes that he had made. While the activity changes seemed small, they actually added up to some important changes. Alex completed *Worksheet 2.15: A measure of my health and well-being through activity and participation* again and his responses showed that he had indeed made changes in areas he considered meaningful. He had more regular social contacts with important people, was moving towards activities that would bring him a bit more money and he also had more physical activity in his life. Through all of these changes he was also accessing more community environments and developing new skills. Alex used some of the money he earned to purchase his sister's daughter a gift to give her at the family birthday party. At the peer centre, Alex saw a notice for an upcoming bus trip to another city and said that maybe he would like to do something like that in the future. This trip would certainly give him something to include in his e-mails to his cousin.

Focused Questions:

1. What communication practices does Jamie use to support Alex's activity and participation efforts? What other practices might you use?
2. How can service providers support involvement in activities and participation where they have little or no experience or personal interest?
3. What complementary interventions might enable Alex to be successful in his new activities and participation efforts?

This chapter includes the following worksheets:

Worksheet 6.1: Reflecting on practices of supporting change in activity and participation patterns (service provider version)

Worksheet 6.2: Enabling sustained commitment by supporting performance in activity and participation (service provider version)

Worksheet 6.3: Enabling sustained commitment by supporting positive activity and participation experiences (service provider version)

DOI: 10.4324/9781003111368-6

6.1 Supporting Sustained Investment in Activity and Participation Patterns

In this intervention approach attention is directed to defining and providing support to sustain the momentum of change. While our vignettes are simplified for the purposes of illustration, in practice, service providers can expect to find change processes are less linear, and subject to bumps, often requiring revision. Here are just a few considerations related to sustaining commitment for change:

- New activity and participation patterns will present new opportunities that, while potentially rewarding, will bring with them new demands and challenges to be addressed. For example, Alex's connection to the peer centre introduces him to an opportunity for some travel. That opportunity might bring the need to consider saving money or accessing new sources for funding, the social connections that could support his involvement, etc.

- Changes to one aspect of daily activity and participation patterns can be expected to influence other aspects of daily activity and participation routines. Alex's involvement in casual work may shift his self-care and sleep patterns in ways that need to be considered, particularly given that he resides in a group living situation. Will he, for example, be able access meals provided through his residence, gain access to bathroom facilities to suit his new schedule, have the quiet he might need to go to sleep earlier, etc.?

- People can experience flare ups of symptoms of mental illnesses, including acute or intensive forms of care that impact activity and participation. This can be experienced by individuals as a derailment, obstructing their intentions for a particular course of action and change. This has the potential to damage the sense of hope, and possibility. Sustaining investment might be supported in this case by normalizing 'bumps along the way', and focused efforts to reduce disruptions to the return to activity and participation.

- Like everyone, individuals can find that they change their minds about their intended changes in activity and participation patterns. It may be, for example, that they don't find meaning or satisfaction in their planned changes, or that they discover other options that are more aligned with their needs, wants, and expectations.

Supporting sustained commitment to positive changes in activity and participation patterns is a challenging and complex practice skill. Central to this is the service provider's awareness of their own response to the shifts and bumps in the process. It is common for providers to find their own sense of hope and possibility challenged. Where such feelings of frustration emerge, the risk is always that the response of the service provider will be less than helpful in supporting sustained investment in change. At their worst they can convey negative attitudes to the individual served – such as assumptions that they are not making an effort. Service providers who engage in frequent critical self-reflection around the purpose and methods of supporting actions will be at less risk of falling into these unhelpful attitudes and practices. ***Worksheet 6.1: Reflecting on practices of supporting changes in activity and participation patterns (service provider version)*** offers a structured opportunity to pose critical questions related to practices applied in the work with any individual.

6.2 Enabling Sustained Change by Supporting Effective Performance in Activity and Participation

Supporting performance refers to practices focused on assisting the person to carry out the elements of specific activity and participation that are fundamental to their successful execution. These include performance demands integral to the tasks, social interactions, and procedural aspects of activity and participation. Standards for 'success' in performance tend to be dynamic, context specific, and flexible. Although a prior analysis of any planned activity and participation will go a long way in anticipating and preparing for performance expectations, the demands of any activity are never fully known until they emerge within the actual context and within real-life conditions. For example, Alex's venture into casual work with the peer centre may begin with explicit expectations related to performance (for example, expectations related to hours worked, quality of work performed, job duties), but emerge to be more flexible and open to adaptation once on the job. Similarly, opinions about performance will need to include the persons own perspective. For example, Alex's father may be less concerned about his son's fishing abilities and more interested in the social aspects of their exchanges that might help to build the father-son connection. Alex, on the other hand, may have a wider range of performance concerns – taking the bus to the family home, re-establishing his skill in fishing, and connecting with his father.

Ongoing support directed to facilitating the capacity to effectively meet performance demands, expectations, and desires can include a range of skills, but should always be developed in collaboration with the individual. Examples of support efforts directed to performance are provided below, while ***Worksheet 6.2: Enabling sustained commitment by supporting performance in activity and participation (service provider version)*** provides the opportunity to consider specific practices collaboratively with the individual. The worksheet can provide the opportunity for reflection by the service provider, but also an open discussion with the individual receiving services about how services enable participation. These practices include:

- Balancing difficulties encountered with attention to the person's strengths and capacities that emerge in activity participation.

  The tendency, in working with individuals with serious mental illness, can be to focus on identifying problems in performance, with a view to addressing or minimizing these problems. A strengths approach considers directly the relevant strengths of an individual, capitalizes on these, and balances these with attention to areas of difficulty (see for example, Rapp & Goscha, 2012).

- Refining or modifying the processes, structures or conditions of activities and participation to promote success and well-being.

  Changes in processes, structures or conditions of activity and participation opportunities can often be constructed in a way to make opportunities more accessible without changing their fundamental nature. In many jurisdictions, these practices are referred to 'accommodations' to promote access to employment and education (McDowell & Fossey, 2015). However, the practices are actually applicable across the full range of human activities and participation, with a view to facilitating the 'fit' between the person and the context of performance. This requires service providers' attention to the nature of performance demands, and how they might be adapted to facilitate access to the opportunity.

- Developing supports to enhance performance.

  Developing supportive relations can facilitate effective performance in a range of ways. Support can offer information and real life exemplars, material, and other instrumental resources and emotional support to sustain a sense of efficacy in the face of challenges. Central to this approach is a focus on supports that are 'natural', and not dominated by professional mental health services.

- Accessing material resources that will enhance and sustain performance.

  As individuals engage in activities and participation that are located within the broader community context, it can be expected that their needs related to material resources will change and evolve. For example, with increased activity and participation opportunities, can come resource demands related to transportation, clothing, nutrition, self-care products, technology, information, etc. All of these can impact both the ability to perform the demands of activity and participation, and also the experience of

dignity, inclusion, and acceptance in these opportunities. While any service provider can feel powerless to change the conditions of poverty and dependence that characterize the life of so many people with serious mental illness, there is much that can be done to address material resources in relation to specific activity and participation opportunities. This does depend on the service provider expanding their knowledge related to things like targeted programs to address specific resource needs.

Jamie and Alex, for example, were faced with ongoing challenges related to material resources. Alex found that his participation in the work activities at the peer centre were challenged by the cost of bus transportation. They considered if there were any targeted programs that might address this issue. Through their research they found that aligned with his government disability pension was a funding opportunity to support costs associated with work activities. They also found out that the city offered reduced fare monthly bus passes based on income. Together they weighed the pros and cons of both alternatives and decided to access the local city option. Alex liked that this option was available to the general public.

- Supporting the learning of new skills or the reestablishment of previously held skills.

  Given that involvement in activities and participation is dynamic, the need for new, and often unexpected, skills will emerge and challenge performance and sustained investment. Where individuals experience positive advancements in their daily activities and participation, it can be expected that their personal capacities for managing such challenges will be improved (for example, gaining confidence, sustaining hope, coping skills, etc.), as will the conditions and contexts of their engagement (e.g., supportive people, material resources, safety, etc.). However, events and demands can occur that compromise, and even derail these advancements. For example, Alex made great strides in improving his comfort in social situations and developing skills to deal with social situations. However, in the context of his new activity and participation involvements he will experience new social relations and situations (e.g., work supervisors, customer relations, and other public contacts) that make new types of demands on his performance.

6.3 Enabling Sustained Change by Supporting Positive Experiences with Activity and Participation

Supporting positive experience refers to efforts directed to the affective, emotional, and psychological processes that sustain commitment to activity and participation.

They are efforts that highlight and expand the personal experience of well-being associated with activity, while minimizing those experiences of distress, apprehension, or unease. Despite their potential for influencing positive experiences of well-being, new activity and participation patterns pose inherent risks, and the potential benefits may not be immediately apparent to individual who has lived with significant disengagement from activity. Furthermore, some people with serious mental illness experience a dampening of the emotions and feelings associated with enjoyment, contentment, and other forms of simple happiness. They can also experience heightened feelings of distress in response to stressful emotions, like anxiety and frustration, that can have important adaptive value in relation to activity and participation. For all of these reasons, ongoing support directed to the experiences in activity and participation is important.

Worksheet 6.3: Enabling sustained commitment by supporting positive activity and participation experiences (service provider version) focuses on enabling efforts for direct application. The worksheet can provide the opportunity for reflection by the service provider, but also an open discussion with the individual receiving services, about how services enable participation. Here are some other examples of enabling efforts:

- Convey an attitude of experimentation – an attitude where there is no failure, only new learning and growth.
- Listen to stories about the individual's activity and participation with genuine interest. Convey genuine empathy, spirit and humour, happiness, etc. in response to these narratives.
- Decrease the assistance of formal supports in activities and participation as the natural benefits of activities emerge and the individual gains confidence.
- Make explicit the benefits the individual experiences with changes in activity and participation patterns. Refer back to discussions about values, meaning, and the dimensions of well-being through activity and participation to assist.
- Highlight any positive impacts on important friends, family, and other social connections that emerge in the context of new activity patterns.
- Validate and address difficult emotional experiences such as anxiety and help to equip the individual with the knowledge and skills to manage these emotions (e.g., anxiety management techniques).
- Continue to identify and address situations that leave the individual vulnerable to trauma or victimization.
- Assist with refining activities and participation patterns to match individual needs through periods of instability of mental health. For example, building in additional periods of rest or decreasing stimulation may facilitate activity and participation through periods of more acute illness.

- Provide ongoing support to refine activities and participation so that they most closely reflect the meaning and purpose that the individual associates with the activity.
- Validate concerns related to stigma and discrimination and assist the individual with developing personal disclosure plans and ways to manage social evaluations or judgments in activities.
- Build in ways to celebrate achievements in the process of changing activity patterns.

In the vignette of Alex, the service provider poses questions about the knowledge underlying fishing, a question which can elicit storytelling, enjoys a laugh with Alex about his cousin's travel adventures, and collaborates with Alex to see if his feelings of sluggishness can be reduced. These are all examples of practices meant to ensure that Alex would experience the benefits and meanings of his involvement in activities and participation as intended.

6.4 Evaluating Change as a Way to Sustain Commitment and Consider Future Plans

This intervention approach focuses on achieving the well-being outcomes that are associated with activity and participation. Person-centred evaluation of outcomes is an important component of the intervention process, both to ensure that services are actually achieving intended outcomes, and also to assist with the ongoing refinement of plans related to activity and participation patterns (Brown et al., 2019).

6.4.1 Timing of Evaluation Activities

The formal evaluation of activity and participation changes require the time necessary to allow for intended changes to occur. When an individual's life has been characterized by profound disconnection from activity and participation, even small changes can be monumental with respect to the effort they require and the meaning they hold for the individual. But these small changes can be difficult to capture in formal evaluation. Evaluation should consider both the time required to realize and consolidate intended changes in activity patterns. For example, evaluation at a three-month interval may be a reasonable timeframe to expect meaningful change.

6.4.2 Defining Outcomes

The activity and participation patterns detailed in Chapters 1 and 2 of this workbook provide examples of possible areas of focus for evaluation. These areas include: variety in activities and participation; balance; alignment with values, belief, family, and cultural context; and changes in specific health and well-being dimensions.

Areas that were prioritized during planning for changes could be the focus of specific attention, since these reflect particularly desired changes. However, examining change across all areas is still recommended, since changes in one prioritized area can be associated with positive (or negative) changes in other unanticipated areas. For example, for Alex, the changes in social interactions contributed both to his experience of increased physical activity and increased access to community environments. Similarly, the termination of one previously valued activity involvement may not detract significantly from experiencing positive dimensions of health and well-being. For example, Sol's (see Appendix) involvement with substance-related activities may be less important to him given his growing investment in other activities.

6.4.3 Methods for Evaluation

Evaluation in this intervention approach focuses on identifying meaningful changes in activity and participation patterns. Historically, evaluation activities have been considered as separate and distinct from the enabling process (a type of external check on progress being made). Current thoughts on evaluation have considered it to be an integral element of the change process, involving collaboration with the individual served. These 'participatory' forms of evaluation stress that both health service providers and the individuals they serve have a 'stake' in evaluation findings, and that both parties will ultimately need to collaborate on interpreting findings and making decisions about how to proceed (see for example, Patton, 2008). In short, evaluation activities are not meant to frame individuals as the 'objects of evaluation' but rather to construct evaluation processes to enable their involvement. *Worksheet 6.4: Identifying changes in my activity and participation patterns* and *Worksheet 6.5: Thinking about changes in my activity and participation patterns* provide an opportunity for taking stock of changes.

6.4.4 Qualitative Approaches to Evaluation

Qualitative methods for evaluation will focus on the way activity and participation patterns are experienced or 'lived' by individuals. Qualitative methods are rich in description and provide opportunities to access the voices of people served. Activity and participation patterns can serve as the focus of collecting information about lived experience.

Several innovative methods have been developed for accessing this lived experience in a way that can support evaluation of activity and participation changes and be cited to document these changes. Examples of qualitative methods include:

- Collecting narratives of the experience of activity patterns.

- Journal entries focusing on activity and participation related experiences.
- The use of photographs or other forms of expressive media that capture the individual's changing experiences of activity. Expressive media can encourage access to personal experience for people who are less likely to reflect on their experience verbally.

Qualitative evaluations can often be integrated into and support the change process. For example, many individuals who give voice to their experiences of changing activity and participation have used these narratives to support and mentor others who are undertaking similar journeys, or to influence the training of service providers in the health care arena (see for example, Alvidrez et al., 2010). In essence, the transparency and dissemination of their lived experience can transmit powerful messages of hope and potential to others while reinforcing personal changes made.

6.4.5 Quantitative Approaches to Evaluation

Quantitative evaluations provide an 'objective measure' of the change process. In this intervention approach, the measurement of change in activity and participation patterns is recommended through repetition of the *time-use log (Worksheet 2.1)* and repeated ratings of *Worksheet 2.15: A measure of my health and well-being through activity and participation*. The provider can encourage the individual to reflect back on some of the concerns that led to previous ratings for each of the dimensions and to consider if their efforts have led to changes. In this way, it is possible to reflect on how their experiences in these areas had improved over time – subsequently moving their ratings in each of these areas to show this improvement.

Worksheet 6.6: Measuring changes in my activity and participation patterns over time provides the opportunity to keep track of changes across the various dimensions of activity participation over time and to consider the meaning of these changes. The worksheet offers a simple but structured format for evaluating change. While the form suggests a simple format for identifying change (i.e., *yes – change has occurred over time* or *no – change has not occurred over time*), the form can be modified to provide a more descriptive measure of change. In the example offered immediately above, change in physical activity might be represented as a 2+ to describe the nature (positive) and extent (two rankings) of change.

6.5 Key Competencies

The key competencies associated with this chapter are those related to sustaining an individual's investment in realizing activity and participation patterns that are meaningful and bring well-being. The competencies are based on the expectation that for people with serious mental illness who have been disengaged from meaningful and positive activity and participation, commitment can be expected to fluctuate in response to a broad range of factors. These key competencies include:

- Developing and sustaining a relationship that conveys a genuine respect for the potential of activity and participation to contribute to well-being and the individual's capacity to experience this potential.
- Recognizing the dynamic nature of activity and participation and responding accordingly in a timely and effective manner.

- Analyzing and responding to the multiple factors that influence performance of activity and participation, using recognized practices.
- Attending equally to both person-level factors and the conditions and contextual factors that influence performance.
- Eliciting in the individual the emotional experiences that can sustain investment in activity and participation.
- Engaging the individual in evaluation of change in activity and participation using both qualitative and quantitative approaches and focusing on a range of meaningful outcomes.

Reflecting on practices of supporting activity and participation change (service provider version)

Name of service recipient: _____ **Date:** _____

1. **What knowledge/evidence do I have to assure me that the planned activity changes hold personal meaning for the individual?**

   _____

   _____

   _____

   _____

   _____

2. **From my knowledge of this individual, I think my support actions will need to be sensitive to the following issues:**

   _____

   _____

   _____

   _____

   _____

3. **How will I deliver my practice efforts so that they are attentive to these sensitivities?**

   _____

   _____

   _____

   _____

   _____

4. **How will I ensure that my efforts to support change with this individual are collaborative and person-centred?**

   _____

   _____

   _____

   _____

   _____

Enabling sustained commitment by supporting performance in activity and participation (service provider version)

Name: _____ **Date:** _____

The framework provides an opportunity to consider how specific enabling processes to support the positive <u>performance</u> of activity are implemented with an individual. The information gained can be used to make explicit these enabling processes for discussion with the individual, other health service providers, and for documenting and recording.

Supporting Activity Performance	*Specific Efforts/Date*
Balance difficulties that emerge, with attention to the person's strengths and capacities that emerge in activity participation	
Build on strengths and capacities rather than focusing on personal weaknesses or inabilities	
Refine or modify the context or conditions of the activities to promote success and well-being	
Develop additional human supports to support performance, with particular attention to engaging the support of people that also participate in the activity or 'natural supports'	
Access new material resources that will enhance performance	
Identify and support the learning of new knowledge and skills needed to perform the activity well	

Worksheet 6.3

Enabling sustained commitment by supporting positive activity and participation experiences (service provider version)

The following checklist provides an opportunity to consider how specific enabling processes to support the positive experience of activity are implemented with an individual. The information gained from this worksheet can be used to make explicit these enabling processes for discussion with the individual, other health service providers, and for documenting and recording.

Name: _____ **Date:** _____

Support Action	*Examples*
Convey an attitude of experimentation – an attitude where there is no failure only new learning and growth	
Decrease the assistance of formal supports in activities as the natural benefits of activities emerge and the individual gains confidence	
Make explicit the benefits the individual experiences with changes in activity patterns. Use the dimensions of health through activity to identify and expand upon benefits	
Validate and address difficult emotional experiences and help to equip the individual with the knowledge and skills to manage these emotions	
Identify and address situations that leave the individuals vulnerable to trauma or victimization	
Assist with refining activities and activity patterns to match individual needs through periods of instability of mental health	
Provide ongoing support to refine activities so that they most closely reflect the meaning and purpose that the individual associates with the activity	
Validate concerns related to stigma and discrimination and assist the individual with developing personal disclosure plans and ways to manage social evaluations or judgments in activity	
Build in ways to celebrate achievements in the process of changing activity patterns	

Identifying changes in my activity and participation patterns

Look back at the areas of change you prioritized. Are these areas being improved by your participation in these new activities? Fill in the chart below.

Area of Activity Engagement That I Wanted to Work On…	My Activity Changes That Target This Area…	What Changes Have I Actually Experienced in This Area? How Has This Area Changed?
1.		
2.		
3.		

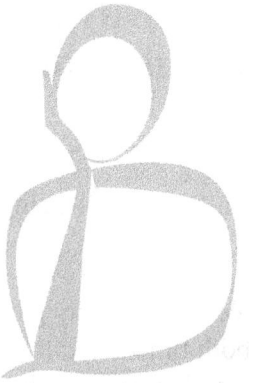

Thinking about changes in my activity and participation patterns

Name: _____ Date: _____

Think about the activity changes you have been working on over the past _____ (time period). How would you answer these questions?

The most <u>difficult</u> change to make in my daily activities was:

_____

It was difficult because: _____
_____

I managed these challenges by: _____
_____

The easiest change to make in my daily activities was: _____

It was easy because: _____
_____

The most <u>enjoyable</u> change I made to my activities was:

_____

It was enjoyable because: _____
_____

What <u>benefits</u> did I experience as a result of these activity changes?

_____

_____

Is there anything about my activity changes that I have been unhappy or concerned about? If so, what are these concerns?

_____

Measuring changes in my activity and participation patterns over time

Name: _____   **Date:** _____

This form is meant to be used along with Worksheet 2.15: A Measure of my health and well-being through activity and participation.

Use this form to keep track of the change in your ratings on the different aspects of your activity patterns over time. List the ratings given for each of the dimensions of activity for both time 1 and time 2. Examine these ratings to identify changes. In the final column, note if positive change (a higher ranking) has occurred.

	Time 1 Ratings Date Completed _____	**Time 2 Ratings Date Completed** _____	**Positive Change: Yes or No**
1. Balance and range of activities			
2. Living values and beliefs			
3. Taking care of myself			
4. Activating my mind and senses			
5. Physical activity and movement			
6. Expressing identity			
7. Developing knowledge, abilities, potential			
8. Having pleasure and enjoyment			
9. Connecting with others			
10. Contributing to society/ community			
11. Building security/prosperity			
12. Accessing community environments			

7 Raising the Profile of Activity and Participation in Mental Health Service Delivery

Jamie considered how prevalent issues of activity and participation were across the population being served by the program. If the issues were prevalent, Jamie thought that the service might benefit from a more integrated, evidence-informed approach. Jamie engaged the commitment of a colleague, Afsanah, who also had a particular interest in, and training, related to health and well-being through activity and participation. With their service leader's approval, they reviewed the records of 60 people who were currently being served. Using *Worksheet 1.1: Making appraisals about activity and participation explicit* and *Worksheet 1.2: Evaluating the benefits experienced through current activity and participation patterns*, they estimated that 24 people (or 40% of people being served) had activity and participation patterns that might seriously limit their experience of health, well-being, and inclusion. Jamie and Afsanah secured time at a regular meeting of the service to present this information. To help focus discussions they presented a list of initial thoughts about how the service might move forward. These ideas included: adding questions about activities and participation in routine information collected when people first entered the service; using public health promotion strategies to inform people about the importance of activity and participation; meeting with key stakeholder groups, such as the client advisory committee, a local peer support group, and family representatives, to gather their perspectives and to engage their assistance; researching and implementing best practices in the area; and finally, building in ongoing processes for the evaluation of outcomes related to activity-health. Overall, the members of the service were on board, agreeing that addressing these issues was consistent with the mission of the service's focus on supporting community integration. However, there were mixed opinions about the scope of their role, whether they had the related training to address these issues, and they were also concerned about the time pressures they were already experiencing in their service delivery. It was agreed that any development of this focus on activity and participation would need to consider how it would effectively be integrated into the structure of the service.

Focused Questions:

1. Jamie and Afsanah estimated how common activity and participation issues are among the population served by their program. How common do you think these issues are among the people served by your program? How might you determine the actual prevalence in your context?
2. Jamie and Afsanah used a team meeting to engage other service providers in a discussion of the relevance of activity and participation. What avenues do you have to raise this discussion with other service providers?
3. The team raised several concerns about integrating a focus on activity and participation into routine service delivery. What concerns do you expect would be raised in your program?

This chapter includes the following worksheets:

Worksheet 7.1: Structures that influence delivery of practices related to activity and participation: Mission and goals

Worksheet 7.2: Structures that influence delivery of practices related to activity and participation: Advancing leadership related to activity and participation

Worksheet 7.3: Structures that influence delivery of practices related to activity and participation: Taking stock of resources

Worksheet 7.4: Structures that influence delivery of practices related to activity and participation: Program processes and operations

Worksheet 7.5: Structures that influence delivery of practices related to activity and participation: Partnerships

DOI: 10.4324/9781003111368-7

7.1 A Conceptual Framework to Support Program Level Activity and Participation Practice

While this text largely focuses on practices directed to working with *individuals*, the ideas and materials can also be applied towards program-level efforts to achieve positive changes in the activity and participation patterns of the *population* served. A central assumption of the approaches detailed in this book is that achieving health and well-being through activity and participation is a population-health issue that has particular meaning and relevance for people with serious mental illness. Advocacy and action at the service and system level is required to raise the profile and the commitment to this issue.

Mental health services designed to meet the needs of people with serious mental illness are complex interventions. They are complex in that they are often faced with addressing multiple challenges related to health and well-being – from acute illness, multiple morbidities, and risk of death to a broad range of social concerns. Addressing these challenges calls for the coordination and integration of services. For example, recovery-oriented practices will depend on the integration of interventions addressing symptoms of illness, and those addressing activity and participation. How well they negotiate these various challenges and interactions will be influenced by many factors including the source of funding, government policy and priorities, and the availability of evidence-informed practices. Thankfully, there is a growing body of work directed to describing and providing guidance on how to advance complex interventions (O'Cathain et al., 2019) and their specific practices (Eldredge et al., 2016).

Programs are guided in their choices and priorities related to their specific approaches by the ways they view the needs of the people they serve. Integrating a focus on activities and participation in any service or program will be strengthened where there is an explicit commitment to a conceptual framework aligned with this focus. Recovery, as a conceptual framework, is an example of this; recovery-oriented practice stresses the importance of activity and participation to health and well-being.

Another conceptual framework that can be helpful at the program level is that proposed by the Capabilities Framework (Nussbaum, 2003; 2011; Sen, 2000). The Capabilities Framework is a justice framework concerned with what Nussbaum refers to as 'a world in which all human beings have what they need to live a life with human dignity' (Nussbaum, 2004, p. 12). Capabilities are essentially the freedoms that people have to participate in the activities that they value and to become who they might want to be. 'Not denying' access to an opportunity or resource is not the same as guaranteeing capabilities. Rather, active support or facilitation for capabilities is the process whereby these freedoms can be achieved.

The framework is based on the notion that humans should be entitled some degree of the fundamental capabilities (i.e., opportunities, resources, power, etc.) that constitute a decent life. Nussbaum identifies ten fundamental human capabilities, itemized in Table 7.1. Evaluations of what constitutes an acceptable level will vary across contexts. In this way, mental health services and programs can consider the daily lives of the people they serve and evaluate the extent to which they, within their broader social context, are afforded the opportunities

Table 7.1 Fundamental human capabilities

1. **Life.** Being able to live to the end of a human life of normal length
2. **Bodily health.** Being able to have good health, including reproductive health; being adequately nourished; being able to have adequate shelter
3. **Bodily integrity.** Being able to move freely from place to place; being able to be secure against violent assault, including sexual assault; having opportunities for sexual satisfaction and for choice in matters of reproduction
4. **Senses, imagination, thought.** Being able to use the senses; being able to imagine, to think, and to reason – and to do these things in a way informed and cultivated by an adequate education; being able to use one's mind in ways protected by guarantees of freedom of expression with respect to both political and artistic speech and freedom of religious exercise; being able to have pleasurable experiences and avoid non-beneficial pain
5. **Emotions.** Being able to have attachments to things and persons outside ourselves; being able to love those who love and care for us; being able to grieve at their absence, to experience longing, gratitude, and justified anger; not having one's emotional developing blighted by fear or anxiety
6. **Practical reason.** Being able to form a conception of the good and to engage in critical reflection about the planning of one's own life
7. **Affiliation.** Being able to live for and in relation to others, to recognize and show concern for other human beings, to engage in various forms of social interaction; being able to imagine the situation of another and to have compassion for that situation; having the capability for both justice and friendship; being able to be treated as a dignified being whose worth is equal to that of others
8. **Other species.** Being able to live with concern for and in relation to animals, plants, and the world of nature
9. **Play.** Being able to laugh, to play, to enjoy recreational activities
10. **Control over one's environment.** (a) Political: being able to participate effectively in political choices that govern one's life; having the rights of political participation, free speech and freedom of association; (b) material: being able to hold property (both land and movable goods); having the right to seek employment on an equal basis with others

Nussbaum, M. (2003). Printed with permission

to live a life of decency and dignity. The relevance of the Capabilities Approach to mental health services has been highlighted by others (Davidson et al., 2009; Hopper, 2007; Sacchetto, Ornelas, Calheiros & Shinn, 2018). The Capabilities Approach is well aligned with ideas of occupational justice, a social justice construct which focuses on access to opportunities for meaningful activities and participation. Efforts have been directed to describing different expressions of occupational injustice, including alienation, deprivation, imbalance, and marginalization (Townsend, 2012).

While it could be argued that evaluating the capabilities afforded people with serious mental illness is beyond the role and scope of mental health services, it should be considered that this highly marginalized population often have few people, beyond family and service providers, who are routinely engaged with them in daily life. The question then arises: 'if mental health services and systems do not take on an advocacy and action role, then who will?'

7.2 Service Structures That Influence Delivery of Activity and Participation Practices

While the delivery of competent direct services related to activity and participation is necessary, the extent to which these practices are supported at the program level will have a large impact on their actual delivery. Service providers interested in raising the profile of practice related to activity and participation need to consider how it might be integrated into important service structures and process. Direct service providers may not function as administrators of programs and services, but they are important stakeholders who can take active and leadership roles in helping programs to evolve. In this section we identify several program structures that need to be considered.

7.2.1 Linking Activity and Participation Outcomes to Mission and Goals

The mission and goals of a program formally state the service's intentions. Attention to activity and participation is more likely when it is recognized that service efforts in this area will help achieve the service's mission and goals. The link between mission/goals and activity and participation will not always be clear and may need to be clearly defined and articulated. For example, a service may have an overarching mission of 'enabling recovery' or 'full community participation'. These are broad and complex constructs, and the shared understanding of their meaning among service providers and administrators may not automatically include activity and participation. The relationship between these constructs and activity and participation will need to be specified and highlighted. For example, in one service with a mission to enable

recovery, several service providers and administrators defined 'recovery' as freedom from symptoms, and thus prioritized treatments designed to reduce symptoms of illness, and hospitalizations. Other service providers, however, highlighted that engagement in meaningful activities and participation in the community were central elements of recovery and provided current literature and evidence to support this claim. These differences of opinions led the team to discuss and clarify how the mission was to be understood and what this meant for service delivery. *Worksheet 7.1: Structures that influence delivery of practices related to activity and participation: Mission and goals* has been developed to guide service providers in reflecting upon the mission and goals, with a view to clarifying formal intentions of their program or service.

7.2.2 Advancing Leadership in the Area of Activities and Participation

Leaders are people who have influence over the evolution of service development and delivery. As such, they can influence the extent to which practice related to activity and participation is embraced by the organization and integrated into routine practice. Formal leaders are those with authority and explicit responsibility for administration, management, and supervision. In mental health services, psychiatrists are not always the designated formal managers or supervisors, but they do hold a high level of authority for the nature of the services that individuals will receive. Informal leaders are those people who, without formal responsibilities or authority, have the ability to influence other service providers and the nature of service delivery. Leadership activities can evolve when connections are made between service providers to advance particular goals, knowledge, and practices. These kinds of connections depend on service providers moving beyond competition and strict role boundaries to advance ideas of how service practices can be integrated to promote health and well-being through activity and participation. *Worksheet 7.2: Structures that influence delivery of practices related to activity and participation: Advancing leadership related to activity and participation* provides guiding questions to reflect on leadership in the program/service.

7.2.3 Taking Stock of Program Resources

The integration of practices related to activity and participation depends on identifying and mobilizing potentially supportive material resources. These resources can include the allocation of human resources who may have special interest and advanced knowledge and training in the area. The allocation of funds to engage in these practices will also be important. For example, funds for community visits will be necessary. The allocation of time to related practices will be important. Mental health programs will often recognize and acknowledge those activities where there is direct contact between a provider and person served, but not provide the time resources required for community assessment and capacity building – activities that may advance the program mission and goals in the long run. *Worksheet 7.3: Structures that influence delivery of practices related to activity and participation: Taking stock of resources* provides the opportunity to reflect on how allocation of and access to resources impacts the delivery of practice related to activity and participation.

7.2.4 Considering Program Processes and Operations

Supportive program processes can include, for example, sanctioned activities, policies, and documents that organize and govern service delivery. These can include job descriptions, service meetings, processes for supervision, training and certification, service standards, policy documents, routine program-level data collection, and service evaluation activities and reports. Each of these can be considered for the extent to which they can be used, modified, or developed in a way that can support the integration of activity and participation approaches and outcomes. Such program processes have been central to the development of fidelity measures for the integration of specific intervention approaches in mental health service delivery. For example, the strengths-based model of case management has a well-developed fidelity measure focused on both direct service therapeutic processes and organizational structures and operations to ensure that intervention approaches are being delivered as intended (Fukui et al., 2012).

Worksheet 7.4: Structures that influence delivery of practices related to activity and participation: Program processes and operation provides an opportunity to reflect on these aspects of the program that might be strengthened to promote activity and participation-oriented practice.

7.2.5 Building Partnerships

The opening vignette illustrates how the program and service connected with a range of other people and organizations to advance the practices, goals, and outcomes of activity and participation-oriented practice. The vignette suggests that the service did not simply 'hand over' responsibility through processes such as referrals, but rather considered how they might work together to advance a shared interest and vision. Partnerships that are likely to advance activity and participation goals are those that are explicitly grounded in the investment in recovery as a guiding vision. Current efforts have identified key elements of effective partnerships in recovery-oriented community mental health, including inclusive identification of key stakeholders, development of a shared vision, mutual

respect, and the appreciation of differences, good communication, the involvement of service users and families, clear governance structures, and inclusion of multiple sectors (Ng et al., 2013).

Worksheet 7.5: Structures that influence delivery of practices related to activity and participation: Partnerships provides an opportunity to reflect on current and potential partnerships of the service that can promote practice and health and well-being outcomes.

7.3 Tips for Raising the Profile of Activity and Participation at the Program Level

There are also some relatively simple efforts that can raise the profile of health and well-being through activity and participation and perhaps help to prepare for program-level changes. Here are a few examples:

- Displaying relevant posters, pamphlets, newsletters etc. in prominent service delivery sites can be part of a focused effort to raise awareness about the importance and relevance of activities and participation to mental health and well-being.
- Identifying and publicizing educational opportunities related to activity and participation with a view to increasing the knowledge and skills required to enable changes in this area.
- Creating and disseminating narratives of how people with serious mental illness served by the program have realized health and well-being outcomes through activity and participation.
- Collecting and distributing competency standards related to promoting health and well-being through activity and participation.
- Sharing published research and other forms of scholarship that highlight the relevance and underlying evidence base for practices related to activity and participation.
- Organizing and implementing speakers' training, support, and events so that individuals with serious and mental illness can tell their recovery stories about activity and participation.
- Identify and share examples of initiatives of other services initiatives that have focused on and developed innovations related to activity and participation.

7.4 Key Competencies

The competencies underlying this chapter are those that have service providers move beyond direct service practice, to understand and influence the broader program context within which they operate. These competencies include:

- Participating in efforts that contribute to the effectiveness of the program/service to deliver practices that will achieve outcomes related to health and well-being through activity and participation.

- Promoting open dialogue about activity and participation practices at the program level.
- Incorporating the perspective and efforts of service users to influence the design and development of program practices related to activity and participation.
- Incorporating the perspective of family members and family organization to influence the design and development of program practices related to activity and participation.

- Promoting dialogue and supporting efforts to reconcile service level tensions related to activity and participation practice.
- Supporting the program/service in the identification of key stakeholders (individuals and groups/organizations) who could be enlisted to support practices, goals, and outcomes related to activity and participation.
- Advancing program/service involvement in advocacy efforts related to activity and participation.

Structures that influence delivery of practices related to activity and participation: Mission and goals

1. **What are the mission and goals of my program/service?**

   _____
   _____
   _____
   _____

2. **Are the mission and goals of my service/program consistent with attending to the activity and participation patterns of people served? Why or why not? What specific concepts or ideas in the mission and goals are consistent with attention to activity and participation?**

   _____
   _____
   _____
   _____

3. **Does the philosophy underlying the service mission and goals support attention to activity and participation patterns?**

   _____
   _____
   _____
   _____

4. **Are values espoused by the service or program consistent with a focus on activity and participation?**

   _____
   _____
   _____
   _____

5. **How do other people working for or with this program/service understand the mission and goals? Is their understanding aligned with health and well-being through activity and participation?**

   _____
   _____
   _____
   _____

6. **What service priority goals may compete with efforts directed to activity and participation as a means to health and well-being?**

   _____
   _____
   _____
   _____

Structures that influence delivery of practices related to activity and participation: Advancing leadership

1. **Who are the 'leaders' in this service who are in a good position to influence the acceptance and integration of practices focused on activity and participation?**

   Formal leaders –_____

   _____

   Informal leaders –_____

   _____

2. **What information and evidence can I share with these leaders that will raise the profile of activity and participation in practice?**

   _____

   _____

   _____

   _____

3. **What ideas can I share about how attention to activities and participation might be developed as a fundamental part of service delivery?**

   _____

   _____

   _____

   _____

4. **How might the link between activity and participation and the mission and goals of the service be explained in order to secure support?**

   _____

   _____

   _____

   _____

5. **Which service providers have an interest, knowledge, and expertise related to promoting practices related to activity and participation? How might these people work together to promote practice in this area?**

   _____

   _____

   _____

   _____

Structures that influence delivery of practices related to activity and participation: Taking stock of resources

1. Who are the people connected to this service who will have a particular interest, and commitment to activity and participation? Does the overall make up of staff in the program support a commitment to activity and participation?

_____

_____

_____

_____

_____

_____

2. Is program funding allocated to service approaches related to activity and participation? What are examples of this allocation? What are some examples where practices are limited because of funding constraints?

_____

_____

_____

_____

_____

_____

3. Is time recognized and allocated for both direct service and community-capacity building practices related to activity and participation? Provide some examples of how this happens and/or does not happen.

_____

_____

_____

_____

_____

_____

Structures that influence delivery of practices related to activity and participation: Program processes and operations

1. What service activities do or could be used to increase awareness of and commitment to activity-health approaches and outcomes? (For example, service meetings, communications, educational sessions, supervision)

_____

_____

_____

_____

2. What written documents do or could provide support for an activity and participation oriented approach? (For example, service descriptions, job descriptions, annual reports, intake assessments)

_____

_____

_____

_____

3. Are there any program policies that impede the delivery of approaches directed to activity and participation?

_____

_____

_____

_____

4. Does the service participate in any advocacy activities to improve the experience of activity and participation, empowerment, inclusion, and citizenship of the people served? If not, why not?

_____

_____

_____

_____

Structures that influence delivery of practices related to activity and participation: Partnerships

1. **What partnerships does your program currently have? Do they have the potential to advance practices and goals related to activity and participation?**

_____
_____
_____
_____

2. **How are service users currently involved in the design and delivery of services?**

_____
_____
_____
_____

3. **How are family networks currently involved in the design and delivery of services?**

_____
_____
_____
_____

4. **What partnerships with people/organizations might be developed to support practices, goals and outcomes related to activity and participation?**

Peer/service users –

Family –

Neighbourhood –

Volunteers –

Primary care/community health/public health –

Social welfare –

Housing –

Employment –

Education –

Media –

Nongovernmental organizations –

Other –

8   Evaluation of Activity and Participation to Inform Service Development

As part of their efforts to integrate practices related to activity and participation into routine service delivery, Jamie and Afsanah's program agreed to include these efforts into their program evaluation efforts.

Jamie and Afsanah took the lead in collecting completed responses from *Worksheet 2.15: A measure of my health and well-being through activity and participation*, for all individuals who received services focusing on their activity and participation patterns over a two-year period. They used the assistance of students involved in the program, both to increase the resources available to them and to develop student competencies in program evaluation.

They first compiled the responses into a format that provided an easy to understand description of these responses at baseline (the initial completion of the activity measure). In total they had responses for 40 people. This represented about 20% of the total population of people who were served by their program in this time period.

The responses at baseline were consistent with a picture of individuals who experience their activity and participation patterns as lacking in important dimensions of health and well-being.

The measure was re-administered at six months and one year for these individuals. Only 34 people actually completed both follow-up periods. Jamie and Afsanah calculated the means for each dimension across the three time periods. They noted that in each dimension, ratings either improved or stayed the same. Positive change was particularly noticeable in the areas of making social connections, physical activity, developing knowledge and skills, balance/variety, and values and beliefs.

Jamie and Afsanah presented these results at a service meeting. Excited by the changes, there was interest in adapting the scale to allow for examining the statistical significance of change. The service member responsible for program evaluation agreed to work with Jamie and Afsanah to develop this. Discussions also focused on some of the areas with limited change and how specifically these were being addressed by the service. The need for more training and supervision in areas was discussed. Jamie and Afsanah were charged with taking these evaluation findings out to people using the service and their families to get their impressions of the findings and the implications for the services. For example, discussions amongst family and service users suggested the need for developing other partnerships and raised possibilities for new initiatives.

Focused Questions:

1. The service in this vignette has an established program of evaluation. If there was no such established program, what strategies might Jamie and Afsanah use to go about implementing program-level evaluation related to activity and participation?
2. What other measures might be used by a program to determine the nature of the activity and participation changes of the people served?
3. The program in this vignette is open to using evaluation results to inform their practice. What barriers do services experience in using evaluation results? What strategies could be used to promote the use of such evaluation information in program development?

This chapter includes the following worksheet:

Worksheet 8.1: A framework for presenting program-level information about activity and participation

This chapter includes the following resource:

Resource 8.1: A framework for presenting program-level information about activity-health (example).

DOI: 10.4324/9781003111368-8

8.1　The Potential Benefits of Program-Level Evaluation of Activity and Participation

Program evaluations are systematic processes for the collection, synthesis, and interpretation of information about the quality of particular aspects of services. There are many types of program evaluations, constructed for a variety of purposes. Of particular relevance to the Action Over Inertia approach are what Patton (2008) describes as utilization-focused evaluation – those that are 'done for and with specific primary users for specific, intended uses' (p. 37). Utilization-focused evaluations are constructed in a way that is sensitive to the needs and commitments of the primary users of the evaluation information, provide relevant information about the consequences of service efforts, and encourage consideration of 'what is working' and what adjustments or modifications might be made to improve service delivery.

Program evaluation related to activity and participation patterns stand to make an important contribution to supporting recovery-oriented practice. For example, psychosocial domains frequently included in program evaluations in community mental health include employment status and ratings of overall community functioning. While these are important domains, they may not capture important dimensions of health and well-being that can be realized through other forms of activity and participation. A subset of the population served could, for example, be 'unemployed', but still be engaged in meaningful and health-promoting activity and participation patterns, while others could score high on overall community function while leading daily lives bereft of health-promoting activity and participation. Often outcome measures are related to activity and participation, but do not directly promote understanding of the experiences of individuals – experiences such as inclusion and empowerment.

There is good reason to include systematic evaluation of service efforts to meaningfully impact the activity and participation patterns of service users. As outlined in Chapter 7, the integration of activity and participation-oriented practices into routine service delivery can be a complex endeavour. Implementing and sustaining these practices, particularly in the face of the multiple competing demands on services, resource limitations, and established routines, can be enhanced when evidence can be used to reflect on the nature of the changes, intended and unintended consequences, and potential solutions to issues encountered.

The development of a full-scale evaluation process is beyond the scope of this text, but this chapter offers ideas for some relatively simple ways to begin to collect and synthesize evidence about activity and participation patterns as a means to influence continuous program improvement.

8.2　Program-Level Evaluation Focuses on Activity and Participation Patterns

The interventions and approaches described in this workbook highlight the need for program-level evaluation that will more fully describe health and well-being through activity and participation. In this case, the evaluation questions might, for example, be stated as

- *Are individuals served by this program experiencing activity and participation patterns that are consistent with health and well-being?*
- *Do the activity and participation patterns of individuals served demonstrate access to a broad range of opportunities, balance, and alignment with personal values and beliefs?*
- *Do the activity and participation patterns of individuals served demonstrate inclusion, empowerment, and citizenship?*

Evaluation methods can be *qualitative* or *quantitative* in nature. Program-level qualitative evaluation activities might take the form of individual interviews, focus groups, or the analysis of documents such as health-related records, with a view to developing a rich description and understanding of how the services related to activity and participation are experienced by service recipients, their alignment with their personal beliefs and values, and how they contribute to their health and well-being. In this way they give a window to understanding the meanings associated with activity and participation.

Qualitative evaluation is particularly good at capturing the complexities associated with change in a way that can inform good service delivery. For example, focus groups might reveal some common themes around challenges experienced by individuals in their efforts towards achieving health and well-being through activity and participation, or specific problems they encounter in their use of services. They can also reveal how services are particularly enabling and reveal unexpected sources of strength that can be mobilized in future efforts.

The wide range of methods for collecting information in qualitative approaches can potentially be translated into meaningful activity opportunities. For example, the use of photography, or other forms of art in evaluation can capture experiences of recovery including those not easily translated in to words and can create a meaningful opportunity for activity and participation (Casey & Webb, 2019; Mizock et al., 2015).

Quantitative evaluations focus on the objective measurement of status and change. Several of the worksheets provided in this workbook can be adapted to provide measures of change over time. For example, ***Worksheet 2.1: Daily time-use logs*** can be repeated over time to demonstrate changes in activities and participation, and in particular shifts in the range of opportunities accessed and balance.

Worksheet 2.15: A measure of my health and well-being through activity and participation can be used to provide program-level information, as well as information about individual change. In this case, the measure might provide an overview of the status of individuals served with regards to the health and well-being dimensions of activity and participation patterns, and, with repeat administrations of the measure, demonstrate the extent to which changes in activity and participation patterns occur among the population served.

Analyzing and interpreting data is facilitated within an evaluation framework that presents collected information in an easy to understand format. The process should encourage dialogue among multiple stakeholders to provide multiple perspectives. For example, qualitative data collected might be organized around key themes that are supported by many direct quotes from the data.

Quantitative data can be organized using tables and other visual illustrations that identify the areas measured and link the data clearly to the population served. *Worksheet 8.1: A framework for presenting program-level information* and *Resource 8.1: A framework for presenting program-level information (example)* demonstrate how information collected related to *Worksheet 2.15: A measure of my health and well-being through activity and participation* might be presented to show change over time. This framework can be adapted to provide more information as required. For example, baseline measures can be adapted to include summary data that provides findings as a percentage of all people served. Change over time measures can be adapted to include information about standard deviations, and statistical significance of change reported.

Interpretation is also enhanced when probing and meaningful questions are posed of the information gathered. For example, services will need to consider how they will define meaningful change in the area of activity and participation, and health and well-being. They might also consider how these are experienced across different sub-groups of the population served, or if particular groups appear to be more likely to access and benefit from these services. For example, concerns related to differences based on gender, age, disability levels, race, ethnicity, and sexual orientation might all be considered.

8.3 Using Program-Level Evaluation of Activity and Participation to Inform Continuous Service Improvement

The goal of continuous improvement related to activity-health is to use evaluation to facilitate an ongoing process of informed service development and refinement. It is meant to engage service providers and other stakeholders in the services, including people receiving services, in reflecting on findings. Potential questions to be posed include:

- What has been learned about health and well-being through activity and participation among service recipients?
- How are these findings consistent or inconsistent with the goals and intentions of the service or program?
- How do these findings compare with other relevant information in the mental health field?
- What information do we have about how services related to activity and participation were actually delivered? Which aspects of the intervention were delivered routinely and which were not delivered? Why?
- What can be learned from other initiatives or service efforts that could help with service development?
- What service activities appear to be effective in promoting activity and participation aligned with health and well-being?
- Are there particular dimensions of activity and participation patterns that require direct attention?
- Are there particular sub-groups served that benefit most or least from practices related to activity and participation? What might this mean for service delivery practices?
- What service-level initiatives might be implemented to address specific areas requiring attention?

This last question is perhaps particularly important in continuous improvement. The question moves the service beyond the work of any one service provider with any one client, to consider and organize activities and structures that could be accessed across the population of people served. For example, if evaluation findings suggest that individuals served are experiencing a lack of opportunity to contribute to their community, the service might commit to the development of partnerships with the local senior centre, places of worship, social services, charitable organizations, and other community organizations to provide a range of real opportunities for this type of engagement. In this way, it might also lend support to the notion that program activities related to assessing and developing community capacities has merit and promote consideration of how program resources might be allocated to this.

8.4 Key Competencies

The competencies associated with this chapter are related to the attitudes, knowledge, and skills underlying the service providers ability to engage in program-level evaluation of activity and participation practices, and to promote the program's use of evaluation methods and findings to inform ongoing service development. Competencies related to program evaluation in this area also highlight the engagement of key stakeholders, and the values underlying activity and participation practices. These competencies include:

- Collaborating with existing program evaluation processes and resources to advance evaluation related to activity and participation patterns.

- Framing program evaluation questions consistent with the values and practices of activity and participation-oriented service delivery.
- Choosing types of program evaluation methods that are relevant to and possible within the program context.
- Contributing to the design, data collection, interpretation, and sharing of findings for program evaluation focused on activity and participation.
- Promoting continuous improvement of practice related to activity and participation using program evaluation.
- Engaging key stakeholders, including service users and their families, in the evaluation process.
- Planning and designing of service-level initiatives focused on addressing issues raised in program evaluation of activity and participation.

A framework for presenting program-level information about activity and participation

Baseline status based on *Worksheet 2.15: Measure of health and well-being through activity and participation*. Total number completing measure: N=_____

I Could Benefit from More of the Following in My Day…	---Ratings: Number of People---									
	1	*2*	*3*	*4*	*5*	*6*	*7*	*8*	*9*	*10*
1. Balance and variety										
2. Living values and beliefs										
3. Taking care of myself										
4. Activating mind and senses										
5. Physical activity/ movement										
6. Expressing identity										
7. Developing knowledge/ abilities										
8. Having pleasure/ enjoyment										
9. Connecting with others										
10. Contributing to society/ community										
11. Building security and prosperity										
12. Accessing community										

Worksheet 8.1

Tracking change over time

Total number of people: _____

I Could Benefit from More of the Following in my Day….	Baseline Evaluation (Mean)	Follow-Up Evaluation at _ Months (Mean)	Follow-Up Evaluation at _ Months (Mean)	Difference between Baseline and Last Follow-Up: (Check all that Apply) -ve = 2 or more point decrease Neutral = no change +ve = 2 or more point increase
1. Balance and variety				( ) –ve ( ) Neutral ( ) +ve
2. Living values and beliefs				( ) –ve ( ) Neutral ( ) +ve
3. Taking care of myself				( ) –ve ( ) Neutral ( ) +ve
4. Activating mind/ senses				( ) –ve ( ) Neutral ( ) +ve
5. Physical activity/ movement				( ) –ve ( ) Neutral ( ) +ve
6. Expressing identity				( ) –ve ( ) Neutral ( ) +ve
7. Developing knowledge/abilities				( ) –ve ( ) Neutral ( ) +ve
8. Having pleasure/ enjoyment				( ) –ve ( ) Neutral ( ) +ve
9. Connecting with others				( ) –ve ( ) Neutral ( ) +ve
10. Contributing to society/community				( ) –ve ( ) Neutral ( ) +ve
11. Building security/ prosperity				( ) –ve ( ) Neutral ( ) +ve
12. Accessing community				( ) –ve ( ) Neutral ( ) +ve

A framework for presenting program-level information about activity-health (example)

Background:

I. Baseline Status of Measure of Health and Well-Being through Activity and Participation.

Total number: N = 40

I Could Benefit from More of the Following in My Day…	*Ratings: Number of People*									
	Very True 1	*2*	*3*	*4*	*5*	*6*	*7*	*8*	*9*	*Not True 10*
Balance/variety	7	8	8	10	6	1	0	0	0	0
Living values/beliefs	6	8	10	6	10	0	0	0	0	0
Taking care of myself	2	2	5	7	7	5	7	4	1	0
Activating mind/senses	7	9	8	10	4	2	0	0	0	0
Physical activity/movement	5	6	10	10	6	1	2	0	0	0
Expressing identity	5	7	6	8	10	2	2	0	0	0
Developing knowledge/abilities	5	8	10	10	6	1	0	0	0	0
Having pleasure/enjoyment	6	9	7	7	10	0	0	1	0	0
Connecting with others	6	6	6	7	5	1	3	4	2	0
Contributing to society/community	7	7	7	6	5	3	4	1	0	0
Building security/prosperity	12	10	5	10	0	3	0	0	0	0
Accessing community	3	3	5	5	10	5	4	2	2	1

II. Tracking Change over Time

Total number of people: N = 40 N=38 N=34

	Baseline Evaluation (Mean)	*Follow-Up Evaluation at 6 Months (Mean)*	*Follow-Up Evaluation at One Year (Mean)*	*Difference between Baseline and Last Follow-Up: (Check all that Apply)* *-ve = 2 or more point decrease* *Neutral = no change* *+ve = 2 or more point increase*
1. Balance/variety	3.1	5.4	5.7	( ) –ve ( ) Neutral (x) +ve
2. Living values/ beliefs	3.2	5.2	5.3	( ) –ve ( ) Neutral (x) +ve
3. Taking care of myself	5.1	5.6	6	( ) –ve (x) Neutral ( ) +ve
4. Activating mind/ senses	3.0	4.2	4.5	( ) –ve (x) Neutral ( ) +ve
5. Physical activity/ movement	3.4	5.2	5.1	( ) –ve ( ) Neutral (x) +ve
6. Expressing identity	3.6	4.1	4.3	( ) –ve (x) Neutral ( ) +ve
7. Developing knowledge/ abilities	3.2	5.8	5.9	( ) –ve ( ) Neutral (x) +ve
8. Having pleasure/ enjoyment	3.3	4.0	4.8	( ) –ve (x) Neutral ( ) +ve
9. Connecting with others	4.2	5.3	6.2	( ) –ve ( ) Neutral (x) +ve
10. Contributing to community/ society	3.6	3.7	3.9	( ) –ve (x) Neutral ( ) +ve
11. Building security/ prosperity	2.6	2.9	3.2	( ) –ve (x) Neutral ( ) +ve
12. Accessing community	4.9	5.5	5.5	( ) –ve (x) Neutral ( ) +ve

Bibliography

Alvidrez, J., Snowden, L. R., & Kaiser, D. M. (2010). Involving consumers in the development of a psychoeducational booklet about stigma for black mental health clients. *Health Promotion Practice*, *11*(2), 249–258. https://doi.org/10.1177/1524839908318286

Anand, P., & Ben-Shalom, Y. (2014). How do working-age people with disabilities spend their time? New evidence from the american time use survey. *Demography*, *51*(6), 1977–1998. http://dx.doi.org/10.1007/s13524-014-0336-3

Ashcraft, L. (2013). Community interdependence: The path to sustained recovery: To end stigma, people in recovery must give back to their communities. *Behavioral Healthcare*, *33*(1), 8–11.

Aubry, T., & Myner, J. (1996). Community integration and quality of life: A comparison of persons with psychiatric disabilities in housing programs and community residents who are neighbours. *Canadian Journal of Community Mental Health*, *15*(1), 5–20. https://doi.org/10.7870/cjcmh-1996-0001

Barbic, S., Krupa, T., & Armstrong, I. (2009). A randomized controlled trial of the effectiveness of a modified recovery workbook program: Preliminary findings. *Psychiatric Services*, *60*(4), 491–497. https://doi.org/10.1176/ps.2009.60.4.491

Barris, R., Kielhofner, G., & Hawkins Watts, J. (1988). *Occupational Therapy in Psychosocial Practice*. Slack.

Bartholomeusz, C. F., Allott, K., Killackey, E., Liu, P., Wood, S. J., & Thompson, A. (2013). Social cognition training as an intervention for improving functional outcome in first-episode psychosis: A feasibility study. *Early Intervention in Psychiatry*, *7*, 421–426. http://dx.doi.org/10.1111/eip.12036

Bejerholm, J. Hansson, L. & Eklund, M. (2006). Engagement in occupations among men and women with schizophrenia. *Occupational Therapy International*, *13*, 100–121.

Brown, E. V. D., Muñoz, J., & Pan, A. W. (2019). Person-centred evaluation. In C. Brown, V. C. Stoffell, & J. P. Muñoz (Eds), *Occupational Therapy in Mental Health: A vision for participation* (pp. 47–68). FA Davis.

Brown, L. D. (2012). *Consumer-Run Mental Health: Framework for Recovery*. Springer.

Casey, B., & Webb, M. (2019). Imaging journeys of recovery and learning: A participatory arts-based inquiry. *Qualitative Health Research*, *29*(6), 833–845. https://doi.org/10.1177/1049732318804832

Chen, S., Krupa, T., Lysaght, R., McCay, E., & Piat, M. (2014). Development of a recovery education program for inpatient mental health providers. *Psychiatric Rehabilitation Journal*, *37*(4), 329–332. https://doi.org/10.1037/prj0000082

Chen, S., Koller, M., Krupa, T., & Stuart, H. (2016). Contact in the classroom: Developing a program model for youth mental health contact-based anti-stigma education. *Community Mental Health Journal*, *52*(3), 281–293. https://doi.org/10.1007/s10597-015-9944-7

Cho, S. H., Torres-Llenza, V., Budnik, K., & Norris, L. (2016). The integral role of psychoeducation in clinical care. *Psychiatric Annals*, *46*(5), 286–292. http://dx.doi.org/10.3928/00485713-20160329-01

Christiansen, C., & Townsend, E. (2004). *Introduction to Occupation: The art and Science of Living*. Prentice-Hall.

Clarke, S. P., Crowe, T. P., Oades, L. G., & Deane, F. P. (2009). Do goal-setting interventions improve the quality of goals in mental health services? *Psychiatric Rehabilitation Journal*, *32*(4), 292–299. https://doi.org/10.2975/32.4.2009.292.299

Colori, S. (2020). The meaning of my diagnosis. *Schizophrenia Bulletin*, *46*, 1032–1033.

Cook, J. A., Copeland, M. E., Corey, L., Buffington, E., Jonikas, J. A., Curtis, L. C., Grey, D. D., & Nichols, W. H. (2010). Developing the evidence base for peer-led services: Changes among participants following wellness recovery action planning (WRAP) education in two statewide initiatives. *Psychiatric Rehabilitation Journal*, *34*(2), 113–120. https://doi.org/10.2975/34.2.2010.113.120

Corrigan, P. W., Morris, S. B., Michaels, P. J., Rafacz, J. D., & Rüsch, N. (2012). Challenging the public stigma of mental illness: A meta-analysis of outcome studies. *Psychiatric Services*, *63*(10), 963–973. https://doi.org/10.1176/appi.ps.201100529

Davidson, L., Ridgway, P., Wieland, M., & O'Connell, M. (2009). A capabilities approach to mental health transformation: A conceptual framework for the recovery era. *Canadian Journal of Community Mental Health*, *28*(2), 35–46. https://doi.org/10.7870/cjcmh-2009-0021

Davidson, L., Shahar, G., Lawless, M. S., Sells, D., & Tondora, J. (2006). Play, pleasure, and other positive life events: "Non–specific" factors in recovery from mental illness? *Psychiatry*, *69*(2), 151–163. https://doi.org/10.1521/psyc.2006.69.2.151

Deegan, P. E. (2020). The journey to use medication optimally to support recovery. *Psychiatric Services, 71*(4), 401–402. https://doi.org/10.1176/appi.ps.201900506

Deegan, P. E. (2002). Recovery as a self-directed process of healing and transformation. *Occupational Therapy in Mental Health, 17*(3–4), 5–21. https://doi.org/10.1300/j004v17n03_02

Deegan, P. (1996). Recovery as a journey of the heart. *Psychiatric Rehabilitation Journal, 19*(3), 91–97. https://doi.org/10.1037/h0101301

Deegan, P. (1988). Recovery: The lived experience of rehabilitation. *Psychiatric Rehabilitation Journal, 11*(4), 11–19. https://doi.org/10.1037/h0099565

Degnan, A., Berry, K., Sweet, D., Abel, K., Crossley, N., & Edge, D. (2018). Social networks and symptomatic and functional outcomes in schizophrenia: A systematic review and meta-analysis. *Social Psychiatry and Psychiatric Epidemiology, 53*(9), 873–888. https://doi.org/10.1007/s00127-018-1552-8

De Waal, M. M., Dekker, J. J., Kikkert, M. J., Christ, C., Chmielewska, J., Staats, M. W., Brink, W., & Goudriaan, A. E. (2019). Self-wise, other-wise, streetwise (SOS) training, an intervention to prevent victimization in dual-diagnosis patients: Results from a randomized clinical trial. *Addiction, 114*(4), 730–740. https://doi.org/10.1111/add.14500

Drake, R., Bond, G., & Becker, D. (2012). *Individual Placement and support: An Evidence-Based Approach to Supported Employment*. Oxford University Press.

Drake, R. E., & Whitley, R. (2014). Recovery and severe mental illness: Description and analysis. *Canadian Journal of Psychiatry, 59*(5), 236–242. http://dx.doi.org/10.1177/070674371405900502

Ecker, J., & Aubry, T. (2017). A mixed methods analysis of housing and neighbourhood impacts on community integration among vulnerably housed and homeless individuals. *Journal of Community Psychology, 45*(4), 528–542. https://doi.org/10.1002/jcop.21864

Edgelow, M., & Krupa, T. (2011). A randomized controlled pilot study of an occupational time use intervention for people with serious mental illness. *American Journal of Occupational Therapy. 65*(3), 267–276. http://dx.doi.org/10.5014/ajot.2011.001313

Eklund, M., Leufstadius, C., & Bejerholm, U. (2009). Time use among people with psychiatric disabilities: Implications for practice. *Psychiatric Rehabilitation Journal, 32*(3), 177–91. http://dx.doi.org/10.2975/32.3.2009.177.191

Eldredge, L. K., Markham, C. M., Ruiter, R. A., Kok, G., Fernandez, M. E., & Parcel, G. S. (2016). *Planning Health Promotion Programs: An Intervention Mapping Approach*. Jossey-Bass.

Enam, A., Konduri, K. C., Eluru, N., Ravulaparthy, S., & Srinath, G. (2018). Relationship between well-being and daily time use of elderly: Evidence from the disabilities and use of time survey. *Transportation, 45*, 1783–1810. http://dx.doi.org/ 10.1007/s11116-017-9821-z

Fitzgerald, P. B., De Castella, A. R., Filia, K. M., Filia, S. L., Benitez, J., & Kulkarni, J. (2005). Victimization of patients with schizophrenia and related disorders. *Australian and New Zealand Journal of Psychiatry, 39*(3), 169–174. https://doi.org/10.1080/j.1440-1614.2005.01539.x

Fossey, E., Krupa, T., Davidson, L. (2016). Occupation and meaning. In T. Krupa, B. Kirsh, D. Pitts & E. Fossey. *Bruce & Borg's Psychosocial Frames of Reference: Theories, Models, and Approaches for Occupation-based Practice* (4th ed., pp. 75–92). Slack.

Fukui, S., Goscha, R., Rapp, C. A., Mabry, A., Liddy, P., & Marty, D. (2012). Strengths model case management fidelity scores and client outcomes. *Psychiatric Services, 63*(7), 708–710. https://doi.org/10.1176/appi.ps.201100373

Gelkopf, M. (2011). The use of humor in serious mental illness: A review. *Evidence-Based Complementary and Alternative Medicine, 2011*, 342837. https://doi.org/10.1093/ecam/nep106

Gewurtz, R. E., Moll, S. E., Letts, L. J., Lariviere, N., Lavasseur, M., & Krupa, T. M. (2016). What you do everyday matters: A new direction for health promotion. *Canadian Journal of Public Health. 107*(2), e205–e208. http://dx.doi.org/10.17269/CJPH.107.5317

Gearing, R. E., Alonzo, D., Smolak, A., McHugh, K., Harmon, S., & Baldwin, S. (2011). Association of religion with delusions and hallucinations in the context of schizophrenia: Implications for engagement and adherence. *Schizophrenia Research, 126*(1–3), 150–163. https://doi.org/10.1016/j.schres.2010.11.005

Gibson, R. W., D'Amico, M., Jaffe, L., & Arbesman, M. (2011). Occupational therapy interventions for recovery in the areas of community integration and normative life roles for adults with serious mental illness: A systematic review. *American Journal of Occupational Therapy, 65*(3), 247–256. https://doi.org/10.5014/ajot.2011.001297

Golden, S. D., & Earp, J. L. (2012). Social ecological approaches to individuals and their contexts: Twenty years of health education & behavior health promotion interventions. *Health Education & Behavior 39*(3), 364–372. DOI: 10.1177/1090198111418634

Haselden, M., Dixon, L. B., Overley, A., Cohen, A. N., Glynn, S. M., Drapalski, A., Piscitelli, S., & Thorning, H. (2018). Giving back to families: Evidence and predictors of persons with serious mental illness contributing help and support to families. *Community Mental Health Journal, 54*(4), 383–394. https://doi.org/10.1007/s10597-017-0172-1

Hiday, V. A., Swartz, M. S., Swanson, J. W., Borum, R., & Wagner, H. R. (1999). Criminal victimization of persons with severe mental illness. *Psychiatric Services, 50*(1), 62–68. https://doi.org/10.1176/ps.50.1.62

Highton-Williamson, E., Priebe, S., & Giacco, D. (2014). Online social networking in people with psychosis: A systematic review. *International Journal of Social Psychiatry 61*(1), 92–101. https://doi.org/10.1177/0020764014556392

Höhl, W., Moll, S., & Pfeiffer, A. (2017). Occupational therapy interventions in the treatment of people with severe mental illness. *Current Opinion in Psychiatry, 30*(4), 300–305. https://doi.org/10.1097/yco.0000000000000339

Holley, L. C., Tavassoli, K. Y., & Stromwall, L. K. (2016). Mental illness discrimination in mental health treatment programs: Intersections of race, ethnicity, and sexual orientation. *Community Mental Health Journal, 52*(3), 311–322. https://doi.org/10.1007/s10597-016-9990-9

Holmes, E. P., Corrigan, P. W., Stephenson, J., & Nugent-Hirschbeck, J. (1997). Learning street smarts for an urban setting. *Psychiatric Rehabilitation Journal*, *20*(3), 64–66. https://doi.org/10.1037/h0095361

Hopper, K. (2007). Rethinking social recovery in schizophrenia: What a capabilities approach might offer. *Social Science & Medicine*, *65*(5), 868–879. https://doi.org/10.1016/j.socscimed.2007.04.012

Jaremka, L. M., & Sunami, N. (2018). Threats to belonging threaten health: Policy implications for improving physical well-being. *Policy Insights from the Behavioral and Brain Sciences*, *5*(1), 90–97. https://doi.org/10.1177/2372732217747005

Jaiswal, A., Carmichael, K., Gupta, S., Siemens, T., Crowley, P., Carlsson, A., Unsworth, G., Landry, T., & Brown, N. (2020). Essential elements that contribute to the recovery of persons with severe mental illness: A systematic scoping study. *Frontiers in Psychiatry*, *11*. https://doi.org/10.3389/fpsyt.2020.586230

Katz, P., & Morris, A. (2007). Time use patterns among women with rheumatoid arthritis: Association with functional limitations and psychological status, *Rheumatology*, *46*(3), 490–495. http://dx.doi.org/ 10.1093/rheumatology/kel299

Kessler, D., & Graham, F. (2015). The use of coaching in occupational therapy: An integrative review. *Australian Occupational Therapy Journal*, *62*(3), 160–176. https://doi.org/10.1111/1440-1630.12175

Kidd, S., Herman, Y., Barbic, S., Ganguli, R., George, T. P., Hassan, S., McKenzie, K., Maples, N., & Velligan, D. (2014). Testing a modification of cognitive adaptation training: Streamlining the model for broader implementation. *Schizophrenia Research*, *156*(1), 46–50. http://dx.doi.org/10.1016/j.schres.2014.03.026

Kiepek, N. C., Beagan, B., Rudman, D. L., & Phelan, S. (2019). Silences around occupations framed as unhealthy, illegal, and deviant. *Journal of Occupational Science*, *26*(3), 341–353. https://doi.org/10.1080/14427591.2018.1499123

Kinoshita, Y., Furukawa, T. A., Kinoshita, K., Honyashiki, M., Omori, I. M., Marshall, M., Bond, G. R., Huxley, P., Amano, N., & Kingdon, D. (2013). Supported employment for adults with severe mental illness. *Cochrane Database of Systematic Reviews*, *9*. http://dx.doi.org/ 10.1002/14651858.CD008297.pub2

Krupa, T. (2016). The drive and motivation for occupation. In T. Krupa, B. Kirsh, D. Pitts & E. Fossey (Eds.), *Psychosocial Frames of Reference: Theories, Models and Approaches for Occupation-Based Practice* (4th ed., pp. 93–106). Slack.

Krupa, T., Kirsh, B., Pitts, D., & Fossey, E. (2016). *Psychosocial Frames of Reference: Theories, Models and Approaches for Occupation-Based Practice* (4th edition). Thorofare: Slack.

Krupa, T., Edgelow, M., Chen, S. P., Mieras, C., Almas, A., Perry, A., Radloff-Gabriel, D., Jackson, J., & Bransfield, M. (2010). *Action Over Inertia: Addressing the Activity-Health Needs of Individuals with Serious Mental Illness.* CAOT Publications.

Krupa, T., Woodside, H., & Pocock, K. (2010). Activity and social participation in the period following a first episode of psychosis and implications for occupational therapy. *British Journal of Occupational Therapy*, *73*(1), 13–20. https://doi.org/10.4276/030802210x12629548272628

Kukla, M., Strasburger, A. M., Salyers, M. P., Rollins, A. L., Lysaker, P. H. (2020). Psychosocial outcomes of a pilot study of work-tailored cognitive behavioral therapy intervention

for adults with serious mental illness. *Journal of clinical psychology*, 1–8.

Leamy, M., Bird, V., Le Boutillier, C., Williams, J., & Slade, M. (2011). Conceptual framework for personal recovery in mental health: Systematic review and narrative synthesis. *British Journal of Psychiatry*, *199*(6), 445–452. https://doi.org/10.1192/bjp.bp.110.083733

Lecomte, T., Corbière, M., Giguère, C. E., Titone, D., & Lysaker, P. (2020). Group cognitive behaviour therapy for supported employment–Results of a randomized controlled cohort trial. *Schizophrenia Research*, *215*, 126–133. http://dx.doi.org/10.1016/j.schres.2019.10.063

Lester, H., & Tritter, J. Q. (2005). 'Listen to my madness': Understanding the experiences of people with serious mental illness. *Sociology of Health and Illness*, *27*(5), 649–669. https://doi.org/10.1111/j.1467-9566.2005.00460.x

Li, H., Pearrow, M., & Jimerson, S. R. (2010). *Identifying, Assessing, and Treating Early Onset Schizophrenia at School.* Springer Science & Business Media.

Lipskaya-Velikovsky, L., Bar-Shalita, T., & Bart, O. (2015). Sensory modulation and daily-life participation in people with schizophrenia. *Comprehensive Psychiatry*, *58*, 130–137. http://dx.doi.org/10.1016/j.comppsych.2014.12.009

Lipskaya-Velikovsky, L., Krupa, T., Silvan-Kosovich, I., & Kotler, M. (2020). Occupation-focused intervention for in-patient mental health settings: Pilot study of effectiveness. *Journal of Psychiatric Research*, *125*, 45–51. https://doi.org/10.1016/j.jpsychires.2020.03.004

Lucksted, A., Drapalski, A., Calmes, C., Forbes, C., DeForge, B., & Boyd, J. (2011). Ending self-stigma: Pilot evaluation of a new intervention to reduce internalized stigma among people with mental illnesses. *Psychiatric Rehabilitation Journal*, *35*(1), 51–54. https://doi.org/10.2975/35.1.2011.51.54

Lukyanova, V. V., Balcazar, F. E., Oberoi, A. K., & Suarez-Balcazar, Y. (2014). Employment outcomes among African Americans and whites with mental illness. *Work*, *48*(3), 319–328. https://doi.org/10.3233/wor-131788

Mahlke, C. I., Krämer, U. M., Becker, T., & Bock, T. (2014). Peer support in mental health services. *Current Opinion in Psychiatry*, *27*(4), 276–281. https://doi.org/10.1097/yco.0000000000000074

Marrone, J., & Golowka, E. (1999). If work makes people with mental illness sick, what do unemployment, poverty, and social isolation cause? *Psychiatric Rehabilitation Journal*, *23*(2), 187–193. https://doi.org/10.1037/h0095171

Marshall, C. A., Lysaght, R., Krupa, T. (2018). Occupational transition in the process of becoming housed following chronic homelessness. *Canadian Journal of Occupational Therapy*, *85*(1), 33–45. http://dx.doi.org/10.1177/0008417417723351

McDowell, C., & Fossey, E. (2015). Workplace accommodations for people with mental illness: A scoping review. *Journal of Occupational Rehabilitation*, *25*(1), 197–206. https://doi.org/10.1007/s10926-014-9512-y

McGinty, E. E., Baker, S. P., Steinwachs, D. M., & Daumit, G. (2013). Injury risk and severity in a sample of Maryland residents with serious mental illness. *Injury Prevention*, *19*(1), 32–37. http://dx.doi.org/10.1136/injuryprev-2011-040309

McKnight, J. L., & Kretzman, J. P. (2012). Mapping community capacity. In M. Minkler (Ed.), *Community Organizing and*

Community Building for Health and Welfare (pp. 171–186). Rutgers University Press.

McLean, K. C., & Syed, M. (2015). Personal, master, and alternative narratives: An integrative framework for understanding identity development, *Human Development*, *58*(6), 318–349. http://dx.doi.org/10.1159/000445817

Mizock, L., Russinova, Z., & DeCastro, S. (2015). Recovery narrative photovoice: Feasibility of a writing and photography intervention for serious mental illnesses. *Psychiatric Rehabilitation Journal*, *38*(3), 279–282. https://doi.org/10.1037/prj0000111

Moll, S. E., Gewurtz, R. E., Krupa, T. M., Law, M. C., Lariviere, N., & Levasseur, M. (2014). Do-live-well: A canadian framework for promoting occupation, health, and well-being. *Canadian Journal of Occupational Therapy*, *82*, 9–23. http://dx.doi.org/10.1177/0008417414545981

Mueser, K. T., Corrigan, P. W., Hilton, D. W., Tanzman, B., Schaub, A., Gingerich, S., Essock, S. M., Tarrier, N., Morey, B., Vogel-Scibilia, S., & Herz, M. (2002). Illness management and recovery: A review of the research. *Psychiatric Services*, *53*(10), 1272–1284. https://doi.org/10.1176/appi.ps.53.10.1272

Mueser, K., & Roe, D. (2016). Schizophrenia disorders. In J. Norcross, G. VandenBos, D. Freedheim, N. Pole (Eds.), *APA Handbook of Clinical Psychology* (pp. 225–251). American Psychological Association.

Nelson, G., Lord, J., & Ochocka, J. (2001). *Shifting the Paradigm in Community Mental Health: Towards Empowerment and Community*. University of Toronto Press.

Ng, C., Fraser, J., Goding, M., Paroissien, D., & Ryan, B. (2013). Partnerships for community mental health in the Asia-Pacific: Principles and best-practice models across different sectors. *Australasian Psychiatry*, *21*(1), 38–45. https://doi.org/10.1177/1039856212465348

Nussbaum, M. (2003). Capabilities as fundamental entitlements: Sen and social justice. *Feminist Economics*, *9*(2–3), 33–59. http://dx.doi.org/10.1080/1354570022000077926

Nussbaum, M. (2004). Beyond the social contract: Capabilities and global justice. *Oxford Development Studies*, *32*, 3–18. http://dx.doi.org/10.1080/1360081042000184093

Nussbaum, M. (2011). *Creating Capabilities: The Human Development Approach*. Harvard University Press.

O'Cathain, A., Croot, L., Duncan, E., Rousseau, N., Sworn, K., Turner, K. M., Yardley, L., & Hoddinott, P. (2019). Guidance on how to develop complex interventions to improve health and healthcare. *BMJ Open*, *9*(8), e029954. https://doi.org/10.1136/bmjopen-2019-029954

Ory, M. G., Jordan, P. J., & Bazzarre, T. (2002). The behavior change consortium: Setting the stage for a new century of health behavior-change research. *Health Education Research*, *17*(5), 500–511. https://doi.org/10.1093/her/17.5.500

Patton, M. Q. (2008). *Utilization Focused Evaluation* (4th ed.). Los Angeles: Sage.

Pentland, W. E., & McColl M. A. (2007). Application of time use research to the study of life with a disability. In W. E. Pentland, M. Powell Lawton, A. Harvey, & M. A. McColl (Eds), *Time Use Research in the Social Sciences* (pp. 169–183). Springer.

Pentland, W. E., & McColl, M. A. (2008). Occupational integrity: Another perspective on "life balance". *Canadian*

Journal of Occupational Therapy, *75*(3), 135–138. http://dx.doi.org/10.1177/000841740807500304

Perez-Cruzado, D., Cuesta-Vargas, A. I., Vera-Garcia, E., & Mayoral-Cleries, F. (2017). Physical fitness and levels of physical activity in people with severe mental illness: A cross-sectional study. *BMC Sports Science, Medicine and Rehabilitation*, *9*(1), 1–6. https://doi.org/10.1186/s13102-017-0082-0

Ponce, A. N., Clayton, A., Gambino, M., & Rowe, M. (2016). Social and clinical dimensions of citizenship from the mental health-care provider perspective. *Psychiatric Rehabilitation Journal*, *39*(2), 161–166. https://doi.org/10.1037/prj0000194

Quinn, N., Bromage, B., & Rowe, M. (2020). Collective citizenship: From citizenship and mental health to citizenship and solidarity. *Social Policy & Administration*, *54*(3), 361–374. http://dx.doi.org/10.1111/spol.12551

Rapp, C. A., & Goscha, R. (2012). *The Strengths Model: A Recovery-Oriented Approach to Mental Health Service Delivery (3rd ed.)*. Oxford University Press.

Rees, E. F., Ennals, P., & Fossey, E. (In press). Implementing an action over inertia group program in community residential rehabilitation services: Group participant and facilitator perspectives. *Frontiers in Psychiatry (Section: Social Psychiatry and Psychiatric Rehabilitation)*.

Rosenbaum, S., Tiedemann, A., Sherrington, C., Curtis, J., & Ward, P. B. (2014). Physical activity interventions for people with mental illness: A systematic review and meta-analysis, *Journal of Clinical Psychiatry*, *75*(9), 964–974. http://dx.doi.org/10.4088/JCP.13r08765

Rosenheck, R. A., Estroff, S. E., Sint, K., Lin, H., Mueser, K. T., Robinson, D. G., Schooler, N. R., Marcy, P., & Kane, J. M. (2017). Incomes and outcomes: Social security disability benefits in first-episode psychosis. *American Journal of Psychiatry*, *174*(9), 886–894. https://doi.org/10.1176/appi.ajp.2017.16111273

Rummel-Kluge, C., & Kissling, W. (2008). Psychoeducation in schizophrenia: New developments and approaches in the field. *Current Opinion in Psychiatry*, *21*(2), 168–172. http://dx.doi.org/10.1097/YCO.0b013e3282f4e574

Russinova, Z., Rogers, E. S., Cook, K. F., Ellison, M. L., & Lyass, A. (2013). Conceptualization and measurement of mental health providers' recovery-promoting competence: The recovery promoting relationships scale (RPRS). *Psychiatric Rehabilitation Journal*, *36*(1), 7–14. https://doi.org/10.1037/h0094741

Saccheto, B., Orenelas J., Calheriros, M. M., & Shinn, M. (2018). Adaptation of Nussbaum's capabilities framework to community mental health: A consumer-based capabilities measure. *American Journal of Community Psychology*, *61*(1–2), 32–46.

Seeman, M. V. (2017). Identity and schizophrenia: Who do I want to be? *World Journal of Psychiatry*, *7*(1), 1. https://doi.org/10.5498/wjp.v7.i1.1

Sen, A. (2000). *Development as freedom*. Anchor.

Sells, D. J., Rowe, M., Fisk, D., & Davidson, L. (2003). Violent victimization of persons with co-occurring psychiatric and substance use disorders. *Psychiatric Services*, *54*(9), 1253–1257. https://doi.org/10.1176/appi.ps.54.9.1253

Sharma, S., & Sharma, M. (2010). Self, social identity and psychological well-being. *Psychological Studies*, *55*(2), 118–136. http://dx.doi.org/10.1007/s12646-010-0011-8

Shiers, D., Rosen, A., & Shiers, A. (2009). Beyond early intervention: Can we adopt alternative narratives like 'woodshedding' as pathways to recovery in schizophrenia? *Early Intervention in Psychiatry*, *3*(3), 163–171. https://doi.org/10.1111/j.1751-7893.2009.00129.x

Slade, M., Amering, M., Farkas, M., Hamilton, B., O'Hagan, M., Panther, G., Perkins, R., Shepherd, G., Tse, S., & Whitley, R. (2014). Uses and abuses of recovery: Implementing recovery-oriented practices in mental health systems. *World Psychiatry*, *13*(1), 12–20. https://doi.org/10.1002/wps.20084

Spaniol, L. J., Koehler, M., & Hutchinson, D. (2009). *The Recovery Workbook: Practical Coping and Empowerment Strategies for People with Psychiatric Disabilities*. Boston University Art Gallery.

Statistics Canada. (2019). *General Social Survey– Time Use (GSS)*. Retrieved January 2021, from http://www23.statcan.gc.ca

Strauss, G. P., Visser, K. F., Keller, W. R., Gold, J. M., & Buchanan, R. W. (2018). Anhedonia reflects impairment in making relative value judgments between positive and neutral stimuli in schizophrenia. *Schizophrenia Research*, *197*, 156–161. https://doi.org/10.1016/j.schres.2018.02.016

Sullivan, W. P., & Carpenter, J. (2010). Community-based mental health services: Is coercion necessary? *Journal of Social Work in Disability & Rehabilitation*, *9* (2–3), 148–167. https://doi.org/10.1080/1536710X.2010.493483

Tallon, D., McClay, C. A., Kessler, D., Lewis, G., Peters, T. J., Shafran, R., Williams, C., & Wiles, N. (2019). Materials used to support cognitive behavioral therapy for depression: A survey of therapists' clinical practice and views. *Cognitive Behavior Therapy*, *48*(6), 463–481. http://dx.doi.org/10.1080/16506073.2018.1541927

Tøge, A. G., & Bell, R. (2016). Material deprivation and health: A longitudinal study. *BMC Public Health*, *16*(1), 747. https://doi.org/10.1186/s12889-016-3327-z

Townsend, E. A. (2012). Boundaries and bridges to adult mental health: Critical occupational and capabilities perspectives of justice. *Journal of Occupational Science*, *19*(1), 8–24. https://doi.org/10.1080/14427591.2011.639723

Townsend, E. A., Beagan, B., Kumas-Tan, Z., Versnel, J., Iwama, M., Landry, J., Stewart, D., & Brown, J. (2007). Enabling: Occupational therapy's core competency. In E. A. Townsend & H. J. Polatajko (Eds.), *Enabling Occupation II: Advancing an Occupational Therapy Vision for Health, Well-Being & Justice Through Occupation* (pp. 87–134). CAOT Publications.

Townsend, E. A., & Polatajko, H. J. (2007). *Enabling Occupation II: Advancing An Occupational Therapy Vision for Health, Well-Being and Justice Through Occupation*. CAOT Publications.

Vagnia, G., & Cornwell, B. (2018). Patterns of everyday activities across social contexts. *Proceedings of the National Academy of Sciences of the United States of America (PNAS)*, *115*, 6183–6188. https://doi.org/10.1073/pnas.1718020115

Velthorst, E., Fett, A. J., Reichenberg, A., Perlman, G., Van Os, J., Bromet, E. J., & Kotov, R. (2017). The 20-Year longitudinal trajectories of social functioning in individuals with psychotic disorders. *American Journal of Psychiatry*, *174*(11), 1075–1085. https://doi.org/10.1176/appi.ajp.2016.15111419

Wade, D. (2009). Goal setting in rehabilitation: An overview of what, why and how. *Clinical Rehabilitation*, *23*, 291–295

Wagman, P., & Håkansson, C. (2014). Introducing the occupational balance questionnaire (OBQ). *Scandinavian Journal of Occupational Therapy*, *21*(3), 227–231. http://dx.doi.org/10.3109/11038128.2014.900571

Wasserman, D. (2006). Disability, capabilities and distributive justice. In A. Kaufman (Ed.), *Capabilities Equality: Basic Issues and Problems* (pp. 214–234). Routledge.

Wilcock, A. A. (1998). *An Occupational Perspective on Health*. Slack.

Williams, J., Stubbs, B., Richardson, S., Flower, C., Barr-Hamilton, L., Grey, B., Hubbard, K., Spaducci, G., Gaughran, F., & Craig, T. (2019). 'Walk this way': Results from a pilot randomised controlled trial of a health coaching intervention to reduce sedentary behaviour and increase physical activity in people with serious mental illness. *BMC Psychiatry*, *19*(1), 1–10. http://dx.doi.org/10.1186/s12888-019-2274-5

Wilton, R. (2004). Putting policy into practice? Poverty and people with serious mental illness, *Social Science & Medicine*, *58*, 25–39. https://doi.org/10.1016/S0277-9536(03)00148-5

Wolf-Powers, L. (2017). Food deserts and real-estate-Led social policy. *International Journal of Urban and Regional Research*, *41*(3), 414–425. https://doi.org/10.1111/1468-2427.12515

World Health Organization. (2001). *International Classification of Functioning, Disability and Health (ICF)*.

World Health Organization. (2013). *ICF Application Areas*. Retrieved January 2021, from http://www.who.int/classifications/icf/appareas/en/index.html.

World Health Organization. (2016). *MhGAP Intervention Guide for mental, neurological and substance use disorders in nonspecialized health settings*. Retrieved January 2021, from http://apps.who.int/iris/bitstream/handle/10665/250239/9789241549790-eng.pdf;jsessionid=81BFEA8B6CB87AE808F24E6C28B9BE2D

Wykes, T., & Spaulding, W. D. (2011). Thinking about the future of cognitive remediation therapy – what works and what could we do better? *Schizophrenia Bulletin*, *37* Supplement 2, S80–S90, https://doi.org/10.1093/schbul/sbr064

Xia, J., Merinder, L. B., & Belgamwar, M. R. (2011). Psychoeducation for schizophrenia. *Cochrane Database of Systematic Reviews*, *6*. https://doi.org/10.1002/14651858.CD002831.pub2

Zimolag, U., & Krupa, T. (2009). Pet ownership as a meaningful community occupation for people with serious mental illness. *American Journal of Occupational Therapy*, *63*(2), 126–137. https://doi.org/10.5014/ajot.63.2.126

Appendix A: Additional Vignettes

Vignette 1 – Sol

Sol (47 years old) has spent the last several years staying at shelters, with friends, and on the street when not receiving mental health care in a hospital setting. He has just recently moved into a new subsided housing complex. The apartment complex is all single units (no roommates) with shared common areas for socialization and group programming by the mental health staff that support individuals in their apartments.

Most of Sol's days are spent walking the local streets and in parks. The community mental health team knows the areas frequented by Sol and will seek him out to engage with him. Sol is not particularly interested in their help but enjoys the coffee that comes with the visit. He often expresses that there is nothing they can do for him as they are the same as hospital staff – 'you all just tell me what to do'.

Kyrie, Sol's service provider, has concerns about his daily activities. Kyrie notes that he has little structure to his day and that there has been little change in Sol's daily routine since his move into his own apartment.

Kyrie has observed Sol yelling in the street, appearing to respond to voices he is experiencing. The team is concerned that he is vulnerable to drug dealers and will often 'do jobs' for them to obtain money or cigarettes. When Kyrie meets with Sol his personal care is unattended to and Kyrie is concerned how this may impact his integration into the social community of his apartment complex.

During their most recent meeting, Kyrie explored how Sol is adapting to living in his new apartment. Responding to Kyrie questions, Sol expressed that he is bored in his apartment and states that he doesn't have any social interactions with other residents in the complex. Kyrie has the sense that Sol continues to live like he is 'homeless but housed'.

Kyrie discusses the challenges Sol is experiencing with the mental health team in order to get their input as well. The team shares a common concern about Sol's activity and participation patterns, his vulnerabilities to drug dealers and others on the street, and his lack of connection within his housing environment. The team discusses the importance of supporting Sol in his adaptation to his new home as they are aware of the challenges of the transition from homelessness to being housed. They agree that attention to his activity and participation patterns might be a perspective that can help him settle into his new surroundings and contribute to his health and well-being.

Preparing for Making Change

At their next meeting, Kyrie shared the team's concerns with Sol regarding his safety and his activity and participation patterns. Kyrie presented their perspectives with sensitivity to his perception that service providers are 'telling him what to do'. Kyrie shared some information on the connection between mental health challenges and activity patterns with Sol and in particular they talked about how his housing situation had contributed. Kyrie told Sol that many first person accounts describe how being homeless can come with a set of daily routines and associated community and social connections. Kyrie described the transition to being housed as an adjustment. Although reluctant, Sol agreed look at his current activity and participation patterns with the support of Kyrie and the team to 'help with his boredom'.

Sol worked with Kyrie to complete the worksheets about his current activity patterns and what benefits he got from them. He was uncomfortable completing the sheets but Kyrie clarified some of the ideas in the worksheets and discussed with him how they might be relevant to him. For example, he was initially not certain about the idea of 'expressing values' through his activities, but following clarification he noted that although he was a loner, he always tried to look out for other people on the street. Kyrie observed that Sol's reflection was similar to the team's. His activities were generally passive and had little meaning for him. Kyrie and Sol agreed to work further together at their next meeting on his activity and participation patterns in way that respected Sol's comfort and needs.

Understanding Personal Activity Patterns

With Kyrie's support, Sol was able to identify how he spent his day as forms of activity. Kyrie reviewed the logs for the two days that Sol completed and noticed gaps in the log or long periods of just walking. First Kyrie asked Sol about his walking and learned that although sometimes he walked without an aim in mind, some of his time was spent walking to drop-ins or shelter areas that he used to frequent. Kyrie also reflected on her knowledge of his past patterns and wondered if perhaps he wasn't reporting some activities that were not legal. Kyrie explained the purpose of the time-use log to Sol as a tool to assist in improving his health and well-being and success in adapting to his apartment. Kyrie reassured Sol that there was no judgement in the process and that the more complete the information the better the outcome of the tool. With Kyrie's support, Sol was able to fill in the gaps and identified when he delivered drugs in return for cigarettes and included panhandling activities as well.

During supported reflections on his activities, Sol was able to identify the risks in some of his activities, but was unsure if he wanted to change this, particularly given the income/resources he received. He noted that his day did lack structure and stated 'The day is pretty much like it was when I didn't have this apartment'. Most of his time was spent in activities which did not have much direction or purpose, beyond the immediate time.

Kyrie noted that even though Sol interacted with others during his walks, most of his activities were alone. In reviewing his daily time-log, Sol commented on how limited his activities were and acknowledged this contributes to his boredom. Kyrie also noted that Sol's rest largely occurred throughout the day, with activities in the evening and at night.

When exploring the dimensions of his activities and participation through the worksheets, Sol found that he experienced little pleasure in his activities and participation; he lacked connection to his community and did not have the opportunity to express himself. Sol did note that he values helping others and that during his walks he checks in with others to ensure they are okay and assists if needed.

While completing the reflection worksheets Sol mentioned that he looked forward to his weekly calls with his brother, and that his brother would like him to get more involved in some of the activities at the groups at the apartment complex and maybe get back into some sports like he did in high school.

Making a Quick Change

Kyrie felt Sol's trust was increasing and wanted to keep the momentum going. Kyrie used the opportunity of Sol expressing boredom to discuss the role of activity and participation to one's mood and satisfaction. Kyrie suggested Sol try to add one new activity to his routine to assist with his boredom. Sol had difficulty identifying a new activity to try adding to his routine. Kyrie shared information on potential quick changes to his routine and offered that perhaps trying a sports activity as suggested by Sol's brother. Sol had noticed a basketball net in the courtyard of the apartment complex but said it wasn't possible as he could not afford a ball. Kyrie offered to speak with the staff at the complex to see if they had a basketball that Sol could borrow. Sol was reluctant as he hadn't played in years but agreed for Kyrie to explore. Kyrie and Sol spoke with the staff who were happy to loan Sol a basketball and they offered to join him in a game. Sol thought it might be nice to have someone to play with.

Kyrie noticed that the courtyard did not have good lighting around the basketball court area and suggested to Sol that given it gets dark earlier now that he may need to consider playing in the afternoon when the sun is still out. Kyrie also noted that there were some running shoes at the thrift shop if Sol found he needed different footwear for the court.

At their next meeting Sol reported he had played basketball with the staff twice that week and was surprised he had retained some skills. He had also noted others from the apartment complex watching them play. Sol did comment that the years of smoking made it physically harder for him to play. Sol thought he might try to decrease his smoking and Kyrie offered the support of the team if he wanted to explore further.

They talked more about Sol's experience of the activity change. Sol indicated he started sleeping less during the day in order to play in the sunlight and he enjoyed the physical activity. He described a sense of feeling 'more like his old self'.

Providing Education about Activity and Participation, Health and Mental Illness

Kyrie continued to support Sol in exploring new ways to change his activity and participation patterns. Sol reported that a few other residents had joined in the basketball games. Kyrie noted that Sol appeared more comfortable with his peers at the apartment. Reflecting on the positives from the quick change activity, Sol and Kyrie explored other opportunities to add activities to Sol's routine.

Kyrie used the success of the quick change to provide Sol with information on the benefits of activity and participation on health and well-being. Kyrie shared some of the resource sheets on the benefits of activity and Sol commented that basketball had provided him more than 'just something to do'. Sol enjoyed that others had joined the games and he now was engaging with them in the hall when he saw them. Physically he described feeling better and was showering more frequently after the games. Kyrie discussed that many others have experienced multiple benefits for changes in their activity and participation and they agreed that exploring more activity experiments could have benefits as well.

Making Longer Term Changes

Kyrie and Sol continued to meet regularly, and Kyrie offered support for his efforts to increase his activity. Sol reported that several residents in the apartment complex are now joining the games and that with the help of the staff they have hung signs around the building to invite others to the games.

Kyrie and Sol reviewed his routine as compared to when they first completed the time use diaries. As he was getting to know a few more residents through the games Sol reported spending more time at the apartment and socializing with a few residents. His sleep routine is more balanced with more time up during the day and rest in the night. His self-care activities had increased, and he reported doing laundry regularly. They discussed how Sol could continue to build on these successes by setting longer term goals for changes. They used the worksheets to plan and prioritize his activity and participation changes. Kyrie did not want to stress or overwhelm Sol with too many changes and supported his lead in the process.

Sol was pleased with his increased self-care activities, increased physical activities and positive socialization at the apartment complex. He identified getting to knowing the community around the apartment and volunteering as his next goals. Kyrie and Sol discussed ways he could get to know the community around his apartment. Sol thought with his new friendships with a few residents that he could ask them to walk different routes in the area to see what was around them. Kyrie suggested the look up maps of the area on the common area computer to plan the routes.

Kyrie asked Sol about his ideas for volunteering. Sol recalled that in his youth volunteers had helped his sports teams at the games and tournaments. They discussed that volunteer opportunities may require a police reference check and have expectations of time commitment. They agreed that in Sol's exploration of the area he would look for community centres that may have youth volunteer opportunities. Sol was also going to ask his brother for ideas of local sports leagues that he may be able to volunteer at. They planned to explore opportunities on the internet as well.

Sol had also noticed that there was space for a community garden. He asked Kyrie for ideas on how they could raise money to buy gardening tools and supplies. After discussing possible solutions they decided to have a basketball free-throw competition with residents obtaining pledges for their efforts. The money obtained would be used to buy equipment that residential staff could loan out to residents to assist in gardening.

At the next team meeting Kyrie reported Sol's successes and longer term goals. The team was encouraged by Sol progress of integration into his housing environment and believed this would contribute to longer term housing stability for him.

Supporting Sustained Changes in Activity and Participation Changes

Kyrie and the team continued to regularly visit with Sol. The visits now took place at his apartment or in the community surrounding it. The team continued to support the positive changes that Sol had made and offer assistance for ongoing changes. Sol had begun walking with a friend he had made at the apartment and had noticed a community centre nearby. Sol was not comfortable exploring the services offered there so Kyrie accompanied him to see what programs were offered. Kyrie assisted Sol in obtaining a subsidized membership so he could attend the centre which would be particularly helpful in the colder months for his physical activities. Kyrie asked if Sol had seen anything interesting in his walks around the community and Sol shared the story of seeing a family of geese that were nesting at the side of a building.

Sol had noticed that the community centre had a youth basketball league. They set up an appointment to meet with the volunteer coordinator at the centre to explore the requirements and expectations of volunteering at the centre. They planned to review the information at their next meeting and determine if this would meet Sols needs.

Sol updated Kyrie on the basketball free-throw competition. They raised just over $200 for gardening tools and supplies. Sol and interested residents prepared the garden and planted the seeds. Kyrie asked Sol how long before they could eat the fruits of their labour.

Kyrie and Sol reviewed the changes he had made over the last several months and used the *Worksheet 6.6: Measuring changes in my activity and participation patterns over time* to evaluate the dimensions of his experience through his activity changes. Sol reported positive change in the areas of physical activity, connecting to others, contributing to society, and taking care of oneself. He also noted that he was happy to be involved in activities that were of interest and he considered important.

Sol was pleased with the changes he had made over time to improve his health and well-being and felt encouraged to continue to identify and try new changes. Kyrie reinforced his positive change and all his efforts.

Vignette 2 – Ananthi

Ananthi is a 23-year-old woman who lives in a suburb of a large urban city. She lives with her parents and brother in the family home. Ananthi's daily activities are largely structured around her helping with the family grocery mart. Ananthi has limited activities outside her work in the family business.

Ananthi had been an academically strong and social student in high school and had always planned to attend university to study health sciences. She had begun the program after completing high school but experienced difficulties with concentration and integration of the concepts. She had previously enjoyed studying and learning new concepts but found university work more challenging and felt she 'didn't fit in'. Her parents were disappointed that she left university after one semester and their expectation was that she would live at home and work in the family business until she was married. It frustrates her that her brother does not have to work in the store as he is attending university. Ananthi feels that she must abide by the family expectations and her brother does not have to.

Ananthi experiences symptoms of her mental illness that interfere with her ability to interact with customers, and similarly she feels uncomfortable in social interactions. She prefers to complete jobs in the grocery mart that do not involve interacting with customers and tends to spend her time in the back stocking inventory. Ananthi's father would like to see her spend more time waiting on customers to relieve the burden on her mother who has some health issues of her own. He does not understand her concerns about interacting with customers and believes she should engage in puja (an act of worship) more often.

Ananthi is supported by a team that specializes in first episode psychosis. She is guarded with the service providers and generally meets with them to appease her mother. During visits with service providers Ananthi expresses her frustrations with the customers staring at her and judging her.

Armani is the occupational therapist with the First Episode Psychosis team. The team has recently started working with Ananthi and is beginning to form a relationship with her. Armani is aware of the many challenges that complicate activity and social participation following first episode psychosis. Armani is concerned of the risk of Ananthi's further disengagement from activity and participation patterns that could bring her health and well-being. Armani discussed these concerns with the team at their meeting and the team agreed that the methods employed in Action over Inertia could be helpful.

Preparing for Change

Armani met with Ananthi at the family home. Ananthi, still unsure of the team, asked if her mother could join the meeting. Armani supported the request and thought this might provide an opportunity to gain some understanding of the impact of the illness on Ananthi's previous activity and participation patterns and help in building a relationship with Ananthi and her family.

Armani took the opportunity to discuss some of the challenges that may occur following an episode of psychosis. Ananthi, with the support of her mother, was open to the conversation. Armani inquired if either of them felt there was a change in Ananthi's activity and social participation patterns since the onset of the illness. From the

conversation, Armani learned that in high school Ananthi was a very organized student with a small social crowd and she took pride in her appearance and fashion. Her mother described her as 'happier' then. Ananthi's mother would like to see her daughter get more involved in the community activities and be social again. Her mother described Ananthi practicing traditional Bharatanatyam dance as a child and that she had been an assistant teacher in dance at the local community centre. Ananthi agreed that she has lost interest in many things that she previously valued and found simple things harder to organize and complete.

Armani offered her observations that most of Ananthi's time appeared to be working in the family grocery mart, quiet activities in her room, and rest. Armani reassured them that the decline in participation in previous activities is common for individuals living with a mental illness and that there is evidence that these disruptions can be addressed. With her mother's encouragement, Ananthi agreed to further explore her activity and participation patterns to realize positive change. Armani reassured them the process would be done collaboratively with Ananthi ensuring her comfort with the process and personal needs.

Understanding Personal Activity Patterns

Armani discussed the benefits of collecting information about Ananthi's current activity and participation patterns. They agreed that it would be most helpful to complete a time diary, one for a day she is working and one where she is not, to explore the differences. They agreed to meet in one week's time to review the diaries. Armani offered that Ananthi could contact her if she needed assistance in completing the diaries.

Armani and Ananthi met to review her diaries and reflect on how her activity patterns impact Ananthi health and well-being. On the days when Ananthi worked in the family grocery mart there was little activity outside of the work other than self-care and some reading before sleeping. On her non workdays Ananthi spent most of time in solitary activities such as reading, watching documentaries, preparing meals for the family, and rest. Ananthi seemed saddened by the information, commenting 'she used to be more active'.

Armani and Ananthi together completed the other worksheets related to the dimensions of experience of activity and participation patterns and their connection to health and well-being. Ananthi reported she missed the mental challenges of school and the stimulation and creativity of dance. Ananthi also noted that she would like to connect more to people with similar background and values at the community centre.

They discussed activities that Ananthi previously enjoyed but no longer participated in, such as dance, as an opportunity for working towards positive change and agreed to plan to add a 'quick change' to her routine.

Making a Quick Change

Exploring activities that Ananthi had previously engaged in provided an opportunity for Armani to suggest adding one or two of these activities to Ananthi's routine as an opportunity to engage in activities that Ananthi values. Building on their previous conversations, Armani suggests attending a dance class at the community centre with her old neighbourhood friend as she had done previously. Ananthi indicated the neighbour has reached out regularly however with her increased anxiety Ananthi had not gone with her. Armani offered some suggestions on managing anxiety. Ananthi had always enjoyed her relationship with her neighbour and agreed to try attending the dance class with her neighbour over the next week. Ananthi also states that maybe she will try putting her hair up like she used to at dance class. Armani thinks that a great idea and Ananthi is pleased with setting goals to achieve. They agree to check in next week.

A week later Ananthi reports that her neighbour was pleased to hear from her, and they enjoyed the dance class they participated in at the community centre. They chose a time when the centre was less busy which assisted with Ananthi managing her anxiety. Armani complimented Ananthi on her earrings and makeup.

Providing Education about Activity and Participation, Health and Mental Illness

With Ananthi's interest in healthcare, Armani used this opportunity to provide her with information on first episode psychosis. Ananthi found the information helpful, particularly related to changes in her mental capacities that she has been experiencing and understanding it is part of the illness. Ananthi found comfort in the information that her challenges were consistent with others with mental illness and not a result of personal failings or lack of prayer. Ananthi disclosed that she does not talk about her anxiety and worries about others judging her as she wants to appear 'well'. Armani was able to link the disclosure of her experiences with increased health and well-being in a way that Ananthi could understand. Ananthi was then able to see how hiding her symptoms limited her activities and participation.

With Armani's support and resources Ananthi decided to share information about her mental health and its impact on her life with her neighbour on their next visit. Armani also provided some information on peer support services in her area. Ananthi agreed to review and discuss later with Armani.

Making Longer Term Activity Changes

Ananthi and Armani continued to meet regularly. Ananthi had increased her participation at the community centre with her neighbour to two times per week and she enjoyed their conversations, the dance classes, and her neighbour's sense of humour. Ananthi had also increased her time in self-care and had received a few compliments from her family and her neighbour. Feeling positive about the quick changes Armani and Ananthi discussed possible longer term changes. Ananthi liked the idea of using the worksheets to plan for activity change, as she was anxious about taking on larger changes. Reflecting on previous conversations and activity and participation patterns prior to the illness, Ananthi identified wanting to do more community activities with her neighbour especially shopping for new clothes.

Ananthi also wondered if they could make another goal of exploring college courses for her to try. While employed in the family grocery mart she still hoped to someday obtain alternate employment that she valued and enjoyed more. She missed the stimulation of academics and the sense of purpose and pleasure she derived from it.

Ananthi and Armani explored the options of college programs available through online resources. Armani explained that student services in post-secondary institutions have accessibility services that can support Ananthi's needs in her studies. Armani explained that they can provide extra time on exams and assistance with note taking, to list a few options, and that Ananthi would need to schedule an appointment with the service to review her needs. Ananthi was not aware of the potential support for her studies and was pleased that it was available.

Ananthi also wondered if the accessibility services could help her with obtaining the money to attend school. Armani agreed that in their next meeting they could explore scholarship options and possible supports through pharmaceutical companies to assist with tuition costs.

Armani agreed to bring Ananthi's goals to the team as well so they could share ideas and be supportive.

Supporting and Evaluating Activity Change

Armani and Ananthi met regularly to discuss the changes Ananthi had made in her activity and participation patterns. With the team's assistance, Ananthi was able to manage her anxiety and was able to attend social activities at the community centre. Ananthi and her neighbour continued their shopping together, now focused on finding the best deals. Armani asked for tips on finding the best deals in the local shops. Ananthi's comfort working the grocery mart had improved and she was able to provide some relief from duties for her mother. Her family was pleased with the positive changes she had made.

Ananthi was able to complete an online college course with the support of the Accessibility Services at the college. She was given extra time on exams and extension of due dates on assignments if needed. Ananthi was encouraged by this and was exploring other courses she could take that could lead to employment opportunities outside the family grocery mart. She identified Medical Laboratory Technologist as the program she would like to complete.

Ananthi expressed concern in attending classes, as although she had made progress in managing her anxiety, new situations could still be problematic for her. Armani suggested they explore the possibility of a combination of online and in person classes in order to complete the degree.

Ananthi and Armani used the ***Worksheet 6.6: Measuring changes in my activity and participation patterns over time*** to evaluate the changes Ananthi had made in her activity and participation patterns. Ananthi found this reflection helpful in understanding the challenges she encountered in making changes to her activity and participation patterns but also the benefits she had gained from the changes. Ananthi was pleased with her increased involvement in her community and the enjoyment and stimulation of school.

Armani and the team continue to support Ananthi in identifying changes she would like to make in her activity and participation to build on the positives she had already made.

Focusing on Activity and Participation Health to Inform Service Development

Reflecting on the successes achieved by Ananthi, Armani felt that many of the clients served by the first episode psychosis program could benefit from the exercises and activities in Action Over Inertia approach and a stronger focus by the team on activity and participation patterns. Armani brought this idea to the team's manager. The team's manager was supportive and asked Armani to lead the implementation of this approach.

Armani began with education sessions for the team focusing on the capabilities of the individuals they serve to live the lives that they value. A foundation of the education was the principles of person-centred practice, partnership in practice, respect for diversity, and social inclusion as integral to the mission and philosophy of their program. Armani and clients with positive experience of activity and participation pattern changes formed an advisory group to assist the team in implementation of the approach and tools. The advisory group assisted with the development of program policies and procedures to promote the health and well-being of the individuals they serve through activity and participation.

Armani led mentorship and troubleshooting sessions for all team members to promote discussion and learning as a team in the activity and participation focus for service. This provided the opportunity for team growth and learning related to improving the health and wellness outcomes for the individuals supported by the service.

Appendix B: Activity Engagement Measure (AEM)

The activity engagement measure is the measure of health and well-being through activities and participation developed in the first version of the Action Over Inertia intervention. Psychometric testing suggests that the AEM has good reliability (Chronbach's alpha of .89), test-retest reliability, content validity, and criterion validity. Advancements in the conceptual understanding of activity and participation led to the development of a new measure (Worksheet 2.15) in this second version of the Action Over Inertia approach.

Name: _____ Date: _____

1. **Balance in my life: I could benefit from more balance between my self-care, leisure, productivity, and rest activities.**

Rate how true this statement is for you.

1	2	3	4	5	6	7	8	9	10
Very True				Somewhat True				Not True	

2. **Physical activity: I could benefit from more 'physical activity' activity in my life.**

Rate how true this statement is for you.

1	2	3	4	5	6	7	8	9	10
Very True				Somewhat True				Not True	

3. **Structure/routine: I could benefit from more structure and routine in my day.**

Rate how true this statement is for you.

1	2	3	4	5	6	7	8	9	10
Very True				Somewhat True				Not True	

4. Meaning: I could benefit from more activities that I find meaningful in my day.

Rate how true this statement is for you.

1	2	3	4	5	6	7	8	9	10
Very True				Somewhat True					Not True

5. Satisfaction: I could benefit from more satisfaction from activities in my day.

Rate how true this statement is for you.

1	2	3	4	5	6	7	8	9	10
Very True				Somewhat True					Not True

6. Social interactions: I could benefit from having more social interactions through my daily activities.

Rate how true this statement is for you.

1	2	3	4	5	6	7	8	9	10
Very True				Somewhat True					Not True

7. Accessing community environments: I could benefit from activities that take me to a broader range of community environments.

Rate how true this statement is for you.

1	2	3	4	5	6	7	8	9	10
Very True				Somewhat True					Not True

Ratings

Fill in the scores that you assigned to each area above. A lower score in any area suggests that it could benefit from direct attention and perhaps be given a higher priority for change.

Area of Activity Engagement	*Rating*
Balance	
Physical activity level	
Structure and routine	
Meaningfulness of activity	
Satisfaction derived though activity	
Social interaction	
Accessing community environments	

Appendix C: Other Applications of Action Over Inertia

This appendix includes five sections describing the application of this intervention approach with other populations and practice contexts. These health conditions and practice contexts represent the ones we have most frequently received questions about from service providers in response to the original version of Action Over Inertia. In collaboration with several occupational therapists, resources related to activity and participation for use with people who experience anxiety disorders, chronic pain, mood disorders, and post-traumatic stress disorder were designed, pilot-tested and refined. In addition, resources were developed for group interventions offered in four and ten sessions.

Appendices C1 to C4 expand existing information, worksheets, and resources to address health and well-being through activity and participation for specific populations.

This content complements Chapters 1–6 of this text which will be useful to assess and understand the activity and participation patterns of service recipients, develop plans for change, and to move toward fuller participation in daily life.

Appendices C1–C4 provide tailored psychoeducational content related to specific health conditions and activity participation, expanding the relevance of the content from Chapter 4 to these populations. Each appendix begins with a psychoeducational resource *'How is [health condition] and activity and participation connected?'* which is designed for service providers to anchor their understanding of the impact of each health condition on activity and participation. The *'What do I need to know about activity and participation and [health condition]?'* resource that follows can be used as a take-away of key activity and participation messages. The worksheets that follow these resources are intended for collaborative use with service providers and recipients, increasing the utility of this intervention approach for a variety of populations.

Appendix C5 contains group outlines, suggesting ways the intervention approach can be organized for delivery in a group setting. There is a four-week open group format suitable for in-patient, out-patient, and community settings. There is also a ten-week closed format group suitable for out-patient and community settings.

All of the content from the appendices can be adapted to suit the context where the service provider works and is meant to offer a starting point in adapting the intervention approach. Given the complexity and heterogeneity of the lived experience of mental illnesses, it is expected that the additional information and worksheets in the appendix may be useful across health conditions and contexts.

Appendix C1 – Anxiety Disorders and Activity and Participation

Contributed by Allison Casteels

How are anxiety disorders and activity participation connected? (Service provider resource)

This resource looks generally at the impact anxiety disorders have on activity and participation and quality of life. These are grouped into biomedical, psychological, and social explanations.

People diagnosed with an anxiety disorder often describe changes in the way they experience their daily activities, including:

- Difficulties with feeling motivated and sustaining interest in activity.
- A tendency to avoid or withdraw from situations in which they've had an unpleasant experience.
- Difficulty planning and following through with activities.
- Cognitive changes such as difficulties with problem-solving, working memory, and attention during thinking processes.
- Limited opportunities for activities that hold value and meaning.

These changes can be uncomfortable both for the individual experiencing them, and for their family, friends, and others.

Biomedical Explanations

Biomedical explanations focus on the structures, physiology, and functions of the human body that could account for disruptions in activity and participation patterns for people with anxiety.

Brain Structures

The amygdala and hippocampus are brain structures which have been identified as playing a significant role in most anxiety disorders. The *amygdala* is responsible for processing and interpreting sensory information. This information is projected to the *hippocampus*, which then activates the sympathetic nervous system and a 'flight, fight, or freeze' response is triggered. In response to a perceived threat, adrenal chemicals are released into the bloodstream which activate bodily responses – shaking, flushing, increased heart rate, and an aching chest are all bodily processes designed to increase reaction time and protect the individual from danger. These responses can impact the experience of engagement in activities and participation.

Neurophysiological Changes

Stressful experiences activate a wide range of hormones and neurotransmitters which contribute to the experience of anxiety. When an individual experiences panic or fear, the hormone cortisol is released from the adrenal gland. The role of cortisol is to prepare the body for a fight or flight response, and its release leads to increased blood pressure and blood sugar levels. Dopamine has also been associated with anxiety disorders. Dopamine is connected to the emotions you feel and plays a major role in the sensation experienced when accessing a reward.

The brain's GABA-benzodiazepine receptor system is also implicated in anxiety disorders. GABA supports emotional regulation by producing a calming effect when an individual is faced with a stressful situation. A disruption in the ability of GABA to bind to receptor sites in the brain contributes to anxiety disorders.

Another neurotransmitter that is associated with anxiety is serotonin. Normal serotonin activity is important in maintaining feelings of well-being while deficiencies in serotonin are believed to be related to anxiety disorders.

The Impact of Medications on Activity

Medications taken to treat anxiety may also change the experience of activities and participation. While prescribed medications can be effective in reducing symptoms and avoiding relapses, managing medications may require the development of coping strategies to deal with the impact on activity and participation. Common side effects of medications that impact activity and participation include: feeling tired, lack of motivation and/or energy, difficulty concentrating or feeling 'foggy', weight gain, and changes in body movements.

Psychological Explanations

There are a number of psychological processes which impact how an individual thinks about themselves in relation to activities, and this influences their participation and engagement.
The following are a few ways disruption in motivation for activity can occur:

Avoidance

Individuals experiencing anxiety can feel as though they have lost control of their health and well-being, and also of their present and future lives. As a way to limit the experience of disturbing or unpleasant symptoms, those living with anxiety often choose to withdraw from meaningful activities and participation.

Feelings of Distress

Anxiety is often associated with increased feelings of distress related to activity and participation. Activity participation can provoke feelings of distress such as panic, fear, and dizziness, even when the desire for engagement in a particular activity is present.

Self-Evaluations

Negative experiences with anxiety and activity participation can impact self-confidence and self-esteem and belief in one's own abilities. This self-doubt can lead to caution and even avoidance of activities and participation.

Social Explanations

Social explanations focus on factors 'external' to the individual that can impact activity patterns.

Impact on Families and Support Networks

Families and support networks may limit their engagement with the individual in an effort to reduce their stress, or because they misinterpret their avoidance as a lack of desire to maintain the relationship. Extended hospital stays or time away from the community can make this disconnection from meaningful relationships worse.

Impact on Employment Opportunities

Individuals who experience significant anxiety may experience disruptions to their ability to work. Maintaining or accessing employment opportunities may suffer as a result, particularly where reasonable accommodations are not provided.

Stigma and Disclosure

Stigma has a profound impact on the daily lives of people with a mental health conditions, including decreased opportunities which can, for example limit social connections, material resources, etc. Individuals with concealable illnesses, such as an anxiety disorder, face the dilemma of disclosure. For example, an individual might wonder if disclosing their mental illness may provide them with workplace support needed for success or hinder their chance for promotion.

What do I need to know about activity and participation and anxiety disorders?

(service recipient resource)

- Anxiety disorders can disrupt your daily activities, including self-care, sleep, work, community involvement, leisure, and time spent with other people.
- Sometimes people avoid activities when they're feeling anxious or expect to accomplish so much in a day that it increases their anxiety. This imbalance can make it hard to manage the activities in your day.
- Activity and participation are central to your physical, social, and emotional well-being, and having a balanced daily routine can help you meet your needs and improve your well-being.
- Activities that are connected with personal interests and goals have the potential to reduce your anxiety and provide meaning and satisfaction.
- You can modify your daily activities to help you manage your health. If you're feeling overwhelmed, you can take breaks and split activities into smaller, more manageable tasks.
- Some activities that could help with coping include exercise, meditation and relaxation, artistic activities, or music. These provide value, meaning, and help you connect with who you are, even when you're experiencing anxiety.
- Social activities, especially with groups, can make activity participation easier and give you the support you need to live a full life.
- Being engaged in meaningful work that is a fit for your abilities and interests can broaden your social network and supports and make coping with anxiety easier.
- ***Don't give up and avoid meaningful activities! They will help you cope with your anxiety and are an important part of every person's daily routine.***

Coping and your daily routine

Date: ____ / ____ / ____

Name: _____

We all encounter stressful, difficult, or challenging situations throughout our lives. Coping strategies are the things we do to deal with these challenges. Some strategies will be more helpful than others. For example, avoiding something or using substances might lead to more problems, while exercising or talking about your feelings might be more helpful.

Here are some examples of coping strategies:

- Breathing exercises
- Physical activity
- Writing down your thoughts and feelings
- Calling someone (friend, family, therapist, hotline)
- Mindfulness exercises or meditation
- Doing a relaxing or enjoyable activity
- Spend time with a pet or person you love
- Saying a mantra or affirmation
- Praying or other spiritual/religious practices
- Going to a support group
- Planning and problem solving

Coping strategies are personal and unique for everyone. Come up with a list of coping strategies you can use based on your own strengths and preferences, ranking them from most helpful to least helpful:

1.

2.

3.

4.

5.

When you are stressed or having trouble coping, it can affect your participation in everyday life and meaningful activities. Fill out the tables below to describe how your daily routine might be impacted, how you currently cope, and what healthy coping strategies you could use in the future. Keep the ideas you thought of before in mind while completing the activity.

Morning Routine (getting ready for the day):

I Have Trouble with...	Current Coping	Future Coping
EXAMPLE: Getting out of bed	Avoiding the situation by pressing snooze on my alarm	Saying a mantra to wake up feeling positive, thinking of something you enjoy waking up for (e.g., a cup of coffee), putting your alarm far away so you need to get out of bed to turn it off

Productive tasks (work, education, parenting, housework, etc.):

I Have Trouble with...	Current Coping	Future Coping
EXAMPLE: Cleaning my house. There is too much to do and I become overwhelmed.	Avoid cleaning the house, letting things pile up, which in turn makes me more stressed.	Take 5–10 minutes at the end of every day to tidy up. This seems manageable and things don't pile up.

Leisure Tasks (e.g.; social life, hobbies, etc.):

I Have Trouble with…	Current Coping	Future Coping
EXAMPLE: Telling my friends that I struggle with anxiety.	I don't tell them anything and then they don't support me because they don't understand. I feel unsupported and have stopped having a social life.	I can select a few good friends that I trust and explain the difficulties I am having. If they better understand what I am going through, then maybe they can help me when I'm having challenges.

Other (e.g., cooking, working out, etc.):

I Have Trouble with…	Current Coping	Future Healthy Coping
EXAMPLE: Eating regularly. It is hard for me to motivate myself to cook. I don't know any healthy recipes and don't have time to cook healthy meals.	Avoid cooking. Eating take-out food or microwavable dinners as they are easy to access.	Go online and find some easy step-by-step instructions for healthy meals. I can plan my meals and do some food prep to help manage my time.

Analyzing my activities & anxiety level

Date: ____ / ____ / ____

Name: _____

You may notice patterns in what activities tend to cause you the most worry or make you the most anxious. It can be helpful to break down activities to make them more manageable.

An activity and participation analysis can outline the different components of your daily activities, including the emotional, mental, and physical tasks that are involved. If you can identify one activity that seems to consistently cause you high levels of anxiety, try using that activity and working through the activity analysis questions below.

Outline the whole activity

_____

_____

_____

_____

_____

Identify as many smaller tasks within the activity as you can.

1. _____
2. _____
3. _____
4. _____
5. _____

During the activity what were you thinking and feeling during each of these tasks?

_____

_____

_____

_____

To do this activity I need to…

Mentally	*Emotionally*	*Physically*

Next time I do this activity, what strategies could I use?

_____

_____

Using physical activity to manage anxiety and experience well-being

Date: ____ / ____ / ____

Name: _____

Physical activity can benefit both your overall well-being and has been shown to help people manage anxiety. Physical activity is included in a whole range of activities; walking to the corner store, playing on a sports team, or going to the gym are some examples.

Look back on the last week and consider what kind of physical activity you get each day in the chart below. In the left column, list the type of activity and the duration. In the right column plot out how much physical activity you would ideally like to get in a week. Aim for 30 minutes of physical activity per day!

	Current Activities	*Physical Activity Plan*
Monday		
Tuesday		
Wednesday		
Thursday		
Friday		
Saturday		
Sunday		

What barriers do you see to incorporating more physical activity into your day?

_____
_____
_____
_____

What strategies could you use to overcome these barriers?

_____
_____
_____
_____

Tips to help you get active

- Walk, run, or bike instead of getting a ride.
- Do something you enjoy (run, jump, swim, skateboard, snowboard, ski, skate...).
- Join a recreational sports team.
- Check out yoga, hip-hop, or aerobics classes.
- Try indoor rock climbing, play soccer, ride a bike.
- Take the dog for a walk.
- Dance to your favourite music.
- Rake the leaves, shovel snow, carry the groceries home.
- Set physical activity goals with your friends and family.
- Reduce screen time.
  - Consider walking in place, on a treadmill, or using a stationary bike while watching TV.
  - Take stretch and walk breaks when working on the computer.

References

Brown, C., Stoffel, V., & Munoz, J. (2019). *Occupational Therapy in Mental Health: A Vision for Participation* (2nd ed.). Philadelphia: FA Davis Company.

Canadian Society for Exercise Physiology (CSEP) (n.d.). *Canadian Physical Activity Guidelines: For Adults*, 18–64. http://www.csep.ca/en/guidelines/get-the-guidelines.

Cara, E., & MacRae, A. (2013). *Psychosocial Occupational Therapy: An Evolving Practice*. Clifton Park, NY: Thomson Delmar Learning.

Krupa, T. et al. (2016). *Psychosocial Frames of Reference*, 4 Ed. Thorofare, NJ: Slack Inc.

National Institute of Mental Health. (2014). *Post-traumatic Stress Disorder*. Retrieved from: http://www.nimh.nih.gov/health/publications/post-traumatic-stress-disorder-ptsd/index.shtml

Appendix C2 – Chronic Pain and Activity and Participation

Contributed by Tina Siemens

How are chronic pain and activity participation connected? (Service provider resource)

People who experience chronic pain often describe changes in the way they experience activities and their desire to participate, including:

- Difficulty with feeling motivated and sustaining interest in activities.
- Unpleasant emotions, such as anxiety, associated with activity and participation.
- An inability to engage because symptoms of pain are experienced.

The life changes associated with pain can be uncomfortable both for the individual experiencing them and for their family and friends. The reasons for these changes are complex and are not completely understood, as pain itself is a complex and individual experience

There are several different pain disorders, each with its own set of aetiologies, symptoms, and prognosis. This resource looks generally at the impact pain disorders have on activity participation and overall quality of life. These are grouped into biomedical, psychological, and social explanations.

Biomedical Explanations

Biomedical explanations focus on the structures, physiology, and functions of the human body that could account for the disruptions experienced in activity patterns. The brain does not have a specific 'pain centre', which in part explains the complexity of an individual's pain experience.

Brain Structures

The following outlines the significant areas of the brain associated with pain. The thalamus: known as the 'hub' of information receives sensory input and relays information to applicable areas of the brain.

1. The reticular system: responsible for the autonomic and motor responses to pain and warning an individual to do something immediately, such as a reflexive response.
2. Somatosensory cortex: involved with the perception and interpretation of sensations. It identifies the intensity, type, and location of the pain sensation and relates the sensation to past experiences, memories, and cognitive activities. This area actually identifies the nature of the stimulus before a response can be triggered.
3. Limbic system: responsible for the emotional and behavioural responses to pain, including attention, mood, and motivation. It also processes pain with past experiences of pain.

Neurophysiological Changes

Glutamate is the main neurotransmitter identified with pain transmission and modulation. In high levels, this neurotransmitter may over-stimulate certain regions of the brain leading to chronic pain perception. In contrast, endorphins, which are known as the body's natural painkillers, are most often produced in response to stress, fear, and pain, but also during many daily activities. Endorphins are responsible for our feelings of pleasure and can reduce the perception of pain.

Pharmacological Interventions and Their Impact on Activity

Medications are often prescribed to assist individuals in coping with pain. While medications may assist with pain management they are often only one part of a comprehensive treatment plan with activity and participation being another invaluable component. While medication prescribed for pain management can be effective in reducing pain symptoms, common side effects of medications that can impact activity and participation include: feeling tired, lack of motivation and/or energy, and difficulty concentrating or feeling 'foggy'.

Psychological Explanations

The psychological elements are particularly relevant since pain is an individual experience.

What happens when you focus on the pain?

Focusing on the pain is a powerful psychosocial determinant of negative health outcomes which may lead to the following:

1. Helplessness: the belief that one is powerless to control or decrease their own suffering
2. Magnification: the tendency to exaggerate the threat value of symptoms
3. Rumination: the inclination to excessively focus on symptoms

There is a strong relationship between attention and pain. As the focus on the pain increases, the pain experience may intensify as individuals become less able to divert their attention away from the pain itself. This type of thinking can lead to an increased focus on what is going wrong, potentially leading to the development of anxiety or depression This can impact activity participation by leading to greater activity avoidance, contributing to inactivity, isolation, and an overall decreased quality of life.

Social Explanations

Social explanations focus on factors 'external' to the individual that can impact activity and participation patterns.

Chronic pain is invisible, often with no distinct physical cause, meaning that people may encounter stigmatization and a lack of social support due to misunderstandings about pain.

The following are the most commonly held myths surrounding pain that contribute to stigmatization, along with explanations to help dispel these myths

1. *No pain, no gain*: Knowing one's limits and actively participating within them will help to manage the pain. Overexerting yourself will most likely exacerbate the pain, leading to avoidance.
2. *It's all in your head*: Pain is a complex, individual experience. Pain is a legitimate medical condition that can and should be treated. Pain is invisible but that does not make it any less real.
3. *You just have to live with the pain*: There are several options for pain relief and while a person may not always be able to control their pain experience, there are techniques that can assist in pain management.
4. *Suck it up, pull up your socks*: Seeking treatment is not an admission of weakness but rather one of strength. Pursuing effective treatment strategies can improve quality of life.
5. *People do not want to get better*: Individuals do not enjoy being in pain. Malingering (or 'faking' symptoms) is rare.

What do I need to know about activity participation and chronic pain?

(Service recipient resource)

- Chronic pain disrupts activity and participation in daily life, including self-care, sleep, work, community involvement, leisure, family, social, etc.
- The challenges that chronic pain can create in daily life can happen because of changes to the brain, our thinking, the way we cope, and the way that other people relate to us.
- It is important for people who experience chronic pain to stay active.
- If people avoid activities to manage pain, this can lead to higher levels of disability, depression, and decreased quality of life.
- Activity and participation is important to our physical, social, and emotional well-being, and can often be used as a source of distraction from the experience of pain.
- Experiences that create opportunities for laughing, hugging, and relaxation promote the body to release endorphins, the body's natural painkiller.
- Activities that are connected to a personal goal have increased potential to provide pain relief.
- Modify activity patterns, use strategies like pacing and energy conservation, take breaks and split activities into more manageable tasks. Breaks may be taken on a fixed schedule, by monitoring pain, or upon completing tasks.
- Exercise, meditation, relaxation, and artistic activities provide value, meaning, and promote identity maintenance in times when you may feel a loss of roles and interest due to pain.
- Being engaged in meaningful work that is a fit for your abilities and interests can broaden your social network and supports and make coping with chronic pain easier.
- ***Don't give up and avoid meaningful activities and participation! They will help you cope with chronic pain and are an important part of every person's daily routine.***

Lifestyle strategies to help you cope with pain

There are many strategies that can help you cope with pain during activities and participation. Using these suggestions, can build a personal toolbox of strategies that help you cope with and manage your pain. The aim is to enable you to continue participating in activities that you need or want to do and enjoy. ***Circle or put a star beside the strategies that sound useful to you.***

- **Optimize Your Sleep**
  - Try rebuilding your sleep environment. Do you need a few more or less pillows?
  - Try not to associate your bedroom with working, eating, worrying, and watching television. Your bedroom should be reserved only for sleeping and sexual activity.
  - Have a regularly scheduled bedtime and a set routine to set the stage for sleep.
  - Avoid caffeine, alcohol, and nicotine a few hours before bed.
  - If you find you are unable to fall asleep after 20 minutes, get up and do something you find calming.
- **Communication with Your Healthcare Team**
  - Continue to use any prescribed medications as directed by your doctor and discuss any concerns or side effects with your healthcare team.
  - Ask your doctor for referrals to other healthcare professionals such as psychologists, occupational therapists, and physiotherapists. Pain is experienced physically, psychologically, and socially and should be treated holistically.
- **Daily Schedule**
  - Schedule time for breaks throughout your day (e.g., alternate 25 minutes of activity to 5 minutes of rest/break).
  - Structure and pace activities throughout your day so that you do not overextend yourself and become more tired or experience more pain the following day.
  - Schedule activities at times when you tend to feel best.
  - Eat regular nourishing meals.
- **Social Support**
  - Call or visit with friends and family.
  - Invite a friend to your home for a cup of tea.
  - Attend a support group for chronic pain.
  - Play a sport or go for a walk with a friend/family member/pet.
  - Volunteer with an organization that is meaningful to you.
- **Physical Activity**
  - Try attending a yoga class, tai chi, or incorporating stretching throughout the day or during a break between activities.
  - If you are new to physical activity begin by doing short bouts of activity and gradually increase the time or the intensity.
  - Go for a walk.
  - Slowly and gently move your joints through the entire range of motion.

Relaxation activities for pain management

Participating in relaxation activities can be a useful strategy to help manage your pain. ***Circle or put a star beside the strategies that sound useful to you.*** You can add these to your pain management tool-box. Remember: some strategies take three or four times before you can see a noticeable difference.

Relaxation Activity	*What to Do*
• Diaphragm (belly) breathing	Lie on your back or sit tall in a chair with your feet flat on the floor. Place one hand on your stomach and one on your chest. Breathe in slowly through your nose. Your chest should remain as still as possible and your stomach should move out against your lower hand. Try breathing slowly by counting 3-5 seconds in your head. Do this for 3-5 minutes.
• Imagery & visualization	Place yourself in a room or area with minimal distractions. Think of a calming place or relaxing experience. Go through imagining every detail of your relaxing scene.
• Using your senses	This exercise is used to ground you in the present moment. The goal is to use your senses to notice something in your current surroundings. • <u>What are five things you can see?</u> Look around your surroundings. Take note of five things you hadn't noticed before like a wall pattern or painting. • <u>What are five things you can feel?</u> Maybe you can feel the pressure of your feet on the floor or the temperature of the room. • <u>What are five things you can hear?</u> Notice the sounds that you have been filtering out such as birds chirping. • <u>What are five things you can smell?</u> Can you notice any smells like cut grass, laundry, or coffee?
• Progressive muscle relaxation	The idea is to intentionally tense each muscle and then to release the tension. Find a quiet spot where you can sit or lie down comfortably. Start with your hands and make your way down to your feet. For example: • Tense the muscles in your fingers by curling them into your palm, making a fist. Notice how it feels when your hand is tense. Hold the tension for five seconds. • Release the tension from your fingers. Let them relax. Notice how your fingers feel differently after you release the tension. • Tense the muscles all throughout your arm. Hold it for five seconds. Notice the feeling of tension in your arm. • Release the tension in your arm and notice how the feeling of relaxation is different. Follow this pattern of tensing and releasing tension throughout your body. After you are finished with your hands and arms, move up or down going through your neck, head, torso, legs, and feet.
• Other ideas:	Find a relaxation recording (you could download one or find a relaxation app) and listen to it every day until you are able to do this on your own. Join a meditation, yoga, or tai chi class in the community, or find one online you can follow along to.

Record of activity and pain management experiments

Date: _____ / _____ / _____

Name: _____

List your selected activity and pain management experiments, the date, and brief comments about the experiment. Use the 'Lifestyle strategies to help you cope with pain' and 'Relaxation strategies for pain management' resources to help you come up with your experiments or come up with some of your own.

Activity Experiment	*Date*	*Comments about the Experience and Progress Made*
(Example) tai chi and stretching	August 12	Stretching and doing tai chi helped reduce the pain felt. Able to walk ten minutes longer in my afternoon walk

References

American Chronic Pain Association. (2015). *ACPA Resource Guide to Chronic Pain Management & Treatment*. Rocklin, CA: American Chronic Pain Association, Inc.

Chronic Conditions Team. (2012). *7 Common Myths About Chronic Pain: Many Americansdownplay Pain As A Part of Getting Older*. Cleveland Clinic. http://health.clevelandclinic.org/2012/07/7-common-myths-of-chronic-pain/

Coghill, R. (2010). Individual differences in the subjective experience of pain: New insights intomechanisms and models. *Headache, 50*(9), 1531–1535.

Drake, R., Vogel, A. W., & Mitchell, A. W. M. (2009). *Gray's Anatomy for Students 2nd Revised Ed*. London; Churchill Livingstone.

Marieb, E., Mallatt, J., & Wilhelm, P. (2005). *Human Anatomy 4th Ed*. San Francisco: PearsonEducation Inc.

Meldrum, B. S. (2000). Glutamate as a neurotransmitter in the brain: Review of physiology andpathology. *The Journal of nutrition 130*(4S), 1007S–1015S.

Radomski, M. V., & Trombly, C. A. (2014). *Occupational Therapy for Physical Dysfunction 7th Ed*. New York: Lippincott Williams & Wilkins.

Squire, P., Williamson, O., Lau, B., Gromala, D., & Pearson, L. (2011). *The Pain Toolbox*. https://www.painbc.ca

Sullivan, M. J. L., Stanish, W., Waite, H., Sullivan, M. E., & Tripp, D. (1998). Catastrophizing pain and disability following soft tissue injuries. *Pain. 77*(3), 253–260.

Therapist Aid (2016). *Relaxation Techniques*. http://www.therapistaid.com/therapy-worksheet/relaxation-techniques.

Vasey, M. W., & Borkovec, T. (1992). A catastrophizing assessment of worrisome thoughts. *CognitiveTherapy and Research, 16*(5), 505–520.

Waugh, O. C., Byrne, D. G., & Nicholas, M. K. (2014). Internalized stigma in people living with chronic pain. *Pain, 15*(5), 550.e1–10.

Appendix C3 – Mood disorders and Activity and Participation

Contributed by Sara Ubbens and Sarah Goodfield Weinstein

How are mood disorders and activity participation connected? (Service provider resource)

There are a number of different types of mood disorders. The main distinction is between depressive disorders and bipolar disorders.

Depression

Individuals with depression face changes in the way they experience their daily activities and participation including:

- Significantly reduced interest or pleasure in previously enjoyed activities.
- Difficulties associated with lack of sleep or a significant increase in sleep.
- Extreme fatigue or lack of energy.
- Cognitive difficulties such as difficulty with thinking, focusing, or making decisions.

Bipolar Disorder

With bipolar disorder, an individual experiences periods of mania or hypomania along with periods of depression. Mania is described as a period of uncharacteristic and enduring elevated or irritable mood. Hypomania is similar to mania, however the changes in mood are less severe.

Individuals who experience mania also face changes in the way they experience their daily activities and participation including:

- Participation in activities that involve risk and could cause harm.
- Increased energy and restlessness.
- Lack of sleep – feeling as if less sleep is necessary.
- Racing thoughts as well as distractibility.

This resource outlines the biomedical, psychological, and social aspects that are affected by the experience of a mood disorder as well as how activity participation and engagement are impacted by the presence of a mood disorder.

Biomedical Explanations

This section focuses on the structures, physiology, and functions of the human body that could account for disruptions in activity and activity patterns for people with mood disorders.

Brain Structures

Two regions of the brain that have been identified as playing a significant role in mood disorders are the limbic system and the prefrontal cortex. The limbic system consists of the hippocampus, the amygdala, the hypothalamus, and a number of other small structures.

The hippocampus helps us store memories and it works together with the hypothalamus and the amygdala to respond to stressful events by regulating the release of stress hormones. Depression can be worsened or even triggered by stressful life events. Cortisol, which is known as 'the stress hormone', is higher in people with mood disorders. Additionally, the hypothalamus helps control the body's Circadian rhythms. Disrupted Circadian rhythm can be present in both depression and bipolar disorders). Disruptions in the prefrontal cortex due to depression or bipolar disorder can impact someone's ability to take in information, control their emotions, and make decisions about their life.

Neurophysiological Changes

Serotonin, which is lower than normal in people experiencing depression, functions to regulate mood, sleep, and appetite. Many drugs designed to treat depression function by increasing serotonin. Other neurotransmitters, like norepinephrine, glutamate, and GABA, may also be important, but evidence for their involvement varies. For people experiencing a manic episode, increased dopamine may be a factor.

How do biomedical changes impact activity?

When the structures and chemicals in our brain are changed or disrupted, this results in symptoms such as abnormal thoughts, actions, and feelings. For example, lowered levels of neurotransmitters involved with the brain's pleasure and reward systems may be linked to anhedonia (the inability to experience pleasure), a common symptom of depression. This can have a huge impact including the avoidance or ceasing of activity and participation altogether. Additionally, with increased dopamine during a manic episode, people may have an increased drive for activity and participation, but may not be able to fully anticipate the consequences of actions.

The Impact of Medications on Activity and Participation

It is important to consider both the positive and negative effects of medications used to treat mood disorders. For instance, medications can reduce symptoms and help people return to meaningful activities. On the other hand, if someone is feeling nauseous or tired as a result of medication side effects, they may not participate in activities or enjoy activities.

Psychological Explanations

Psychological factors have a profound impact on how humans relate to the world around them.

Coping

Stressful life events have been closely linked with the onset and experience of depression However, the critical link is not just the existence of a stressful life event, but rather the way in which people are able to deal with stressful life events

For individuals with bipolar disorder, stressful life events can often be characterized as schedule-disrupting events and events that involve goal-attainment. These types of events can worsen symptoms of bipolar disorder and may lead to more manic episodes depending on how the individual manages these changes.

Motivation

Mood disorders have a drastic impact on motivation. With regard to depression, a lack of motivation to participate in daily activities is most likely present. Regarding the mania that accompanies bipolar disorders, motivation to participate in activities and to successfully accomplish goals is dramatically increased, while judgment may simultaneously be impaired.

Self-Esteem

Low self-esteem is one of the symptoms typically associated with depression. When people have low self-esteem, they can also feel less effective in managing their daily routine.

On the other hand, individuals who experience mania in relation to bipolar disorder can have an increased sense of self-worth or even experience extreme grandiosity. This increased sense of self-worth is often associated with a boost in activity participation and engagement in activities which could be dangerous or risky. Additionally, once people with bipolar disorder are in remission from mania, they may experience lower self-esteem which could diminish their activity and participation.

Social Explanations

Social Support and Relationships

Relationships and social support networks greatly influence a person's experience of mood disorders. In general, low social support predicts greater severity and frequency of mood disorder symptoms. Positive social supports can be extremely beneficial for those who experience mood disorders, however unhealthy relationships can cause additional stress or hinder recovery.

Stigma

Despite increased awareness and changing attitudes in society, stigma is still prominent surrounding mental health conditions like mood disorders. Anticipation of discrimination or stigma can decrease overall functioning and lower self-esteem, keeping people from participating in meaningful activities. Stigma can limit the ability of people with mental health issues to: get and keep a job, get and keep a safe place to live, be accepted by their family and community, find and maintain friendships and relationships, and take part in social activities. Stigma can also affect whether people with mood disorders seek treatment, take prescribed medications, or attend counselling.

What do I need to know about activity and participation and mood disorders?

(Service recipient resource)

- Mood disorders can disrupt your daily activities, including self-care, sleep, work, community involvement, leisure, and time spent with other people.
- The challenges that mood disorders create in daily life can happen because of changes to the brain, our thinking, the way we cope, and the way that other people relate to us.
- Sometimes people avoid activities when they're feeling down or do too many activities when they're feeling up. This activity imbalance can make it hard to manage the activities in your day.
- Activity and participation is central to your physical, social, and emotional well-being. Having a balanced daily routine can help you meet your needs and improve your well-being.
- Activities that are connected with personal interests and goals have the potential to improve your mood and provide meaning and satisfaction.
- You can modify your daily activities to help you manage your health and well-being. If you're feeling down, you can take breaks and split activities into smaller, more manageable tasks. If you're feeling up, you can also simplify tasks to make sure you stay on track and get things done.
- Sleep is really important to maintaining your well-being when you have a mood disorder. Using structure and activity scheduling can help you have a regular sleep routine.
- Some activities that could help with coping include exercise, meditation and relaxation, artistic activities, or music. These provide value, meaning, and help you connect with who you are, even when you're experiencing symptoms of a mood disorder.
- Social activities, especially with groups, can make activity participation easier and give you the support you need to live a full life.
- Being engaged in meaningful work that is a fit for your abilities and interests can broaden your social network and supports and make coping with a mood disorder easier.
- ***Don't give up and avoid meaningful activities and participation! They will help you cope with your mood disorder and are an important part of every person's daily routine.***

Changing my mood through activity and participation

Date: ____/____/____

Name: _____

Those who experience depression may face low mood while those who experience bipolar disorder can have both highs and lows with their mood. It is important to develop healthy strategies that can help regulate mood. Participating in activities can help target mood and make necessary changes.

In the table below, write down some positive strategies or activities you have tried in the past or want to try to help change your mood when you begin to see changes.

My Mood	*Activities and Strategies for Managing my Mood*	*Comments (Did it work? What was your experience? What might you change?)*
Extremely low mood	*E.g., spending time with a good friend*	*E.g., I was grateful to have such a supportive person in my life. My friend reminded me that engaging socially helps me improve my mood. Next time I begin to feel down I will try calling my friend sooner.*
Low mood	*E.g., Go for a walk and enjoy nature.*	*E.g., Being outside in the sun and getting fresh air was more helpful than sitting in my house. It helped me connect with nature. Next time I will try to add an additional ten minutes to my walk.*
Balanced mood	*E.g., This is the mood I want to maintain. I am going to continue engaging in my daily routine of waking up early, doing something productive that I enjoy, eating healthy and regular meals, and going to sleep at a reasonable time.*	*E.g., Keeping a steady routine really helps me regulate my mood. I'm happy when doing something I enjoy. Engaging in productive activities makes me feel like I am contributing to the world around me. Sleep is also really important otherwise I tend to feel poorly all day.*
Elevated mood	*E.g., Having an emergency plan that includes contact information for family, friends, or health care providers I can contact is important. Also having a family member or friend who sees me often enough they can let me know when they think my mood might be too high.*	*E.g., This allows me to use the supports I have in an effective way. I have people who care about me and want to see me doing well.* *I want to edit my emergency plan to include my supportive aunt.*
Other mood levels and ideas		

Social support, activity and participation

Date: ____ / ____ / ____

Name: _____

For those who experience mood disorders it is important to know what type of support is experienced as helpful. This worksheet outlines some ways that families and friends may offer support to someone experiencing a mood disorder. Take some time to look through these and select the ones that you think might be helpful for you and then add some of your own ideas to the blank boxes. Then, try and communicate your needs to your support network.

Example of Supportive Behaviour	✓	*Add Details*
Provide me with reminders (e.g., about appointments, medications, etc.)		
Help with transportation to activities		
Encourage me to do the activities I like		
Have a meal with me		
Have regular outings with me		
Come with me to my appointments		
Help me work through problems that might emerge with activities		
Help me set goals and be accountable to those goals		
Help me create a plan for what happens when a crisis occurs		
Other ideas:		

Activity, participation and self-esteem

Date: ____ / ____ / ____

Name: _____

Self-esteem is the confidence and satisfaction we feel about ourselves. Self-esteem can be negatively impacted for people with mood disorders. It is important to recognize past and current levels of self-esteem and ways to bolster self-esteem in a healthy way. Fill out the worksheet below to increase your awareness of your self-esteem.

How would you describe your self-esteem the majority of the time?

1	2	3	4	5
Low		Moderate		High

How would you describe your self-esteem currently?

1	2	3	4	5
Low		Moderate		High

Have there been times in the past when you have felt really good about yourself or had high self-esteem? What was going on in your life that made you feel good about yourself?

_____

_____

_____

Are there certain activities that make you feel good and encourage a positive self-image?

_____

_____

_____

List some activities that you would like to start doing, keep doing, or do more of that help you feel good about yourself:

_____

_____

_____

This week I will try the following three activities, record how I felt about myself, and what I want to do in the future:

Activity	How I Felt about Myself:	Plan for the Future:
1.		
2.		
3.		

References

American Psychiatric Association. (2013). *Diagnostic and Statistical Manual of Mental Disorders* (5ᵗʰ ed.). Washington, DC: American Psychiatric Association.

Barlow, D. H., Durand, V. M., & Stewart, S. H. (2012). *Abnormal Psychology: An Integrative Approach* (3ʳᵈ ed.). Nelson Education.

Benson, H., & Klipper, M. (1992). *The Relaxation Response.* Harper Collins, New York.

Blairy, S., Linotte, S., Souery, D., Papadimitriou, G. N., Dikeos, D., Lerer, B., ... & Mendlewicz, J. (2004). Social adjustment and self-esteem of bipolar patients: A multicentric study. *Journal of Affective Disorders, 79*(1–3), 97–103.

Harrison, P. (2002). The neuropathology of primary mood disorder. *Brain, 125,* 1428–1449.

McClung, C. A. (2007). Circadian genes, rhythms, and the biology of mood disorders. *Pharmacology & Therapeutics, 114*(2),22–223.

Miklowitz, D. J., & Johnson, B. S. L. (2009). Social and familial factors in the course of bipolar disorder: Basic processes and relevant interventions. *Clinical Psychology: Science and Practice, 16*(2), 281–296.

Monroe, S. M., & Reid, M. W. (2009). Life stress and major depression. *Current Directions in Psychological Science, 18*(2), 68–72.

Appendix C4 – Posttraumatic Stress Disorder and Activity and Participation

Contributed by Cate Preston and Allie Rogers

How are posttraumatic stress disorder (PTSD) and activity and participation connected?

(Service provider resource)

Posttraumatic stress disorder (PTSD) is a disorder in which people experience a severe and persistent emotional response to a traumatic event or events.

Individuals with PTSD often experience persistent increased arousal, with 'fight, flight, or freeze' reactions. This can manifest itself as sleeplessness, irritability, difficulty concentrating, exaggerated startle responses, or hyper vigilance, all of which can impact the experience of engaging in activity and participation.

This resource provides information about some of the ways that PTSD is believed to impact the experience of daily activities and participation. These are grouped into biomedical, psychological, and social explanations.

Biomedical Explanations

This section focuses on the structures, physiology, and functions of the human body that could account for disruptions experienced in activity and activity patterns for people with PTSD.

In the brain, when the amygdala and hippocampus are over active, a person may be stuck in a constant state of 'fight, flight, or freeze' which is a highly uncomfortable state and can cause responses that are out of proportion. In an effort to avoid distressing or unpleasant experiences, individuals who experience PTSD may stop engaging in activities with others or activities that may trigger a response. For example, they may avoid being in a busy environment with loud sudden noises.

Changes to the hippocampus can also impact memory, as individuals with PTSD may have difficulty recalling specific aspects of a traumatic event or experience vivid and persistent flashbacks. General memory may also be impacted, causing issues with a person's ability to consciously remember and verbalize even emotionally neutral information, such as appointments, conversations, and daily tasks.

Additionally, some of the changes in an individual's hormone regulation due to PTSD may affect the experience of activities by impacting motivation, enjoyment, attention, and energy levels.

The Impact of Medications on Activity

The goal of medical management is to reduce a person's experience of symptoms, allowing them to return to meaningful activities and participation. However, medications may also cause weight gain, drowsiness, nausea, or sexual difficulties, side effects that may impact an individual's self-image as well as their motivation to participate in meaningful activity and participation.

Psychological Explanations

PTSD can influence how humans think about themselves in relation to activities and participation and, in turn, influence their engagement in these.

Flashbacks

For those with PTSD, flashbacks may be associated with certain activities, and the potential of triggering this can further increase panic and fear when participating in activities. A fear of re-experiencing their trauma can overcome an individual's motivation to participate.

Self-Evaluations

Past trauma, and ongoing negative experiences with anxiety can impact self-confidence, self-esteem, and beliefs surrounding one's own abilities. This self-doubt can lead to isolation, and withdrawal from activity, participation, and social and family groups.

Avoidance

Individuals with PTSD typically experience heightened reactions to stimuli. In an effort to control these emotions they may avoid places, activities, people, or even conversations that may cause an emotional reaction to maintain their personal sense of safety by lowering their experience of vulnerability

Social Explanations

Social factors, those external to the individua that can significantly impact activity and participation patterns.

Stigma

Often the stigma of a mental illness such as PTSD can make it difficult for individuals to talk about what they are experiencing with important people their lives. For people who experience work-related PTSD, they may worry that their it will cause them to be treated differently by leaders and colleagues. Stigma can involve others perceiving people with PTSD as weak or cause others to have less confidence in them.

Social Supports and Relationships

PTSD can affect and change the relationships within a family or social group, by impacting communication, community, and roles and/or responsibilities. Avoidance of emotional triggers can be a key feature of PTSD, this includes avoiding conversations or even social situations due to worry about being unable to control emotions. This can lead to social isolation and limiting contact with friends or groups outside of the home.

Significant others or family members often take on a caregiver role for the individual with PTSD (Gerlock et al., 2014). While caregiving has positive intentions an individual with PTSD may experience feelings of resentment toward the caregiver. Caregivers can be an incredibly necessary social support; however, they can also be a reminder to those experiencing PTSD of their self-perceived 'diminished capacity'.

What do I need to know about activity participation and PTSD?

(Service recipient resource)

- PTSD can disrupt your daily activities, including self-care, sleep, work, community involvement, leisure, and time spent with other people.
- The challenges that PTSD creates in daily life can happen because of changes to the brain, our thinking, the way we cope, and the way that other people relate to us.
- Activity participation is central to your physical, social, and emotional well-being. Having a balanced daily routine can help you meet your needs and improve your well-being.
- You can modify your daily activities to help you manage your health. If you're feeling overwhelmed, you can take breaks and split activities into smaller, more manageable tasks.
- Sleep is important to maintaining your well-being when you have PTSD. Using structure and activity scheduling can help you have a regular sleep routine.
- Physical activity helps to manage the symptoms of PTSD. Ask for a friend or family member to join you in physical activity to increase motivation and accountability.
- Work with your team to identify 'triggers' that may aggravate your symptom experience. Understanding your tolerance for activities can allow you to set reasonable goals for how to begin to return to some of your previous activities.
- Participating in small activities can help strengthen connections with your family members and friends.
- Some activities that could help with coping include exercise, meditation and relaxation, artistic activities, or music. These provide value, meaning, and help you connect with who you are, even when you're experiencing symptoms of PTSD.
- Social activities, especially with groups, can make activity participation easier and give you the support you need to live a full life.
- Being engaged in meaningful work that is a fit for your abilities and interests can broaden your social network and supports and make coping with PTSD easier.
- Remember that the first few times you try, activities are probably going to be the most difficult! Starting with small goals and building new activity routines can help to manage this.
- ***Don't give up and avoid meaningful activities and participation! They will help you cope with PTSD disorder and are an important part of every person's daily routine.***

Activity and participation and your loved ones

Date: ____ / ____ / ____

Name: _____

Your mental health may not only be impacting you, or only your own level of activity participation, but also have a big impact on your family members and loved ones too.

Your daily activities that involve your family may be some of the first that you pull away from. These may be simple things like eating dinner with the family, or watching TV in the evening together.

The time-use log below is designed for you to take a closer look at how engaged you are in activities with your family now as opposed to before the onset of your mental illness.

Family Activities You Do Now	*Frequency*	*Family Activities You Used to Partake in*	*Frequency*

Changes in your activity and participation levels with others are a common occurrence with mental illness. You are dealing with new emotions and so is your family as they try to support you. Often family members may feel very guilty about some of the feelings they have, as they try to be there for you. Beginning a dialogue about how you both are feeling can be helpful for you and for them.

What are some conversation starters you can use to begin to talk about these feelings with your loved one?

_____
_____
_____
_____
_____
_____
_____

Re-engaging in the family activities you used to participate in can be helpful in your recovery and crucial in maintaining healthy family relationships and support networks.

Try planning out a weekly schedule where you plan to make sure that you and your family do one activity together a day. These can be small, and over time, you can work up to more challenging activities.

Some activities may take more out of you, going to a soccer game in a busy park, for example. Budget in how much effort each activity will take and include this in your planning, on a scale of 1–10. For example, eating breakfast with your family may be an activity that has an emotional budget of 3, it is an activity that occurs in your own home, with a small number of people, and involves small amounts of conversation. An activity such as going to your child's soccer game may have a budget of 8 or 9 as it involves going out in public, being around groups of people, having to interact socially, and being outside when unexpected things may happen. Be aware of the budget of your activities as you plan your week, spreading out high 'cost' emotional activities.

Examples are provided. At the end of each day try to reflect on how that activity went. This can involve thinking about what your mood was that day, how you felt before and after, and how your loved ones reacted.

What changes will you make for next week?

_____
_____
_____

What activity goals do you have for the future? _____

_____
_____

What activities would your friends and family suggest? _____

_____
_____

	Activities	*Energy Budget*	*How Did It Go?*
Example	Read my son a book Pick up my spouse from work	2 7	
Monday			
Tuesday			
Wednesday			
Thursday			
Friday			
Saturday			
Sunday			

Your activity and participation and your sense of self

Date: ____ / ____ / ____

Name: _____

It can be common for an individual's mental health to have a strong impact on their sense of self and self-efficacy – the belief that they are capable of pursuing and being successful in what they are interested in. Trauma and loss of previous roles can compound this loss of 'self' and lead to development of further symptoms such as depression.

A change in your sense of self and confidence in your abilities can lead to you not feeling able or motivated to engage in activities you once did. It is important to be kind to yourself and try to develop skills and strategies that affirm you and your abilities.

Listing your accomplishments can be a way of focusing on the positive. Spend a few moments and list 5–10 accomplishments that you are proud of. These can be career or family oriented, like 'I have paid off the mortgage of our house' or 'I take good care of my dog'. Try to also include emotional and personal accomplishments, such as 'I have been using deep breathing strategies when I began to get anxious in the grocery store'. You can incorporate some of the activities you have planned and strategies you have learned from other worksheets in this package.

1. _____
2. _____
3. _____
4. _____
5. _____
6. _____
7. _____
8. _____
9. _____
10. _____

Take a moment to look at your list – how does it make you feel?

_____

_____

Was it an easy task to complete? Or was it difficult?

_____

_____

Incorporating positivity and gratitude into your daily life may seem daunting at first. Focusing on what you are grateful for can be very powerful.

Use the chart below and take five minutes at the end of every day for a week to reflect on your activities or accomplishments each day as well as write one thing you are grateful for.

MONDAY
My activities & accomplishments: Today I am grateful for:
TUESDAY
My activities & accomplishments: Today I am grateful for:
WEDNESDAY
My activities & accomplishments: Today I am grateful for:
THURSDAY
My activities & accomplishments: Today I am grateful for:
FRIDAY
My activities & accomplishments: Today I am grateful for:
SATURDAY
My activities & accomplishments: Today I am grateful for:
SUNDAY
My activities & accomplishments: Today I am grateful for:

References

Brown, C., Stoffel, V., & Munoz, J. (2019). *Occupational Therapy in Mental Health: A Vision for Participation* (2nd ed.). Philadelphia: FA Davis Company.

Davis, J., Brown, C., & Stoffel, V. (2011). Anxiety disorders. In C. Brown & V. Stoffel (Eds) *Occupational Therapy in Mental Health: A Vision for Participation.* (167–178) Philadelphia: FA Davis Company.

Gerlock, A., Grimesey, J., & Sayre, G. (2014). Military-related posttraumatic stress disorder and intimate relationship behaviors: a developing dyadic relationship model. *Journal of Marital and Family Therapy, 40,* 344–356.

Gould, M., Adler, A., Zamorski, M., Castro, C., Hanily, N., Steele, N., Kearney, S., Greenberg, N. (2010). Do stigma and other perceived barriers to mental health care differ across Armed Forces? *Journal of the Royal Society of Medicine.* 103(4), 148–156.

Samuelson, K. W. (2011). Post-traumatic stress disorder and declarative memory functioning: a review. *Dialogues in Clinical Neuroscience.* 13(3), 346–351.

Tull, M. T., Barrett, H. M., McMillan, E. S., & Roemer, L. (2007). A preliminary investigation of the relationship between emotion regulation difficulties and posttraumatic stress symptoms. *Behavior Therapy, 38*(3), 303–313.

Zen, A. L., Zhao, S., & Whooley, Cohen, B. E., (2012). Post-traumatic stress disorder is associated with poor health behaviors: Findings from the heart and soul study. *Health Psychology, 31*(2), 194–201.

Appendix C5 – Action Over Inertia Together
(4- and 10-Session Group Outlines)

Contributed by Renee Bucci & Tanya Schoenhals

4-Session Open Group

This 4-session group outline was designed for use at an out-patient mental health program but could also be useful for in-patient settings.

Time: Each of the four sessions lasts approximately 60–75 minutes. A consistent day/time is recommended; it could be run over a period of two to four weeks depending on the duration of stay in out-patient or in-patient settings.

Group Format: The format is an open group format; members may join at any point, and the group runs continuously. Members may take part in only four sessions or continue in order to repeat content as needed. The content has been organized and selected in a way that allows members to begin at any session.

Facilitation: Co-facilitation is recommended. Consider having a peer co-facilitator.

Tips for managing group members who begin and finish the group at different times within the four-week schedule: Facilitators should define or revisit main concepts and their relevance to the session before starting new material. Members who may have participated in previous sessions can provide support and insights on activity and participation to fellow group members.

Session	*Session Name*	*General Description*
Pre-Group	N/A	Facilitators meet with potential group members and screen for group membership. Members complete ***Worksheet 2.15: A measure of my health and well-being through activity and participation***.
1	Understanding Personal Activity and Participation Patterns	Members evaluate their own activity and participation patterns and engage in discussion regarding their experience of activities and participation within their daily routines (time-use log and worksheets in Chapter 1).
2	Balance of My Activities and Participation	Members begin exploring the balance of their activities as well as their engagement in various dimensions of activity and participation (worksheets Chapter 2).
3	Activity and Participation and Well-Being	The connection between activity and participation and well-being is explored, as well as the impact of activity and participation on recovery from mental illness (worksheets and resources Chapter 4).
4	Planning for Long-Term Activity and Participation Changes	Members begin preparing and planning for changes in activity and participation. Members may begin to identify activity and participation patterns that they would like to change, as well as any challenges that may need to be addressed and managed to successfully participate in the activity and participation change (worksheets and resources Chapter 5).
3- and 6-Months Post-Group	Checking-in	The group will discuss their activity change to this point. Members will complete a time-use log, ***Worksheet 2.15: A measure of my health and well-being through activity and participation***, and Prioritizing plans for activity and participation changes worksheets (worksheet Chapter 5).

10-Session Closed Group

This 10-session group outline was designed for use by community mental health programs, but could be used in any setting where it is possible to run ten sessions with the same group of participants.

Time: This group will include 10 sessions, each lasting 90 minutes. It is typically run over ten weeks, with one session per week, but a shorter or longer duration could be considered depending on the setting. A consistent day/time each week is recommended.

Group Format: The closed group format allows the content to covered sequentially and for members to develop and achieve their activity and participation goals together over time.

Facilitation: Co-facilitation is recommended. Consider having a peer co-facilitator.

Session	Session Name	General Description
Pre-Group	N/A	Leader meets with potential group members and screens for group membership. Members complete ***Worksheet 2.15: A measure of my health and well-being through activity and participation***.
1	My Activity and Participation Patterns	Members evaluate their own activity and participation patterns and the benefits of these (worksheets Chapter 1).
2	My Yesterday	Members complete a yesterday time-use log and graph their time-use (Worksheet 2.1, 2.2).
3	Balancing Act	Members use their time-use logs to evaluate well-being aspects of their activity and participation.
4	Using Your Time	Members use their time-use logs to evaluate how their activity and participation patterns provide connection to others and access to community environments and complete ***Worksheet 2.15: A measure of my health and well-being through activity and participation.***
5	An Experiment Anyone?	The group discusses the concept of activity and participation experiments. Members consider several activity and participation experiments they may try in the next week.
6	Education	Leaders provide education on activity and participation, health and well-being, and mental illness (worksheets in Chapter 4).
7	Thinking About Change	Members prepare for and prioritize activity and participation changes (worksheets Chapter 5).
8	Planning For Change	Members create plans for activity and participation change (worksheets Chapter 5).
9	Following Through on Change	Members reflect on supporting and evaluating activity and participation change (worksheet Chapter 6).
10	Putting It All Together	Wrap up session. Members discuss what they learned from the group and their next steps (worksheet Chapter 6). Members complete ***Worksheet 2.15: A measure of my health and well-being through activity and participation.***
3- and 6-Months Post-Group	Checking-In	The group discusses their activity change to this point. Members complete ***Worksheet 2.15: A measure of my health and well-being through activity and participation.***

Index

For Product Safety Concerns and Information please contact our EU
representative GPSR@taylorandfrancis.com
Taylor & Francis Verlag GmbH, Kaufingerstraße 24, 80331 München, Germany

www.ingramcontent.com/pod-product-compliance
Lightning Source LLC
Chambersburg PA
CBHW080132270326
41926CB00021B/4455